Investigating Family, Food, and Housing Themes in Social Studies

Investigating Family, Food, and Housing Themes in Social Studies

Cynthia Williams Resor

ROWMAN & LITTLEFIELD
Lanham • Boulder • New York • London

Published by Rowman & Littlefield
A wholly owned subsidiary of The Rowman & Littlefield Publishing Group, Inc.
4501 Forbes Boulevard, Suite 200, Lanham, Maryland 20706
www.rowman.com

Unit A, Whitacre Mews, 26-34 Stannary Street, London SE11 4AB

Copyright © 2017 by Cynthia Williams Resor

All rights reserved. No part of this book may be reproduced in any form or by any electronic or mechanical means, including information storage and retrieval systems, without written permission from the publisher, except by a reviewer who may quote passages in a review.

British Library Cataloguing in Publication Information Available

Library of Congress Cataloging-in-Publication Data

Names: Resor, Cynthia Williams, 1966- author.
Title: Investigating family, food, and housing themes in social studies / Cynthia Williams Resor.
Description: Lanham, Maryland : Rowman & Littlefield, 2017. | Includes bibliographical references and index.
Identifiers: LCCN 2017029597 (print) | LCCN 2017041118 (ebook) | ISBN 9781475832037 (electronic) | ISBN 9781475832006 (hardcover : alk. paper) | ISBN 9781475832020 (pbk. : alk. paper)
Subjects: LCSH: Social sciences—Study and teaching (Secondary) | Social sciences—Study and teaching (Middle School) | Social sciences—Research—Methodology. | Families. | Food--Social aspects. | Housing.
Classification: LCC H62 (ebook) | LCC H62 .R4625 2017 (print) | DDC 300.71/2—dc23
LC record available at https://lccn.loc.gov/2017029597

∞™ The paper used in this publication meets the minimum requirements of American National Standard for Information Sciences—Permanence of Paper for Printed Library Materials, ANSI/NISO Z39.48-1992.

Cover image credits: Frank A Rinehart, Photographer. Sauk Indian Family, Omaha, Nebraska, ca. 1899. (Courtesy of Library of Congress); Currier & Ives. *Home Sweet Home*, hand-colored lithograph, c. 1856–1907. (Courtesy of Library of Congress); Joachim Beuckelaer. *Market Woman with Fruit, Vegetables and Poultry*, painting, 1564. (Courtesy Wikimedia Commons)

To my grandmothers,
Helen Williams (1912–1998) and Mae Vanhooser (1901–2009)

Contents

	Author's Note	ix
	Introduction	1
Chapter 1	Family: Home Is Where the Heart Is	5
Chapter 2	Housing: Home, Sweet Home	21
Chapter 3	Housework and Domestic Service: A Woman's Work Is Never Done	45
Chapter 4	Food: We Are What We Eat	67
Chapter 5	Home Cooking from Scratch	87
Chapter 6	Education Theories behind the Themes	111
	Works Cited	115
	Index	121
	About the Author	127

Author's Note

Visit the companion website teachingwiththemes.com for the following:

- More primary sources, texts, and images related to the themes of family, food, and housing.
- Information about additional publications by this author.
- A feedback form. Please share your experiences and suggestions using the themes, primary sources, and recommendations in this book.

Introduction

"Is that really a thing?" This commonly heard question conveys our confusion about whether a new trend is really that popular. Modern media barrages us with new things that promise to transform our daily lives: new looks, new diets, new gadgets, new apps, new behaviors, or new slang. Should we jump on the bandwagon to join others who appear convinced this new thing is making their lives better?

Asking "Is that a thing?" communicates more than our desire to be up-to-date; it also reveals an underlying skepticism. Maybe the popularity of this new thing is really an illusion created by its promoters. Someone wants to convince us to join the crowd, but what is in it for them? How do we critically assess what appear to be popular trends in a world filled with conflicting advice? How do we decide if something is really a thing?

These questions are at the core of this book. Messages about how one ought to behave, what one ought to be, do, or buy have existed in every era and every culture. People throughout time have consciously and subconsciously measured themselves against the recommended things of their era. Today, and in the past, people question, analyze, conform, transform, or reject the conventions of their culture.

The following chapters revolve around social history themes related to daily life—family, food, and housing. Family, food, and shelter are realities required by everyone for survival, then and now. But family, food, and home are also subjective concepts with meanings that vary. These words can mean different things, to different people, at different times and places. Often, subjective meanings communicate not what is *real*, but what ought to be an *ideal*. Historians must distinguish between real and ideal, objective and subjective. They must ask, "Was that really a thing?"

On one hand, historians study very real, objective, concrete objects and topics, seeking to reconstruct who was included in historical families, what did their dwellings look like, what foods were eaten. On the other hand, historians study idealized and abstract concepts of family, food, and housing. They ask how descriptions and depictions of home expressed the cultural norms of the dominant group of people. How did table manners and silverware convey social status? How did preparing food transmit messages about what is feminine or masculine?

Historical documents and images, or primary sources, convey objective facts, but they also convey subjective concepts of the author and culture. Documents and images are often *prescriptive*, communicating how people *ought* to act, not necessarily how different groups of people really did act. Most sources represent the reality for some groups, but fail to acknowledge the very different lives of others.

Our students must sort out, or critically assess, messages from the modern media, just as historians analyze primary sources. This book is about examining the past and asking, "Is that really a thing?" and encouraging students to ask the same question about modern culture. What should be believed, what rejected? Who is giving the advice? Why do they want me to adopt that viewpoint? How does it confirm or conflict with my experience and background—my family, my friends, my social class, my ethnicity, my culture, my sex, my gender? How does it confirm or conflict with the person I want to be?

Sometimes we ask, "*When* did that become a thing?" This question reflects how we cope with change in daily life. We live in an era of social, economic, technological, and political change. It's hard to keep up with the newest thing while carrying on with life—school, work, family, friends, and daily routines. It is easy to miss the big shifts in society.

Change over time and the transformation in daily life from the pre-industrial to the modern era is examined in each of the following chapters. Historical time is a long game, hard to imagine when viewed from the perspective of just one human life. For the first five thousand years of recorded pre-industrial history, change was slow and almost imperceptible in daily lives of average people. Nearly every aspect of those millennia was completely different from the daily routines of modern students.

Then, in just three hundred years, from the eighteenth into the twentieth century, the Industrial Revolution altered how humans lived their daily lives. The change came at different rates in difference places. Some people experienced radical change in their lifetime; others continued to live pre-industrial lives into the twentieth century. Some idealized past conventions; others embraced a new way of life.

In the twenty-first century, individuals, groups, and entire societies must come to terms with change quickly. Asking students to analyze historical changes in daily life better prepares them to consider change in their own lives and make informed decisions about the ideals and reality of the next new thing.

How to Use This Book

This book is not a recipe; it is not a step-by-step set of instructions for guaranteed success in the classroom. Instead, it is a resource or idea book for incorporating thematic instruction, essential questions, primary source analysis, social history, place-based education, and culturally responsive teaching into your classroom. While the primary source excerpts are for middle and high school readers, elementary teachers may also find this book useful. Thematic, interdisciplinary instruction has always been the most popular in elementary classrooms, and the following chapters may provide new insight into a familiar instructional approach.

Hopefully you will find inspiration to develop at least one thematic unit for your classroom or adapt existing units to include the themes of family, food, and housing. You may discover connections to other disciplines and be inspired to collaborate with other teachers to develop interdisciplinary thematic instruction. Even if you are unable to overhaul your curriculum, you are sure to find interesting anecdotes, activities, and primary source documents and images in what follows that will make your students look at their everyday lives with new eyes.

Family, food, and housing are enormous fields of academic study and popular topics of discussion in every form of modern media. Books and articles on each topic by social historians number in the hundreds, maybe thousands. Therefore, the focus of this volume had to be narrowed; this was accomplished with essential questions and highlighting a few specific historical eras.

Each chapter opens with essential questions that focus the historical summaries and suggested activities. The essential questions can be used in the classroom to prompt discussion, develop activities, guide writing assignments, or direct culminating projects.

The historical summaries following the essential questions revolve around the similarities and differences in pre-industrial and modern life; the transition in daily life during the industrial era; and distinguishing real from ideal, objective from subjective in historical sources. Details of daily life in ancient and medieval Europe are used as examples for the pre-industrial era; the United States for the eighteenth, nineteenth, and twentieth-century transition.

This emphasis is *not* intended as a statement of the importance of Western European culture over that of the rest of the world. Every culture is important. The trends and diversity from just one small slice of history represent my limitations as a historian and my wish to write an inexpensive book someone might actually buy. If everyone and everything were included, you would be holding a heavy, multivolume encyclopedia. My hope is this book will inspire you to learn more about family, food, and dwellings in your local community, the cultures of your students, and from modern and historical cultures throughout the world.

At the end of each themed chapter are descriptions and suggestions for classroom activities and sets of primary source documents. The primary sources are short excerpts, but teachers and students are encouraged to consult the endnotes for references to the full texts, many of which are available online. I have edited some of the more difficult-to-read primary sources to make them accessible to middle and high school students, but I kept the meaning and language as close to the original as possible.

Throughout the book are primary source images related to family, food, and housing. Teaching students to interpret imagery is just as important as reading texts. These images are also available for easy projection in the classroom at the book's companion website.

The final chapter briefly explores how the pedagogies of place-based education and culturally responsive teaching are related to the themes of family, food, and history. A discussion of the current standards used as a framework for this book is also included.

The book's companion website, teachingwiththemes.com, offers many more ideas and resources for thematic teaching. If this book inspires you to do more research on social history themes of interest to you and your students, you may wish to learn more about the development of social history as a discipline and how to research and create your own thematic units in my previous book, *Exploring Vacation and Etiquette Themes in Social Studies*.

I can't guarantee the suggestions in this book will transform your classroom. I've spent my life in classrooms as a student, a teacher, and a professor and read or heard a lot of advice that made me wonder "Is this really a thing?" Many times someone has tried to sell me an education miracle cure that failed to magically transform my teaching, my classroom, or my school. Thematic teaching of social history themes will not result in magical transformations. But you and your students might see new relationships between current events, academic disciplines, historical and modern cultures, and what you eat, where you live, and your interactions with families. You and your students may seek more answers to the critical question, "Is that really a thing?"

CHAPTER ONE

Family

Home Is Where the Heart Is

Essential Questions
- A normal family—is that really a thing?
- How do we separate ideals about family from reality?

Every student has family, but those families can be very, very different. Often, families are judged as good or bad, traditional and normal, or weird and abnormal. These subjective labels communicate messages about what individuals and a society believe a family ought and ought not be. Powerful forces such as religion, government, media, and reform groups advocate an ideal status and role for families and the children, men and women that make up those families. But upon closer examination, these ideals often fail to represent the daily lives of many families. This chapter examines family on two levels—historical reality and perceived ideals.

First, the historical roles of families within wider social, political, and economic institutions of a society is examined. Over the course of history, the functions of family have shifted and changed. In the past, families, households, and kinship groups performed many of the functions of government and other public and private institutions in the modern world.

Second, the impact of the Industrial Revolution on perceptions of social class and family roles of women, men, and children is examined. A new group, the middle class, emerged in the eighteenth, nineteenth, and twentieth centuries alongside the changing economy. New inventions changed daily life in the home and how households defined work for men, children, and women. According to much of the literature of the nineteenth and twentieth century, the middle class became the new normal. But then, as today, not every family was, or is, middle class. How does one separate the ideals of a popular culture from reality?

Defining Family

What we perceive as normal today or about the past is often misleading or just plain wrong. References made to traditional or normal families usually assume a married man and woman and their children. This model is held up as the ideal model of family, universal across time and cultures.[1] A culture's conception of traditional or normal families shapes behavior, how individuals perceive their own experiences, and influences political and economic policies pertaining to families. But many assumptions about traditional or normal families are based upon nostalgia for a past era, rather than historical reality.

To study the concept of family in the classroom, terms must be clearly defined and distinctions made between individual and cultural perceptions and demographic reality. Modern dictionaries list several definitions of human family. These definitions refer to the relationship between a married man, woman, and their mutual children; or one or more adults of the same or different sexes living together and raising their own or adopted children; or an extended group of people related by blood or marriage; or a group of people living under one roof who may or may not be related by blood or marriage.

Technically, *family* is defined as a kinship or legal unit based on marriage or parent-child linkages. *Kinship* refers to a blood or genealogical relationship among groups of families and *extended family* refers to a group of relatives that are kin, but do not live in the same dwelling. Sociologists describe different types of families. The *nuclear* or *conjugal* family is made up of a husband, wife, and their dependent children. But today and throughout time, the *consanguineal* family of a single parent and children and complex family models such as a family that contains two or more generations are common.[2]

When defining family, different disciplines and different agencies may focus on different roles of family. For example, according to the U.S. Census Bureau, a family is distinct from a household; a household is a group of kin and non-kin sharing a common residence. In other words, a family may or may not live in the same household.[3] For tax purposes, the Internal Revenue Service definition of household becomes complicated, and may include economic dependents living outside of the common residence so tax responsibilities can be assessed.

Anthropologists and sociologists focus on the role of the family in social reproduction of culture, while geneticists focus on biological reproduction. The study of family has been an important focus of social historians in recent decades because families are important in the functioning of political power, the creation of social status and class, and in shaping what is perceived as the ideal or norm in a culture.[4]

Responsibilities of the Family—Then and Now

Definitions and roles of family in the pre-modern world are different from those in the United States today. In the past, government, economic activities, religious instruction and social control, socialization and education, and the care of the young, the sick, and the elderly were the responsibilities of families and kinship groups. The wealthiest and most powerful families governed. Families of monarchs and nobles relied on personal and family ties to control the power

Figure 1.1. Family portraits, historical and modern, convey messages about the power, wealth, and status of the family. Holy Roman Empress Maria Theresa, her husband, Francis I, and their children are depicted in this eighteenth-century painting by Martin van Meytens. Maria Theresa ruled the Hapsburg Empire for forty years. She and her husband had eleven daughters and five sons; five of her children became heads of state in Europe.
(Courtesy of Wikimedia Commons.)

and wealth of their cultures and provided or failed to provide what we expect from modern bureaucratic government at the local, state, and federal levels.

Power in the ancient world was both justified and determined by ancestry. Ancient monarchies were family affairs. Even though democracy in ancient Athens and the bureaucratic government of ancient Rome challenged the concept of ruling as a family business, family ties were still very important in the functioning of the government.

As Roman government declined in the fourth and fifth centuries, Europe returned to local government in which power was dominated by kinship groups such as the Carolingians and the Normans.[5] In medieval Europe (c. 400s–1400s), power was transferred within the family from fathers to sons. Power was based on a military force of knights that took oaths of loyalty to individuals within a ruling family. Wars and feuds were waged between powerful families. Courts and police functions were provided not by a neutral bureaucratic authority, but by people related to or allied with the ruling family. Political alliances were made through marriage between families.

In the pre-industrial world, the household was the center of economic production. All business was essentially a family business; daily work took place where the family lived. The main business of most households was agriculture.

Figure 1.2. This 1936 photograph of an Alabama sharecropper family was taken by Walker Evans, a photographer for the Resettlement Administration of the U.S. Department of Agriculture. The purpose of this family portrait was to document the poverty of rural American families during the Depression to generate support for controversial government resettlement efforts. This is one of several photographs of the family and house of Bud Fields available through the Library of Congress. The two-room house had a wood stove, very little furniture, and few material comforts. Many poor or rural American families lived in pre-industrial homes long after modern home conveniences were available in the late nineteenth and early twentieth centuries.
Walker Evans, Photographer. "Sharecropper Bud Fields and his family at home in Hale County, Alabama." 1936. (Courtesy of the Library of Congress)

The shift from an economy based on agricultural society, driven by changing technology, changed the roles of family, its makeup, and the responsibilities of its members.

In the early modern era (c. 1500s–1700s), as the economy was slowly changing and the governments were centralizing, ruling families were replaced by modern bureaucratic states. The family's role in public life shifted to local, state, and national governments, schools, businesses, corporations, and the mass media.[6] Formal schooling is an example of a function what was provided by families throughout most of history. Wealthy children learned to read and write at home from privately hired tutors or private schools paid for by the family. Governments did not begin to assume the responsibility of providing formal education for all children until the nineteenth century.

In the modern world, the role of the family in society has been reduced to largely private functions. The family is no longer a public unit serving as workplace, school, welfare, and government; its roles are more private. Most adult family of members earn wages or salaries to provide shelter, food, and clothing instead of working on family farms. Government-administered social welfare programs provide needed help to those who cannot care for themselves, relieving the family of their historical responsibilities for those orphaned, disabled, indigent, or elderly.

Families still produce children and are important in the socialization of the children, but support for raising children is provided outside the home by public schools. Emotional bonds are generally viewed as the primary function of the family in the modern world. Throughout the past three hundred years of economic and technological change, the roles and functions of the family and the people within it have shifted, been questioned, and been slowly redefined.

Work and the Household in the Pre-Industrial Era

Modern day-to-day lives are unimaginably different from those of humans through time. Most pre-industrial men, women, and children were engaged in almost constant and physically demanding labor to have the food, clothing, and shelter needed to survive. Males and females had clearly defined and usually distinct roles in the household, but the labor of both was essential. Emotional bonds linked family members, just like today, but in the pre-industrial era, marriage partners were also business partners; children were employees. Households were home and work combined.

The word *household* describes the pre-industrial concept of family as an economic and work unit. The pre-industrial concept of household included kin and non-kin people; houses, other buildings, and land; the power structure of the family and the roles of each person in the family; and the work or business that supported the family. Households included unrelated people such as slaves, servants, apprentices, boarders, all of whom worked within the household for the economic survival the group.

The ancient Greeks and Romans did not have words corresponding to the modern definition of family. Instead, Greek sources refer to *oikos*, or households—groups of people residing together under the authority of the head of the household as well as the property owned by the head of the household. The group of people within a household could include people related by blood or marriage as well as slaves and servants.

In Greece, the science of household management was called *economics*, signifying the merging of household and business. The counterpart of household management in public life was *politics*, or the science of government. In ancient Rome, *familia* was the Latin word for the household in which everything and everyone was under the authority of the head of the house, the *paterfamilias*, usually the father.

Ancient census records, used to determine taxes, are an important primary source for the history of families. These records reveal how family, household, work, and business were combined in a way that seems foreign today.[7] Households of rich and poor had a family at their core, but they were also an economic unit. The wealthiest households included numerous estates, dwellings, and structures used for business, and dependents, laborers, and slaves.

While slaves were counted in the households of their owners, they may have lived with their owners, independently in their own homes, or in huge barracks, depending upon their occupation. Slaves may have formed nuclear family units, but could not be counted as an economic unit, or a household. Small households lived in small apartments or houses with meager belongings and fewer people not related biologically. The nuclear family in ancient times tended to be small at all levels of society. Most families had three or fewer children and Roman emperors tried to encourage an increase in the birth rate by offering special rewards or status to parents who had many children.[8]

How the barbarian peoples in late antiquity defined household is difficult for historians to ascertain. The barbarian nations and cultures had different traditions than the Greeks and Romans. But because the barbarian groups did not write, early surviving documents about their daily lives are by outsiders, Greeks and Romans, who judged these foreign households through their own cultural lenses. By the sixth century, the written laws of Germanic people, a chief source for the history of family and households, had been influenced by Christian and Roman traditions. These sources stressed the importance of kindred groups but the details of how households were arranged are obscured.[9]

Starting in the late seventh century, a new unit of measuring land and counting households appeared in records—the peasant farm. In the late Roman Empire, large landowners, faced with slave labor shortages, were forced to make concessions allowing slaves to marry and live in family units. The workers, serfs, or peasants were required to pay rent or owed labor services, but the land they worked and the individual family dwellings came to be regarded as belonging to the peasant family.[10]

By the late Middle Ages, the nuclear family, with parents and children, served as the core of household at all levels, but wealthy households were much larger than those of average people. Wealthy households included servants, apprentices, and additional family or financial dependents. These households recruited workers for their home or business, usually young men and women, from families with fewer resources.[11] Prosperous households controlled more property and were involved in production on a larger scale—large farms in the country or large commercial or administrative roles in the cities. The households of most working people contained only family members and limited possessions.

Work of the pre-industrial household in Europe and America was divided by sex, but the contributions of both men and women were essential to survival. *Housewives*, a term used as far back as the thirteenth century, and *husbands*, were not just a married couple, they were also the male and female economic partners in the business of survival. Their economic security was achieved by working together and *husbanding*, or carefully managing, their resources. The house and land owned or rented by housewives and husbands were the main resources of those engaged in *husbandry*, or farming.[12] Husbandry generally referred to the work assigned to men; the name for the labor of women was *housewifery* until the nineteenth century.

Even though men and women traditionally performed different tasks, the tasks of both were equally demanding, time-consuming, and necessary. For example, cooking in the pre-industrial era required wood to be cut, chopped, and hauled by men; grain grown and processed by men; fruits, vegetables, and herbs grown and preserved by women; milk or cheese produced by women; and meat from animals tended and butchered by men or women, depending upon the animals. Men built houses. Women produced clothing, a process that required gathering and processing the linen or wool fibers, spinning it into thread or yarn, weaving the cloth, and constructing the clothing. Water had to be hauled to the house by men or women. Women made soap and did the laundry and women tended the children while carrying out their tasks.[13]

Household members varied depending upon the family cycle—the stages in a family from marriage of a man and woman, through the birth and maturing of children, to old age.[14] Children were born, died, grew up, left home; orphaned or elderly relatives may have joined a household. Workers and apprentices changed over time. High death rates, especially for women due to the complications of childbirth, meant many husbands and wives lost a spouse. But most remarried quickly because a partner was needed for the unrelenting responsibilities of work and family survival.

While the organization of family and the work of the household of white colonial American families usually followed that of Europe, the work and family structure of Native Americans and American slaves followed different patterns. Family and household organization varied widely between tribes of Native Americans, but two generalizations can be made. First, economic success in Native American society was not based on private ownership of land as in households of European descent. Second, the roles of Native American men, women, and children often contrasted with the prescribed roles of men, women, and children in white families. For example, in seventeenth-century Powhatan culture, women grew the crops and participated in tribal government, unlike the English settlers in Virginia who viewed farming and government as male roles.[15]

Black families in the seventeenth, eighteenth, and nineteenth centuries followed different patterns due to slavery and the laws and social conventions concerning race. A slave's role in the household was as a laborer; the desires of slaves to form emotional and biological family ties were considered secondary. Initially, newly arrived American slaves created family relationships with other slaves unrelated by birth and from many different backgrounds in Africa. Rules governing slave families—who could marry, the choices allowed to slave men and women, the sale of spouses and children, and slave housing—varied widely between slave owners and the labor required for different crops such as cotton, tobacco, hemp, rice, or sugar cane. Since the labor of individual slaves contributed to the wealth of their owners and not to maintenance of their own spouses or children, slave households and families developed on very different models than those considered normal in white American families.

Figure 1.3. Slave families were affected by the laws and conditions of slavery. In this photo, taken in Virginia in 1862, it is impossible to determine the biological relationship between the five adults and five children. The location of the photograph, in front of what was probably their shared home, and position of the children, on the laps of or very near the adults, still communicate the emotional bonds of family.
G. H. Houghton, Photographer. "Family of Slaves at the Gaines' House in Hanover County, Virginia." 1862. (Courtesy of the Library of Congress)

Women had more voice in the slave family and family members were not always related biologically. For example, slave children were often cared for physically and emotionally by adults in the community to which they were not related by blood. Slave religion also served as a bond, especially when family members were sold. After emancipation, freed slaves sought spouses and children from which they had been separated and defined their freedom by creating nuclear family units and independent households. Husbands sought to define their roles as the heads of the households. But low wages of black husbands and debt accumulated from sharecropping meant black wives often had to work outside the family home as servants to support the family.[16]

Nineteenth-century industrialization slowly changed the nature of economic partnership between husbands and wives. The old word describing this family and economic partnership, *housewifery*, slowly fell out of usage. Over the century, housewifery acquired a new name representing this shift—*housework*. Before the era of industrialization, housework described the work of men, women, and children, since work for survival and economic gain took place in their own houses. But industrialization separated the family's dwelling from the workplace.

People, mostly men until the twentieth century, began to *go* to work away from the house and farm for jobs in factories, stores, or offices, while many women continued to work within the home. The term *housework* shifted to mean the work of a woman in the home to provide for the daily needs of the family members. Slowly, over a period of approximately one hundred years, industrialization changed the labor involved in feeding, clothing, and sheltering a family. The labor-intensive jobs of spinning, weaving, and sewing the clothing; producing, preserving, and preparing food; hauling water; heating the home; or doing laundry changed.[17]

Textile production was one of the first processes to be industrialized in eighteenth-century England, relieving women of the unending chores of spinning and weaving fabric. Affordable manufactured fabrics for clothing and other household needs could be purchased, but women still had to sew clothing by hand. The home sewing machine was not widely available until after the Civil War. In the first half of the nineteenth century, the kitchen stove was invented.

It replaced cooking at a hearth at an open fire, revolutionized how cooking and baking had been done for thousands of years, and required less wood to be chopped and hauled.[18]

Women's work changed slowly, over decades. Throughout the nineteenth and into the twentieth centuries, it made more economic sense for the women to perform the labor at home after marriage. The value of her work in the home was greater than the low wages she may have earned in the workplace, even for many low-income families that needed more than one adult wage earner.[19]

After the Civil War, the pace of new inventions quickened. Life was easier for those who could afford the new innovations. Urban homes of the upper classes were the first to get municipal water and sewer service, gas and electric power, and early household appliances. Working class families and rural farm families often did not have access to water, power, or the financial resources to purchase appliances or new houses with modern conveniences. Many rural areas in America did not have access to electrical power until the 1950s.

Cultural conceptions of a woman's role in the home shifted as more men worked away from the home and women's chores within the home changed. As work within the home slowly ceased to be the business of the entire family, women's work began to lose its economic value in the financial support of the household. The new term, *housework*, came to represent not just the chores related to food, clothing, and shelter, but also something women did because it was natural. Economic changes, religious and intellectual traditions, and pseudo-scientific explanations of the natural differences between men and women joined to justify separate and mutually exclusive roles of men and women in society. Nineteenth- and early twentieth-century women and men were expected to conform to middle class sex, gender, and social class roles defined by an ever-growing number of books, newspapers, and magazines.

Social Class, Social Status, and Family

Families are ranked in society—judged on where they live, what they eat, and how they behave and make a living. The words *class* and *status* are often used interchangeably to describe this ranking, but each has a specific meaning. *Social class* is objective, based on economic position or income. *Status*, on the other hand, is based on subjective factors. Status groups think of themselves as a social community with a common lifestyle and develop common customs related to everyday functions such as table manners, household routines, and roles of family members. These customs, assumptions, and behaviors are used to rank people within the status group, as well as used to exclude people from the group, just as income is used to rank social classes.[20]

Class and status are related. Status is usually determined by class (how much money one has or earns), but individuals or groups of people can shift to a different status by learning new customs or manners. Etiquette books, household manuals, advice in newspapers and magazines and even cookbooks depict the lifestyle and manners of a status group. Prior to the Industrial Revolution, books prescribing proper behavior, or manners, were written by and for an elite audience. Moving up in class and status from the lower classes to the nobility was nearly impossible in a world that defined class by birth, not by wealth.

But as economic opportunity expanded and the middle class grew in the eighteenth and nineteenth centuries, more and more advice was written by the middle class, reflecting the lifestyle of this new status group. These publications served as guides on how to exclude people who did not have the correct manners. Authors of this advice often assumed that a person born in a lower class could move up in the world by adopting the proper manners.

Different words and expressions throughout history have been used to describe the grouping of people in hierarchical categories based on income or lifestyle—estates, rank, order, social class, and socioeconomic class. Depending upon the era or point of reference, different categories have been recognized—bourgeoisie and the proletariat; upper, middle, and lower classes; white and blue collar; and elite and working class are just a few examples. A common misconception is a middle class has always existed throughout history.

In the pre-industrial world, only two social classes predominated: the very small minority of rich or elite, and everybody else. One's place in the world was determined by birth, not income. There were distinctions and hierarchies within the upper and lower classes, but the wide swath of people we call the middle class did not exist through most of history. A very small group of people may have fallen in the middle in some cultures, such as merchants living in towns. They may have had wealth, but in societies in which the elite had to be of noble birth, they were excluded.

The term *middling sort* was first used in seventeenth-century England. The growth of trade and colonialization in the early modern period (c. 1500s–1700s) meant more people were engaged in commerce. By the eighteenth century, these new sources of wealth opened opportunities for the middling sort of people to set themselves apart and possibly even enter the upper status groups. Therefore, applying the modern concept of middle class to groups of people prior to the eighteenth century is an anachronism. Middle class is a very general term for a group of people that has changed in size and composition over the last three hundred years as the economy and social structure shifted from agricultural to industrial (1700s and 1800s) to postindustrial era (1970s to present).

Sex, Gender, and Family
Males and females have distinct roles in a biological family. But historically, the sexual, reproductive roles have merged with cultural expectations for males and females, or gender. Only in the recent decades have the distinctions between sex and gender become prominent. Today, the word *sex* is used to indicate biological differences between males and female. On the other hand, *gender* refers to the characteristics a culture defines as masculine or feminine.

In the history of Western culture, sex and gender were generally seen as one and the same. Men were expected to be masculine; women were expected to be feminine. Lessons in these cultural expectations began in the household and were taught by the family. Individuals who did not conform to these expectations were considered outside the norm and criticized, ridiculed, or worse. Separating the concepts by using different words only began in the United States in the mid-twentieth century.[21]

Qualities considered masculine and feminine are not consistent over time and place. Definitions of masculine and feminine evolved as the roles of men, women, and children changed during the eighteenth, nineteenth, and twentieth centuries. Three assumptions about sex and gender are consistent throughout the span of Western history. While these assumptions are questioned more and more in the twenty-first century, they have certainly not disappeared.

First, men and women are often considered psychologically opposite, an assumption known as gender polarization. A gender-polarized society expects men to always be masculine, women to always be feminine, and any person or behavior crossing these lines is characterized as problematic—unnatural or immoral in the eyes of religious authority or biologically abnormal or pathological from a scientific perspective. Both men and women are made to feel insecure and vulnerable, constantly working to prove they are "real" men or women. Men who cross boundaries, often referred to as sissies, are punished more often than women, or the tomboys, who cross gender boundaries.[22]

Second, throughout history, most cultures have assumed men are inherently the dominant or superior sex. This male-centered perspective assumes the male experience is the neutral standard or norm and the female experience is a deviation from this norm. In Western culture, in both pre-Christian Greek and Roman societies, and Christianized Europe, men did hold most of the economic, legal, and political power.[23]

Finally, the belief that men are dominant and superior is often confirmed by a third argument—"it has always been that way" and is therefore assumed to be correct and true, or natural. In Jewish, Christian, and Muslim faiths, God was viewed as male, the leadership was traditionally male, and religion used to justify women's inferior status. Even after the advent of scientific research and reasoning, male dominance is often assumed.[24]

Students may suppose because the roles of males and females have changed so much when compared to the past that all is equal in modern society. But closer analysis often proves this wrong; modern ideals of the equality of the sexes conflict with daily realities in the home and workplace. Debates about gender identity issues demonstrate that many Americans view masculine and feminine as essential opposites. Challenge students to examine the assumptions of their own culture about the roles of men and women.

While examining the themes and primary sources, continually ask *why* women were expected to act one way, men in another manner, and if gendered roles in the family and home continue to exist today. Press students to analyze how the messages have changed or stayed the same. For example, both men and women can prepare food, clean the home, maintain an automobile, or mow the lawn. But cleaning products and household appliances are still marketed mainly to women while advertisements for lawn tools and automobiles are focused on men.

New Family for a New Era—The Nineteenth-Century Middle Class Family
Two ideals dominated how people thought about femininity, masculinity, and the roles of men and women in the family from the late eighteenth century into the twentieth century—*republican motherhood* and the *cult of true womanhood* or *cult of domesticity*. Republican motherhood is a modern phrase coined by historian Linda Kerber to describe the Enlightenment influence on the role of the ideal American women of the 1790s.

Republican motherhood prescribed a civic duty for women to become virtuous mothers who trained their sons to be model citizens for a new nation.[25] Even though women's work was required within the family for survival, men were assumed to be the natural leader and authority within the family. Women, viewed as morally superior and free of the worldly urges, were the natural choice for raising children in a religious home environment; men's natural role was to govern and earn money in a cutthroat world.

The ideals of republican motherhood merged with what was labeled the cult of true womanhood or the cult of domesticity in advice literature published between 1820 and 1860. A true woman was to be judged by her religious piety, sexual purity, submissiveness to her husband, and domestic accomplishments in the home.[26] Men and women were supposed to live in *separate spheres* of influence. Nineteenth century men were to display the masculine traits of rationality, power, domination, and drive to earn wages away from home. Women were expected to be the opposite—compassionate, humanitarian, and unsuited for the aggressive and sinful world outside the home, but the primary force within the home and in raising the children.

In marriage, the two opposites, men and women, were believed to be a perfect and complimentary whole.[27] Women were restricted from public roles in government and were not allowed to enter professions dominated by males. Outside the home, middle and upper class women were largely restricted to charitable efforts and religious and reform movements because these roles were compatible with their perceived feminine personalities and abilities.

Essays, sermons, novels, poems, and manuals offering advice reflecting these ideals began to flood the market in 1820s and 1830s and continued to be published throughout the following century. These publications focused upon the role of the mother, principles for raising children, the role of women in society, the appropriate types of education for women, and specific advice on appropriate manners of men and women.[28] Numerous domestic advice books and magazine articles were published defining the ideal home and described how a woman could create it through correct cooking, cleaning, decorating, managing her time and servants, and every other aspect of home construction and household management. Families that could afford it hired domestic workers to help the wife with daily chores, freeing her to dedicate more time to the children, leisure pursuits, and charity work in the community.

The cult of true womanhood and domestic advice literature for cooking and household management reflected the expectations of the middle class. Domestic advice of any era does not always describe the actual behavior of an era, but instead, the dominant code of behavior that was expected. It falls into a wider category called prescriptive literature, writing that instructs the reader how life should be conducted, a how-to book. This type of writing can reflect actual behavior but usually the advice is representative of the reality of one group of people and may have very little relationship to the lives of people of different social classes, sexes, races, regions, or age groups.

Was everyone in the nineteenth century middle class? No, just as everyone today is not middle class. But when one norm predominates in the media of an era, it is easy to be misled. One must be careful not to assume everyone *was* middle class, or everyone *wanted to be* middle class. The advice on behavior given in prescriptive literature creates a cultural expectation of how one should act, a standard used to measure one's own behavior and that of others. Over time, individuals accept (or reject) these rules and assume they are the norm without question. In other words, assumptions about behavior, learned from one's culture, become the reality of what people see and do.

By the late nineteenth century and first half of the twentieth century, the middle class grew and this status group became more defined. In the nineteenth century, doctors, lawyers, business entrepreneurs, and bankers and their wives and children were the most prosperous members of the middle class. These professionals had excellent incomes but were often at risk of financial disaster in an economic downturn, which was common in the late 1800s. Ministers, skilled craftsmen, small businessmen, newspaper editors, teachers, and well-established farmers earned a wide range of incomes, but their families were also considered middle class.

By 1915, the growth of large corporations, mass retailers, and the government bureaucracy created a new, large group of white-collar, middle class employees distinguished from the working class by better education and salaried jobs that did not require manual labor. This group included factory supervisors and technicians, clerks, salespeople, bookkeepers, middle managers, and civil servants. But incomes of those in the middle class widely varied depending on sex, age, race, location, and occupation.[29]

How did men feel about the nineteenth-century idealization of domesticity and the role of women within the home? Before the nineteenth century, the father was the head of the household—the chief executive officer of the workplace and the people in it. The masculinity of a man was measured by his ability to establish, protect, provide, and control a well-functioning and productive household that included work and family. In the nineteenth century, when the workplace and men began to be separated from the household, the traditional masculine role in the home was undermined.

Figure 1.4. The ideal nineteenth-century woman, as portrayed in essays, sermons, and household advice literature, was a white, middle class wife and mother. In this advertisement from 1904, the words and image reinforce this ideal and suggest the mother is the heart of this comfortable home and must purchase products to demonstrate her love for her children.
Advertisement, Pear's Soap. *Munsey's Magazine*, Vol. 31, no. 3 (June 1904), Advertising Section.

Domesticity, the sphere of women, transformed the household into a place dominated by women. Many men fully endorsed it in publications, letters, and diaries and the ideal was especially promoted within Evangelical Christianity. From the 1830s to the 1870s, many men seemed to believe middle class men had time for the domestic life with their family, needed it, and should embrace it. Upon closer examination, men were not as supportive of the ideal as it appeared. The new expectation of spending time at home with the wife and children conflicted with male traditions of spending time with other men in clubs, taverns, and male-only committees and civic associations.

Domesticity also conflicted with the traditional expectation that men should be heroic and adventurous. How could a man be a masculine soldier, sailor, or explorer when he was expected to spend very un-masculine evenings at home with his wife and children? And what would happen to sons raised in the very feminine environment recommended as the ideal domestic home?

After the 1870s, domesticity lost some of its appeal. Publications of the era began portraying it as unfulfilling for men and a threat to masculinity.[30] Men came to resent and question female leadership of temperance, female suffrage, and other reform movements. For example, the temperance movement attacked the male culture of drinking alcohol and saloons, claiming temperance protected women and children. Suffragettes were threatening the male domain of politics.[31]

Views of childhood also shifted in nineteenth-century middle class households. In medieval Europe until the eighteenth century, most children began to share in the work and life of adults around the age of seven. Education for the majority did not consist of formal schooling. Instead, children learned the skills needed for survival and for their trade from family members or through apprenticeships.[32] As production moved away from the household, children ceased to be viewed as laborers needed for the survival of the household.

In the ideal middle class home children were to be nurtured and educated to become ideal citizens—model wives for girls, professional careers for boys. On average, the number of American children per family declined from seven to three. The concepts of childhood and adolescence were invented, defining new special stages in life focused on play and schooling. Children no longer were expected to work to help support the family. Middle class mothers were instructed on how to properly raise children, and by the late nineteenth century publishers were creating magazines and books especially for young people. Manufacturers and advertisers created and marketed more and more products especially for children—toys, bicycles, and special foods.[33]

This middle class family pattern was not followed by all nineteenth-century American families. Religious and utopian communities followed different and often controversial arrangements. The Shakers family was a household of adult men and women living communally as brothers and sisters instead of husbands and wives. The Oneida Community members practiced what they called complex marriage in which the adults were forbidden to have exclusive sexual relationships and children were raised by the entire community instead of only by their biological parents.

The Hutterites, a European religious group that originated during the Radical Reformation of the sixteenth century and immigrated to the northern Great Plains in the nineteenth century, still live in individual family houses but own property, work, and dine communally. The work of both men and women contribute to the economic success of the community, but men and women work in roles traditionally assigned to their sex.

Working class families also followed different family patterns, often due to economic hardship. Immigrant and African American families faced additional challenges such as long-term separations and racism. Urban working class and farm families continued to function as cooperative economic units.[34] For example, many urban women and children in the late 1800s did piece work for clothing manufacturers in their homes for low wages while the men in the family worked in traditional industrial settings. Many rural and frontier families, men, women, and children, continued to live a pre-industrial life.

By the twentieth century, the middle class domestic ideal of a working husband and stay-home wife, recommended widely advice books, popular novels, magazines, and newspapers, was an American badge of economic success. Over the first half of the twentieth century, as women gained the right to vote and more women entered the workforce, the important status of being a housewife steadily declined.

Mass-produced appliances, smaller home sizes, and the availability of processed food made the work of maintaining the home and feeding the family easier. By the 1950s, many middle class housewives, while economically secure, felt isolated and unappreciated, a feeling Betty Freidan identified as "the problem that had no name" in *The Feminine Mystique* in 1963. The women's movement of the 1960s and 1970s viewed the ideal of domesticity as oppressive and out-of-style and even though housework was still required, it was often despised.[35]

Figure 1.5. In this 1912 photograph, a mother and three sons, ages 5, 7, and 12, are manufacturing clothing for Campbell Kid dolls in their small apartment. Campbell Kid dolls advertised Campbell's Soup. While middle class children of the era were attending school and had free time for play, this family resembled the pre-industrial era when the work of everyone in the household was required for survival. This and other documentary photographs of Lewis Hine changed views on child labor in the United States.
Photograph, Lewis Wickes Hine, Photographer. "New York Tenement Family, March 1912." (Courtesy Library of Congress)

In three hundred years, the shift from agricultural to an industrial to the twenty-first century post-industrial economy has revolutionized daily life. Households have become consumers, not producers. Economic and technological changes transformed the meaning of family and household, the nature of work in and outside the home, and the roles of the men, women, children, and families, and definitions of masculine and feminine. The history of houses, homes, food, and cooking demonstrate these shifts.

In the Classroom

Essential Question

A normal family—is that really a thing?

Family is a concept. A concept is a general idea, derived from specific experiences and assigned various attributes that range from concrete objects to complex ideas. The following concept development activity asks students to explore how their individual concept consists of many different personal experiences and attributes related to family. At the same time, students compare and contrast their concept of family with those of other students.[36]

First, display the word *family* on the board and ask students to brainstorm, individually, a list of words and short phrases related to family. Explain to the students these lists will be used in an activity on the following day. Gather, compile, and edit the lists so words and phrases are not repeated. Add the words *normal*, *traditional*, and *non-traditional* if students did not include these words. Additional words and phrases related to family homes and food such as home sweet home, family room, or home cooking can also be added.

On the following day, distribute the lists of words and phrases to pairs or small groups of students. Instruct students to cut the words and phrases apart and reassemble them in categories. Do not provide names of categories; explain to the students that they must decide what categories are the most appropriate. Provide blank slips of colored paper to be used for category labels. After the words have been sorted into categories, ask groups to share the categories they created and explain why they placed various words or phrases in the categories.

Next, explain the meanings of subjective and objective and provide students with a simple definition. For example, objective words have fact-based definitions everyone can agree upon. Subjective words are interpreted differently by different people and involve individual emotions or feelings. Then ask students to sort the words in each category into subcategories labeled subjective and objective.

Finally, explore subjective meanings of normal, traditional, and non-traditional family. Question students and provide hints so they conclude that a normal family may be defined differently from person to person and in different cultures and time periods. Ask students if concepts of family reflect only twenty-first-century families or if they could also apply to families in previous historical eras. Student answers will vary, but encourage students to reexamine their concepts of family by providing historical facts about families in the past.

Depending upon the focus of the units or lessons that follow, students could be asked to re-sort the words using new categories. For example, students could sort the words related to family into male and female or masculine and feminine categories for discussion about how cultures define specific family roles for men and women.

Normal and Average Using U.S. Census Data

Normal is subjective; its meaning is different from person to person and across time and culture. Norms are cultural principles that guide or regulate the behavior of the members of a group.[37] Average is objective and quantifiable. In math, averages can be obtained by adding a set of numbers and dividing but the number in the set. In this activity, students contrast the subjective concept of a normal to the objective concept of average using modern and historical U.S. Census data.

Introduce the lesson by projecting one or more images of families and ask students to explain how the image represents or contradicts conceptions of a normal family. Images can be historical or modern. For example, an image of a current popular television, movie, or celebrity family might be projected first, as a starting point for discussion. Formal family portraits or snapshots described in the following activity may also be used.

After discussing how the projected images represent normal, ask students to consider where quantifiable information about average families might be obtained. If needed, explain the difference between cultural norms and mathematical averages. Introduce students to the history of the U.S. Census Bureau, its website, and the wealth of data provided about families and households since the first American census in 1790. Ask students to explore the summaries of demographic data about families and households collected over time by the U.S. Census Bureau[38] and make conclusions about changes in families over time and the causes and impact of those changes.

Essential Question

How do we separate ideals about family from reality?

In eras before industrialization, family portraits represented wealth and power. But by the eighteenth century, portraits of middle class families began to appear and the invention of the camera in the nineteenth century made a family portrait possible for almost everyone.

Assemble a set of family portraits from a range of historical eras or a specific historical era and ask students to analyze how the images represents both ideals and realities of family. Remind students that social historians analyze many different primary sources from a historical era and make conclusions about a culture based on repeated patterns over time, rather than only concentrating on one unique example from the past. Encourage students to see the similarities in the set.

As a contrast, provide a set of modern family portraits to stimulate discussion. Use an internet image search for "family portrait" and project the numerous results; students will be able to quickly identify key similarities and difference.

Prompt discussion, through questioning, encouraging students to conclude what has changed, what has stayed the same, and what may account for these patterns of change or continuity over time.

Formal family portraits convey many different meanings. A close study of the clothing and setting can provide details about fashions of an era and the social status of the family. The individuals portrayed in the family communicate information about who is considered a part of a family unit or household. Who is portrayed and what is their relationship? Are additional household members included such as maids or pets? How the people are arranged in a photograph indicate positions of power or influence. The head of the household is often in the center of a photograph; less powerful members are on the edges. Viewed as a set, family portraits also convey what was popular in an era, and messages about wider cultural norms.

But paintings and photographs can also deceive. Is the setting and background really the home or property of the family? Or has the setting been chosen because it is popular at the time or chosen to convey wealth or status? Is the family portrayed as they really are, or how they wish to be perceived? Consider what information is invisible in a portrait. Does a viewer really know the relationships between family members, or assume based on his or her own cultural experience. In other words, what might appear to be traditional might, in fact, be something very different.

Individual experience and modern cultural assumptions shape interpretations of the past. For example, students may assume the serious expressions in historical paintings and photographs indicate negative emotions. In reality, smiling in pictures is a modern practice that began in the early twentieth century when snapshots taken with new small, personal cameras were possible. Before that, smiles in portraits were associated with the lower class, peasants, drunk people, or those with intellectual disabilities.[39]

The agency of the individuals must be considered. A new type of modern portrait, the selfie, can be used to demonstrate agency. A selfie is a visual autobiography; the person taking the picture has complete agency over how he or she is portrayed. Ask students to consider how they edit their own selfies to communicate messages to others.

A formal portrait may communicate more about how the family wants to be perceived than everyday reality. Who chose the clothing worn by the family members? Did each family member choose their own? Or was it chosen by a parent or the artist? Who chose the background? Does the clothing and background communicate specific information about the family portrayed, or styles and expectations about what a family portrait ought to look like in that era?

The subjects of snapshots often have much less agency and snapshots may reveal more about the routines of daily life. Examine the background carefully. What objects appear representing daily life that would not be present in a formal portrait? Keep in mind that family snapshots often portray special occasions, such as vacations or celebrations, rather than daily routines. A very helpful resource that explores the interpretation of visual images in the classroom is *Examining the Evidence, Seven Strategies for Teaching with Primary Sources* by Hilary Mac Austin and Kathleen Thompson.

Families as Measure of Time

Shifts in the roles of the family have taken place over centuries. Changes that are often invisible or barely noticed during the lifetime of an individual are revealed when examined over decades or centuries. Because social trends change over time, it is important students take a wide view of time, rather than one based on specific dates on a timeline. One way to help students comprehend the slow pace of social change is to frame time in *familial generations*. A familial generation is from the birth of a parent to the birth of a child and it was around twenty years for most of history. But this increased to about thirty years from the eighteenth century to today.

During the study of any historical unit, break down the typical timeline into familial generations. For example, the early years of the Industrial Revolution in the United States are seven or eight generations removed from today; when the students' fifth, sixth, or seventh great-grandparents were alive. The Middle Ages spanned approximately one thousand years or fifty familial generations. The time between the Revolutionary War and the Civil War was two or three familial generations. In other words, if one lived during the Civil War, his or her grandparents may have participated in the Revolutionary War.

A *social generation* or a *cohort* is a group of people who were born in the same date range and share the same experiences. In modern historical eras when technological, economic, or intellectual changes have occurred quickly, a generation of young people may have very different life experiences, thus making their daily lives and attitudes different from their parents' or grandparents' generation. The younger generation may have greater opportunities to move to a higher socioeconomic status or to a different region of the country or world and thus adopt different ways of living. On the other hand, in pre-industrial societies the pace of change was generally much slower, so the lives of children, their parents, grandparents, and great-grandparents may have been very similar.

Encourage students to examine the lives of historical figures in the context of contemporary social cohorts. For example, the leaders of the American Revolution did not just represent regional or class interests, they also represented different social generations. Edward Rutledge (1749–1800) was just twenty-six when he signed the Declaration of Independence; Benjamin Franklin (1705–1790) was the oldest signer at seventy years old, old enough to be Rutledge's grandfather or even great-grandfather. Ask students to consider how their opinions differ from their grandparents or great-grandparents and how that might impact political or economic policies.

Family trees, easy to obtain in the era of online genealogy, can assist in illustrating both the distance in time of past eras and how family structure has changed. Many educational resources are available for genealogical research in the classroom, but teachers should always be cognizant that the family structure and history of all students may not allow for traditional genealogy based on biological descent.

Notes

1. Stephanie Coontz, *The Way We Never Were: American Families and the Nostalgia Trap* (New York: Basic Books, 1992, 2000).
2. Steven Mintz and Susan Kellogg, *Domestic Revolutions, A Social History of American Family Life* (New York: The Free Press, 1988), 251–52.
3. Ibid., 251–52.
4. "Family," *Oxford Encyclopedia of American Social History*, vol. 1, ed. Lynn Dumenil (Oxford: Oxford University Press, 2012), 367–69.
5. Stephanie Coontz, *Marriage, A History: How Love Conquered Marriage* (New York: Penguin Books, 2005), 53, 70.
6. Mintz and Kellogg, *Domestic Revolutions*, 251–52.
7. David Herlihy, *Medieval Households* (Cambridge, MA: Harvard University Press, 1985), 2–5.
8. John Stambaugh, *The Ancient Roman City* (Baltimore: The Johns Hopkins University Press, 1988), 158.
9. Herlihy, *Medieval Households*, 2–5, 28–29.
10. Ibid., 59.
11. Ibid., 158.
12. Ruth Schwartz Cowan, *More Work for Mother: The Ironies of Household Technology from the Open Hearth to the Microwave* (New York: Basic Books, 1983), 16–17.
13. Ibid., 21–25.
14. Susan Kellogg and Steven Mintz, "Family Structures," in *Encyclopedia of American Social History*, vol. 3, eds. Mary Kupiec Cayton, Elliott J. Gorn, and Peter W. Williams (New York: Charles Scribner's Sons, 1993), 1927–28.
15. "Family," *Oxford Encyclopedia of American Social History*, 369–71.
16. Ibid., 373–74.
17. Cowan, *More Work for Mother*, 18.
18. Jack Larkin, *The Reshaping of Everyday Life: 1790–1840* (New York: HarperPerennial, 1988), 105–48.
19. Coontz, *Marriage: A History*, 53, 70.
20. Dennis Gilbert, *The American Class Structure in an Age of Growing Inequality*, 9th ed. (Thousand Oaks, CA: Sage, 2015), 1–18.
21. *Oxford English Dictionary Online*, s.v. "gender, n.," June 2016, http://www.oed.com/view/Entry/77468?rskey=ZwrspE&result=1. The first use of the word gender to describe masculine and feminine roles as separate from biological female and male functions appeared in the *American Journal of Psychology* in 1945 and 1950.
22. Sandra Lipsitz Bem, *The Lenses of Gender: Transforming the Debate on Sexual Inequality* (New Haven, CT: Yale University Press, 1993), chapter 4.
23. Ibid., chapter 3. The word *androcentrism* is used to define this concept.
24. Ibid., chapter 2. This concept is referred to as biological and religious essentialism.
25. Linda Kerber, "The Republican Mother: Women and the Enlightenment—An American Perspective," *American Quarterly* 28, no. 2 (1976): 187–205.
26. Barbara Welter, "The Cult of True Womanhood: 1820–1860," *American Quarterly* 18, no. 2 (Summer 1966): 151–52.
27. Coontz, *Marriage, A History*, 155–56.
28. Nancy F. Cott, *The Bonds of Womanhood: "Woman's Sphere" in New England, 1780–1835* (New Haven, CT: Yale University Press, 1997), 63–64, accessed August 2016, eBook Collection, EBSCOhost.
29. Thomas J. Schlereth, *Victorian America: Transformations in Everyday Life, 1879–1915* (New York: HarperCollins, 1991), xiii; Daniel E. Sutherland, *The Expansion of Everyday Life, 1860–1879* (New York: HarperCollins, 1989), xii.

30. John Tosh, *A Man's Place: Masculinity and the Middle-Class Home in Victorian England* (New Haven, CT: Yale University Press 1999), 1–8, accessed September 2017, eBook Collection, EBSCOhost. Tosh's book concentrates on Victorian England, but his conclusions are also applicable to the United States in the nineteenth century.

31. Glenna Matthews, *"Just a Housewife": The Rise and Fall of Domesticity in America* (New York: Oxford University Press, 1987), 66–67.

32. Philippe Ariés, *Centuries of Childhood: A Social History of Family Life*, trans. Robert Baldick (New York: Vintage Books, 1962), 411.

33. Kellogg and Mintz, "Family Structures," 1931–33.

34. Ibid., 1933–37.

35. Matthews, *"Just a Housewife,"* xiii–xiv.

36. Mary Alice Gunter, Thomas H. Estes, and Jan Schwab, *Instruction: A Models Approach*, 3rd ed. (Boston: Allyn and Bacon, 1999), chapter 6, 101–121.

37. Merriam-Webster.com, s.v. "norm." May 2017.

38. U.S. Census Bureau, Families and Households, https://www.census.gov/topics/families/families-and-households.html, accessed May 2017.

39. Cristina Kotchemidova, "Why We Say 'Cheese': Producing the Smile in Snapshot Photography," *Critical Studies in Media Communication* 22, no. 1 (March 2005): 2–3, accessed March 2017, EBSCOhost.

CHAPTER TWO

Housing

Home, Sweet Home

Essential Questions
- How did daily home life of pre-industrial families differ from life today?
- Do houses and their contents represent social class and status? Beliefs about the roles of men and women? Beliefs about family?
- How do historical sources affect interpretations of houses and homes?
- How do we separate the reality of daily life in the past from idealized depictions?

Houses and homes—the first is objective; the second is subjective. Houses are real, measurable, quantifiable, constructed of timber, brick, concrete, or steel. Home is an ideal; it exists in our minds. Homes are defined by a culture and the experiences of an individual. Houses are locations on a map; homes are places in our minds. These two overarching themes—what is real and what is ideal—are central to this chapter and demonstrate both separation and connection between objects and how people think of those objects.

First, housing for ordinary families in the pre-industrial era and during the transitional period of nineteenth and early twentieth centuries is examined. A house is a building for human habitation, historically the place of residence of a family.[1] Surviving historical dwellings or archeological remains, items within a house, tools used to build the house, descriptions, drawings, photographs, and floor plans of houses are a few of the primary sources for the study of historical housing.

Second, home as a cultural construct, an understanding of the world created by a society, is explored. What is home? The answer depends upon who is asked or which primary sources are used. Phrases like "home sweet home," "there's no place like home," and "home is where the heart is" convey a feeling of love and attachment to a dwelling and to belongings, friends, and family associated with home.[2] This sense of place is emotional, nostalgic, mythical, and is conveyed through every sort of historical and modern visual and written media. Artists' depictions of homes, descriptions of what ought to be or not be in a home, and advice about how men, women, and children should act at home are just a few of the primary sources providing insight into the meaning of home.

Historians must sort out the subjective and objective to gain a thorough understanding of the past. Likewise, modern students can learn and practice these critical analysis skills by comparing historical concepts of houses and homes to their own thoughts, experiences, and modern culture.

Architecture of Houses: Mass-Produced or Vernacular?

Modern housing styles are often indistinguishable. Modern houses or apartment buildings in one community are much the same as houses or apartments in any other region of the nation. The most obvious distinctions in modern housing is between the size and luxury of the dwellings for people of different social classes. But homogenous housing styles are relatively new in human history.

Prior to the Industrial Revolution, differences caused by climate, cultures, and available building materials created what is called vernacular housing. *Vernacular housing* is a type of architecture based on local needs, created by local builders, often the owner, and reflecting local traditions. The homogenization of housing began with the Industrial Revolution. Home builders began to use nationally distributed house plans and mass-produced home building materials. New mechanical systems requiring electricity or gas power, prefabricated housing, and large commercial housing developments became the common standard nationwide by the twentieth century.

Buildings fall on a continuum spanning vernacular or folk, popular, and elite architecture. Most houses built today represent a broad popular culture. House designs are chosen from nationally distributed house plan books. Commercial builders prefer popular designs with appeal to a broad range of buyers. These homes can be reproduced as quickly and efficiently as possible using mass-produced and standardized lumber, fixtures, and other commercially available products. But new houses can blend contemporary trends with vernacular elements. For example, new homes in the American southwest are built in a pueblo style, imitating folk adobe homes of the region. In very rare situations will a person or family construct a new home with only locally available materials in an architectural style determined entirely by local tradition and climate. Vernacular older homes from previous eras still survive across the nation, but most have been adapted over time to meet modern needs and fashions.

Of all the world's dwellings, only a tiny proportion, 1 percent or less, have a one-of-a-kind design created by an architect that represent the elite end of the continuum.[3] A completely unique home with hand-crafted elements and fixtures restricts access to a wealthy upper class. Consider the homes designed the famous American architect Frank Lloyd Wright. The best-known example, Fallingwater in Pennsylvania, was designed for the Kaufman family in the 1930s. The family's wealth came from department store chains. The house, built across a waterfall, required a team of engineers and specially designed construction materials.

The lines between vernacular, popular, and elite architecture are permeable. For example, the American bungalow, especially popular from around 1880 to the 1930s, was originally a vernacular style used by British colonists in India. The style was adapted by American architects to create unique vacation homes of the elite. As the style became popular, it was influenced by Louisiana French vernacular homes and Spanish missions of the American southwest. Soon, plans for small bungalows appeared in popular magazines and the bungalow entered popular culture. Any American that could afford to build a house could have a bungalow built from an inexpensive house plan or order a kit from the Aladdin Company or Sears and Roebuck to be delivered by train for on-sight construction.[4]

Houses are historical primary sources representing many different decades or even centuries at once. Generations of occupants adapt and change the house to meet their needs and incorporate new technology or building trends. In 2013, over half of American housing units were over thirty years old; 40 percent were built between 1950 and 1979 and 20 percent before 1950.[5] Over time, houses constructed in the latest fashion fall out of style. These houses are either adapted to meet new needs of successive generations or they fall out of favor and physically decline or get abandoned or destroyed. Filtering and gentrification are modern terms describing the reuse of old homes and neighborhoods.

Filtering, or filtering down, occurs when a housing unit or a neighborhood declines and is occupied by progressively lower-income residents. In many cities and towns, entire neighborhoods, once considered the most stylish and desirable place to live by the middle or upper class, fall out of style. Large mansions are subdivided into apartments; new groups seeking lower rents move in. These new residents are often recent arrivals in the community, immigrants from abroad or poor migrants from other regions of the nation seeking work. But updating old houses to meet the new codes for health and safety is expensive and avoided if possible. Substandard dwellings often contribute to poor health. For example, lead paint and asbestos, banned in the 1970s, may be present in previously constructed homes and both cause health problems if not properly removed or covered.[6]

Homes constructed in the Uptown neighborhood in Chicago in the early 1900s were large, expensive upper middle class houses. By the 1950s, the neighborhood was no longer the most fashionable. The declining houses were subdivided and turned into cheap, run-down apartments for migrants from the south and Appalachia seeking work. The neighborhood became known as Hillbilly Heaven and its residents viewed as a problem population in need of reform (source 6). Today, Chicago's Uptown neighborhood is in the process of gentrification. The homes and neighborhood are being updated to meet the tastes of new middle and upper class residents, displacing the previous low-income residents.

32° BELOW ZERO and comfortable as could be desired

ALADDIN READI-CUT HOUSES SAVE MONEY

ALADDIN BUNGALOW erected at MOOSE JAW SASKATCHEWAN CANADA

Complete Five-Room House   Shipped Anywhere $298

Aladdin houses are real dwellings in every sense of the word. The Aladdin house consists of every item of material necessary for the erection and completion of the building, with the exception of the foundation and chimney. A completed Aladdin house is exactly the same as any first-class dwelling-house.

 Every single piece of material in an Aladdin house is cut in our mill to its proper length, breadth and thickness, and ready to be nailed together without further measuring, sawing or fitting. The Aladdin system of cutting and fitting saves over half the labor required in the erection and completion of the house, and more than cuts the time of erection in two.

100 Designs of Dwellings, Bungalows, Summer Cottages and Farm Buildings

The Aladdin catalog illustrates over one hundred designs of modern dwellings, bungalows, cottages, barns and garages, showing complete photographs, floor plans, specifications and description for each design, together with the prices for the complete buildings. Ask for catalog M.

Shipments made direct from our mills in Michigan, Florida, Texas, Kansas, Oregon and Toronto, Canada

Dwellings of from two rooms to twelve rooms are illustrated with prices from $125.00 up. Aladdin houses are manufactured and shipped from the several greatest lumber-producing sections of the country. High prices are thus eliminated and the material is purchased from the original producer. The price on each house includes material sufficient for the completion of the house as follows: all framing lumber cut to fit; siding cut to fit; flooring cut to fit; all outside and inside finish cut to fit; doors, windows, frames, casings, glass, hardware, locks, nails, paint and varnish for the outside and inside, shingles, plaster board for all rooms, with complete instructions and illustrations for erection, eliminating the necessity of skilled labor. Seven years' success of Aladdin houses have proven their money-saving and time-saving advantages.

NORTH AMERICAN CONSTRUCTION CO., General Offices, BAY CITY, MICHIGAN.

Send stamps for Catalog M   *Quick Shipments*

Figure 2.1. As the house building process was industrialized, home designs were standardized across the nation. By the early 1900s, houses could be selected from a catalog and the complete kit shipped anywhere served by a railroad. This 1912 advertisement offers a catalog of 100 house designs, features the popular bungalow design, and assures readers Aladdin Homes are appropriate for every climate.
Advertisement, Aladdin Homes. *Everybody's Magazine*, Vol. 26, no. 4 (April 1912): 59.

Old houses are reused and adapted for new uses, and these adaptations over time provide insight into change over time. Evolving architectural styles represent changes in the economy, technology, and culture. For example, an open living space is a current popular trend. While the kitchen, living, and dining rooms are one large space, family members each have their own spaces, individual bedrooms, bathrooms, play rooms for children, man caves or craft centers for men and women. Living rooms, dining rooms, individual bedrooms, and bathrooms are historical—these rooms were invented in a specific historical era and represent converging trends of that time. Some of these adaptations tell a straightforward story of technological change, such as availability of indoor plumbing, electricity, gas, telephone, or internet access. But social history, such as changes in family and conceptions of social class, can also be discovered in home architecture.

Life at Home—Then and Now

Pre-industrial houses and lives lived in those houses were completely different from the experience of most modern Americans. From the time humans first began growing crops and settling in permanent locations until the Industrial Revolution, the dwellings of most families contained more people crowded together in smaller and shared spaces used for multiple purposes—work, daily living, household chores, and sleeping.

Pre-industrial dwellings were dirty, dark, and too hot or too cold by modern standards. Average people rarely had access to running water in their home; water had to be carried from outside sources. Washing, cleaning, and bathing were labor-intensive tasks requiring not only hauling, but also heating water. Even soap had to be manufactured by the household. Heating and cooking involved burning some type of fuel that usually required hard labor to collect. The fuel and open fires created dirt, smoke, and burning hazards. Open fires did not provide the warmth in winter expected in homes today. Light was provided by the hearth fire or candles and only the wealthy could afford glass windows that allowed the maximum daylight. Public sanitation services such as sewer systems or garbage pickup were unknown or very limited in pre-industrial cultures. Toilets were separate from the home in privies or outhouses.

Modern standards of privacy were unknown by households in the past. Parents, children, and other household members slept in shared rooms and shared beds, often on pallets on the floor. The piece of furniture we call a bed was a luxury item. The one or two rooms in which pre-industrial households slept and ate also served as the workplace and storage space for the business of the family—agriculture, small scale production of goods, or shops. Amid daily living and work, other important life events occurred in pre-industrial homes. Babies were born and people died in the home, not in a hospital. Marriages and funerals took place in the home; events now associated with churches, funeral parlors, or other public spaces. Overnight guests, family, friends, business associates, boarders, and sometimes strangers, were welcomed in pre-industrial homes; today hotels provide those services.

Households were often larger in the pre-industrial world. Six people lived in the average household of free Americans between 1790 and 1840.[7] In 2013, only 4 percent of the occupied housing units in the United States had six or more people and 27 percent of the households contained only one person.[8] In 2015, the average household had only 2.5 people.[9] Crowded housing is defined by the U.S. Census Bureau as a housing unit with more than one person per room. In 1940, 20 percent of Americans lived in a crowded home, in 2000, only 6 percent.[10]

Pre-industrial homes were crowded with people, but not with furniture and household goods. Furniture, bedding, and clothing had to be manufactured by the household. Most families had only the bare minimum needed and these items were used completely until worn out. Only the well-off could afford extra or luxurious household goods. A few storage chests or boxes and a table served as work areas, storage spaces, and seating. Kitchens were stocked with a few basic tools—a knife, a bowl, a cookpot.

United States Census data provides a stark contrast between modern American dwellings and the living conditions of the pre-industrial era. While most pre-industrial households functioned in small spaces, usually much less than 1,000 square feet with one or two rooms, most modern Americans live in larger spaces, with more rooms, fewer people, and more privacy.

In 2013, only 1 percent of American housing units had one or two rooms and only 25 percent of homes had three or four rooms. Most modern American houses have five or more rooms—57 percent have five, six, or seven rooms and 17 percent of homes have eight or more rooms. Only 23 percent of modern housing units have less than 1,000 square feet and only 1 percent have no indoor bathroom.[11] Most Americans live in homes with electric lights, clean running water, modern plumbing and sewers, mechanical heat and air conditioning, garbage disposal services, and comfortable furnishings—dwellings that are safer, cleaner, and only require the flip of a switch and the money to pay the bills.

Changes in daily life can occur over months, years, decades, or centuries. While change in the pre-industrial era was slower than the modern pace of change, changes in habits and manners of daily living occur at varying paces in different locations among diverse social classes and cultures. The wealthy and those living in cities usually have access to conveniences and new technology first. For example, even though home plumbing systems were available in the late 1800s, nearly half of American homes still lacked complete plumbing systems in 1940.[12] Many homes in the United States did not have access to electric power until after World War II. Furthermore, one must keep in mind that although on average, living conditions in American homes have improved over the last century, many American households still do not have quality homes, food, and other requirements for a safe and healthy life.

Houses of Peasants and Farmers—The Average Working Household

A majority of pre-industrial households depended upon agriculture to make a living. Most peasant and farming households in pre-industrial Europe and America lived in free-standing houses. Therefore, houses of medieval European peasant and the American colonial and nineteenth-century farmer are the focus of this overview. The history of the very poorest groups without permanent homes, urban workers, the wealthy, and those living communally such as nuns, monks, and members of American utopias are very interesting, but space limitations do not allow for a meaningful discussion of those groups.

The experience of modern Americans is somewhat different—fewer work in agriculture, but houses are still the preferred dwelling for families. Today less than 2 percent of Americans work on farms, a decline from 40 percent in 1940 and 74 percent in 1800.[13] Eighty percent of modern Americans live in urban areas.[14] But a majority of Americans continue to live in detached houses (65 percent).[15]

A preference for a detached house is not new in American history; a house has been considered a requirement for successful American families since the colonial era. Today, a slight majority (51 percent) of American adults live in middle-income households[16] and owning a house is considered a badge of middle class status. Since the 1940s, the level of ownership of single-family detached homes has remained at around 60 percent.[17]

Housing in the Ancient World

Recreating the life of the people who worked the land in ancient Greece and Rome is difficult and generalizations about the houses of rural agricultural families in distant cultures should be made with caution. Ancient cultures extend over thousands of years and many different cultures, evidence is fragmentary, and the conclusions made by historians and archaeologists are never final or certain. New evidence can completely change understanding of the distant past. But based on available evidence, one fact is clear: the homes of working people in the ancient world were small compared to modern standards.

Written sources about the lives of ancient working people are meager. Textual references to agriculture are rare and consist of a few laws and agricultural handbooks written by and for wealthy landowners. These say little about the families who did the labor or their dwellings. Even defining the concept of farmer is difficult. Fragmentary sources indicate people called farmers in antiquity could have been wealthy absent landowners who owned slaves or hired day laborers. Or farmers could be renters or small land owners who did the work themselves or used slaves or free laborers. Peasants and farm slaves are depicted in some ancient art, but artists often idealize rural images for religious or political purposes.

Archaeologists have generally focused on urban settings and the large rural villas of the wealthy, not small farmsteads and homes of those who did the labor. Some ancient Greek and Roman rural buildings have been excavated, but because of lack of farm-related evidence at the sites, it is difficult to distinguish the actual purpose of many of these buildings. Many farm implements were made of wood and iron; both have deteriorated over time. In recent decades, landscape and aerial archaeologists are exploring more rural sites.[18]

Ancient farms may have been worked by people living in nearby villages, rather than on the farm itself. In 2009, a group of archaeologists began the excavation of a site believed to be a farmstead in Tuscany, Italy. They discovered a first-century cistern, a building that may have served as a granary, pottery shards, and a few coins. Studies done on remains provided information about the diet of the ancient residents, but the building that served as the dwelling was not located. The scholars speculated the peasantry may have lived in nearby villages, "commuting" to work sites and dwelling in temporary shelters when seasonal work needed to be done. A late fourth-century farmstead was also discovered on the same site. This household reused the walls and materials from the earlier buildings to construct a small house, attached to a larger wooden structure that many have been a barn or stable.[19]

Other excavations of ancient Roman farms have revealed small one- or two-room dwellings. Scholars discovered a first or second century BC two-roomed house, 32 × 36 feet, which also included a forecourt or entrance area and an exterior *dolium*, a large earthenware vase or container used in ancient Roman times for storage or transportation of goods. A single-roomed building, 36 × 5 feet, with a large forecourt and cistern from the era of the Emperor Augustus (27 BC–14 AD) has also been found.[20] Ancient farm households who worked in the fields, whether owners, renters, or slaves, probably lived in small dwellings with few rooms.

Pre-industrial working households often lived in apartment or tenement buildings in urban settings. Then, as now, urban houses and apartments of working people were generally smaller than rural houses because of high property values in towns and cities. In Roman cities during the Republic (509 BC–27 BC) most ordinary people lived in small *tabernae*, attached residences grouped in rows along a street. These one- or two-room buildings were used for the family home, workshops, and businesses. A *taberna* had a wide front door with folding shutters or a grill that could be opened for business during the day and closed for privacy. The front was used for business and commerce; the back room, if the *taberna* had more than one room, was used as a living area for the family. Some may have had small gardens in the rear and a mezzanine, a level inside similar to a balcony, that provided privacy.[21]

As the population of Rome grew, landlords began to construct apartment buildings called *insulae*, some with as many as five or six floors. These usually had storefronts of the first floor, open to the street. Many had an interior courtyard for light and air with a cistern to supply water and one latrine for the entire building. If the first floor was not used entirely for business, the best apartments made up of several rooms were also located there. The apartments got smaller and cheaper as one climbed to the upper floors and may have consisted of only one room. In the small apartments, there are no identifiable kitchens and food was either cooked using charcoal braziers (a small grill) or purchased already cooked from vendors.[22] Quiet and privacy would have been unknown to most working class Romans.

Small domestic structures on the edges of villages and cities, dating from the middle Byzantine period (c. 800–1300), have been found in Greece with one or two rooms for all household activities, business, cooking, sleeping, and storage. Archaeologists look for debris left by daily activities such as cooking to discover how the space in these small dwellings was used. They have concluded the cleaner areas were probably associated with sleeping. There areas were often paved with tile or stone slabs and may have had benches along the walls.[23]

Medieval Peasant Houses
Peasants were small-scale farmers that held subordinate social positions and had low incomes. Even though the medieval rural peasant is often viewed as a single group, a clear socioeconomic hierarchy existed from the lowest serf or unfree farm laborer to independent yeoman or peasant farmers who owned their own land.[24] Furthermore, while the pace of change was slow by modern standards, technological and economic innovations did occur over the one thousand years of the Middle Ages, slowly raising the standard of living and improving the dwellings of many working households.

Excavations have provided little information about individual peasant huts or houses prior to the tenth century. Most early medieval houses in England were very simple, built of rough timber and wattle-and-daub[25] or mud, and have not survived. Evidence of large dwellings, around 80 feet long and 15 to 25 feet wide, with nearby granaries and earthworks survive from the early Middle Ages in northern and western Europe. These served as both housing and protection for groups of peasant families. Livestock may have also been housed in these large dwellings for the security of the animals and the heat they could provide.[26]

The location of the indoor hearth for heating and cooking evolved over time. In ancient times, fire pits were often located at the center of the room with little ventilation to allow for smoke to escape. By the thirteenth century, hearths were against the wall, allowing for a second story. By the fourteenth century, fireplaces with chimneys were common and allowed smoke to escape more effectively.[27]

Communal residences grew smaller by the tenth century and were slowly replaced by small dwellings of one married couple and their household. In England, most homes of rural peasants followed a basic plan with two rooms on the ground floor, commonly called the hall and the parlor, and a loft space above. A byre (cow shed) was connected to the house or separate but located nearby. The hall was the all-purpose general living space. The parlor, also known as the solar or private room, was for the use of the immediate family members and for storage. Additional storage area was in the loft, or located under or in a space adjacent to the house. As the family resources grew, rooms could be added on to the original house or a full second story could be constructed.[28]

A few English houses of ordinary people built between the 1260s and the 1550s have survived. On average, the floor area of the houses is small (average of 880 sq. ft.), with low ceilings and attic or loft space above.[29] These houses belonged to more prosperous peasants, not the poorest. By the fourteenth century, animals were generally housed in separate barns, and prosperous peasants might also have buildings for crop storage, a bake house that could also be used for brewing, and other multipurpose buildings for storage or work.[30]

Houses in America—Pre-industrial to Twentieth Century
The houses of most American colonial families of the 1600 and 1700s were similar to houses of European peasants. For all but the wealthiest elite, houses were small with only a few all-purpose rooms. But very soon after the first colonists arrived, the upper classes built larger houses and with more comfortable furnishings serving not just as shelter and workplace, but also announcing the rank, status, and wealth of the owners. Early houses in different colonial regions—New England, the Middle Atlantic colonies, and the lower South—had distinct vernacular characteristics due to the climate, locally available building materials, and the European culture from which the colonists originated.[31]

Two styles widespread in the mid-section of colonial America were influenced by the English peasant traditions—the hall and parlor and the I house (figures 2.2 and 2.3). These styles were common first in Virginia, New Jersey, Pennsylvania, and Delaware in the seventeenth century and both spread westward and southward in the following two centuries. The floor plans of these two folk forms changed little over time and continued to be the dominant style in the Southeast well into the twentieth century.[32]

Figure 2.2. Hall and parlor house—side view. This West Virginia house was originally a log structure built between 1811 and 1830 with only two rooms and 400 square feet of living space. Wood clapboard siding, the ell, and shed were added later. This house and the I house in figure 2.3 demonstrate how houses are adapted and remodeled over time, representing different time periods, housing styles, and changing concepts of how families should live in their homes.
Photograph of George Judy Farm, Grant County West Virginia, 1933. Historic American Buildings Survey. (Courtesy Library of Congress)

Figure 2.3. I house—side view. This Kentucky I house was built in 1844 when the family remodeled their original log house. The log house was incorporated into the ell on the back. The interior was remodeled in a late nineteenth-century style and in the twentieth century, aluminum siding was added to the exterior. This house and its outbuildings were part of a family-operated farm and mill in central Kentucky. Figures 2.2 and 2.3 are from the Historical American Buildings Survey, a collection of over a half a million drawings, photographs, and histories of 38,600 historic structures and sites, accessible online through the Library of Congress.
Photograph of Guyn House, Woodford County, Kentucky, 1933. Historic American Buildings Survey. (Courtesy Library of Congress)

The simple two-room floor plan called hall and parlor was two rooms wide and one room deep, with a loft above. These houses were often no larger than 16 × 20 feet. The style was so common in the early 1600s in Virginia that it was sometimes called a Virginia house. The I house was similar to the hall and parlor because it was also two rooms wide and one room deep, but incorporated a full second story. The I house and the hall and parlor often had two front doors, one for each room, but the use of one door opening onto a central hallway became common after the mid-1700s.[33]

When homeowners expanded they usually added a front porch and a rearward addition in the form of a shed or an ell. An ell is a wing of a house built perpendicular, and usually behind the main portion of the house, and could have one and a half or two full stories. A shed is a single-story addition. Ells and shed additions were easy to add to an existing structure because they did not interfere with or weaken the original structure. As technology and fashions changed, more additions and details could be added, such the intricate spindles, brackets, and other woodwork of the late 1800s.

The limited space in the houses of colonists and westward-moving frontier families was multipurpose, like the houses of European peasants. In a single room dwelling, the fireplace at one end marked the space for cooking and entertaining; the sleeping area was located at the opposite side of the room. In houses with two ground-floor rooms, the hall was used for eating, indoor work, sitting, sleeping space for children and visitors, and for cooking.

The second room, the parlor or chamber, was the best room. The best bed and often the only bed belonging to the parents and the family's most valuable possessions were in the parlor. This space was reserved for formal entertaining on important occasions. Lofts or the two upstairs rooms in the I-house were used as spaces for sleeping and storage. But household members rarely had their own, private rooms just for sleeping, what we call a bedroom today.

Furniture and other household items were simple and met basic needs. Furniture included a table, often just boards laid across storage barrels or crates. Chairs were luxury items, time consuming to make and most homes only had one or two. People generally sat on benches, stools, or storage boxes. A few communal plates and spoons, often made of wood, metal tools such as a knife and fireplace implements such as pothook, gridiron, pot, and a few crockery items served the needs of preserving, cooking, and serving food. Houses also contained the tools needed for the work of the family—farming, dairying, brewing, spinning, or weaving.[34]

In an age before indoor plumbing, the privy, outhouse, or necessary house was an important part of the pre-industrial home. Placement was important because if it was too close, the household members could smell it, but if it was too far, the journey would be a challenge. Care was also taken to locate the outhouse on ground lower than the well. The connection between polluted drinking water and disease was understood, even if the scientific details were unknown.

On farms where plenty of space was available, the outhouse could be moved when the pit filled. In cities, where space for the outhouse was limited to a small backyard, outhouse pits had to be opened and cleaned out on a regular basis. For those who were unable to make the trip outdoors, or for use during cold nights, homes were often equipped with chamber pots. Emptying and cleaning the chamber pot was a part of the daily routine. Not all households built an outhouse; household members used the nearest patch of woods or brush.[35]

As families became more prosperous, more rooms were added onto the house and more household items were acquired. On prosperous farms, additions were often larger than the original house and could include large kitchens, porches, pantries or storage rooms, and areas for storing firewood. Rooms were designed for specialized chores such as work rooms for making cheese and butter or laundry rooms with separate stoves for boiling water to wash clothing. Large ell additions included extra bedrooms and allowed for light and air on three sides, a real advantage in an age before electric lights and air conditioning. Wells, gardens, and outbuildings such as a chicken house, pigsty, and corn cribs were located near the back of the house for easy access to the kitchen.[36]

Between the seventeenth century and the early twentieth century, the structure of urban and rural houses throughout America gradually changed to reflect new concepts of privacy, family, children, and domesticity. Within the house, new rooms, with new names and purposes, appeared. Even the houses of regular people contained more possessions—more factory-produced furniture and household items. Beginning in the early 1800s in America, mass-produced

Figure 2.4. In this nineteenth-century American genre painting, a guest, the war pension claim agent, is welcomed into a rural home. A bed is a prominent piece of furniture in the main room where the guest is entertained and the three women work at daily chores, sewing and preparing food.
Painting, Eastman Johnson, *The Pension Claim Agent*, 1867. (Courtesy of WikiArt)

consumer goods slowly made life more comfortable and the work of maintaining the household less laborious for more people lower down the scale of wealth and status. The daily habits of the families changed as their houses grew larger and their belongings increased.

The slow shift in where people slept and the history of a piece of furniture—the bed—provide insight into how concepts of privacy have changed since the pre-industrial era. For most of history, people in households of all social classes slept together in a shared space, frequently on stuffed pallets on the floor that could be easily moved out of the way during the day. The piece of furniture called a bed was a luxury item.

Sharing a pallet or a bed with others was common and in the difficult-to-heat homes of the pre-industrial era, provided warmth in the winter. In the modern world, people sharing a bed are often assumed to have a sexual relationship; this was not the case in the pre-industrial era. Unrelated adults shared beds in homes, as houseguests, or while traveling. The husband and wife may have shared the best bed with only each other, but young children often also slept in the parents' bed. Dependent household members shared pallets or beds. Sisters and female domestics slept together and across the room or in another room, brothers, male apprentice or laborers slept together.

The piece of furniture called a bed was a status symbol in the pre-industrial era. Well-to-do Europeans and Americans who could afford a bed on which to sleep and fine bedding displayed this symbol of wealth in the parlor or other rooms used to entertain guests. In the richest households, beds were large and elaborately carved with rich, embroidered curtains and layers of expensive sheets and blankets. Daily business and rituals took place in the very public bedrooms of European kings and queens.

Beginning in the seventeenth-century wealthy British homes, rooms called bed chambers began to be set aside as private spaces segregated by sex and by age. Children were expected to sleep in rooms separate from parents, boys to sleep in rooms separate from girls. In the early nineteenth century, as American families could afford larger homes and more furnishings they adopted these standards of privacy.

Over time, mass production lowered the price of beds and bedding and allowed more people to build additions or new homes with separate bedrooms. The parlor was still used for entertaining guests, but the parents' bed was removed and new furniture and home décor was purchased. Factory-made chairs, upholstered furniture such as sofas, carpets, curtains, printed pictures for the walls, clocks, dishes, and eventually organs and pianos became affordable for the average homeowner.[37]

In the 1830s and 1840s, as beds were moved from the parlor to private bedrooms, the meaning of the words *hall* and *parlor* shifted in meaning. The hall was no longer the all-purpose room; it became passage between rooms and an area where guests were welcomed. Front porches were added to the most up-to-date house plans and existing houses and promoted as public spaces to welcome guests away from the work located in the back of the home.

By the 1860s, specialized pieces of furniture were displayed in the hallways and became badges of middle class status. For example, the hall stand was needed for coats, hats, and umbrellas of guests; elaborate hall tables held card receivers for the visiting cards of respectable upper and middle class people.[38] The public space extended to a front lawn decorated with cast iron furniture, landscaping, and paved walkways.

As space within houses increased, new specialized rooms appeared on house plans and in homes for public and private household functions. Before the nineteenth century, pianos and organs were hand-crafted items and affordable only to the wealthy. As mass production methods produced more affordable parlor organs and pianos, these musical instruments became middle class status symbols. Parlors equipped with an organ or piano demonstrated the family could afford to purchase a large musical instrument, had the leisure time to enjoy it, and the culture and education to play it.

In larger homes, additional rooms designated as libraries and billiard rooms were intended for the use of men, women used morning rooms or boudoirs, children had nurseries. Front parlors were for entertaining guests while sitting rooms or family rooms became new private spaces where parents and their children spent their leisure time together.[39]

The dining room, a room dedicated only to eating, became common, to separate cooking from eating. Dining rooms were meant for guests; kitchens were hidden at the back of the house. Matching sets of tables, chairs, and sideboards and specialized serving dishes furnished these new spaces. The etiquette of serving and eating food became more complex. Families who could afford the expense hired servants to cook and clean. And servants necessitated extra bedrooms and service areas separate from the living and sleeping spaces of family members.[40] Homes with these new rooms sent the message the family had the money for a large home and stylish furnishings, leisure time, a wide social circle to invite into their home as guests, and the proper culture, manners, and education to behave properly.

Figure 2.5. Mass-produced reed organs and pianos were status symbols in parlors of late nineteenth-century and early twentieth-century homes. The stylishly dressed women in this 1909 advertisement are admiring a self-playing piano. The text encourages the reader to trade in the old piano for this new technology everyone in the family could enjoy.

Advertisement, Angelus Player-Piano, *McClure's Magazine* (December 1909): 118.

Free-standing houses in the country or the city were status symbols of those entering the growing middle class of the nineteenth century. As more people moved from farms for employment in towns and cities, the most desirable middle class house was in a suburb, close enough to take the street car, train, or car into the city, but with the advantages of the country—fresh air and green spaces.[41] Tenements in the city were considered suitable only for the poor and workers; the goal of working class households was to own a free-standing house.

Only in the late nineteenth century, as cities grew, population increased, and land prices in urban areas rose, did the middle and upper class consider living in multiple family dwellings socially acceptable. Two apartment houses for the wealthy, Hotel Pelham in Boston completed in 1890 and Stuyvesant Buildings in New York built in 1870, set the standard. The new terms *apartment houses* and *French flats* began to be used to distinguish these homes from the tenements of workers.[42]

Industrialization also changed the outside appearance of houses, construction methods, and materials. First was the shift from local materials such as hand-hewn logs or prairie sod to standardized lumber produced by sawmills. Sawmills began to be constructed in frontier settlements from the late 1700s and through the 1800s. The availability of mass-produced and cheaper iron nails and lumber in standardized sizes allowed home builders to adopt a new construction technique called balloon framing, still used for most free-standing homes today. Balloon framing first appeared in the 1830s in Chicago. Lightweight 2×4 inch boards from sawmills could quickly be nailed together by one or two carpenters to form the frame of the house. The walls are then covered with sawmill-finished planks.

The massive timbers used in most pre-industrial building styles had limited home builders to simple square floor plans, and the amount of hand labor required to construct these homes limited their size for all but the wealthiest. With balloon framing and manufactured materials, nineteenth-century home builders added architectural features imitating elaborate, decorative styles of more expensive mansions. Dormers, bays, wings, and oddly shaped front porches were added to average homes.[43] When a family could afford to build a new house, or enlarge or refurbish their old home, they could use the house plans in books by Andrew Jackson Downing[44] (1815–1852), domestic advisors such as Catharine Beecher (1800–1878), plans from mass-circulation magazines, such as *Ladies' Home Journal,* or mail order catalogs.

Mid and late nineteenth-century railroad expansion also contributed to the dramatic shifts in housing styles. By the early years of the twentieth century, a family could order an entire home kit to be assembled anywhere served by a railroad. Sears, Roebuck and Company, Montgomery Ward & Company, and the Aladdin Company offered mail order home kits. Sears sold more than 41,200 catalog homes between 1908 and 1929.[45] By 1900, the traditional forms for building using local materials and traditional plans survived only in areas isolated from rail service.

Through the nineteenth and into the twentieth century, the homes of average Americans across the nation lost many of their regional differences characteristic of vernacular architecture. Manufactured furnishings and improved construction technology and materials made comfortable homes more affordable to people of average earnings. But many Americans,rural and urban, continued to live small, crowded, and primitive conditions in housing without modern conveniences. Even in the twentieth century, as separate beds and bedrooms, indoor plumbing, sanitary sewage disposal, and gas or electric power became the expected standards of living, these conveniences were still not available or affordable to all Americans.

How Do Historical Sources Affect Interpretations of Houses and Homes?

Imagine a historian in the year 2500, attempting to reconstruct the homes of average families of late twentieth and early twenty-first-century America. Few examples of twenty-first-century dwellings will still exist and those that do will have been remodeled extensively over time to meet new standards and technology. The historian's recreation of the past will be determined by the surviving primary sources selected.

What if the historian uses popular print and media such as *Better Homes and Gardens* magazine and home and garden television shows? Will this future historian really grasp the reality of daily life? This historian will more likely find a version of daily life invented by housing and home goods industries seeking to sell goods to consumers. Historical images and print sources often tell an ideal story rather than reflecting daily reality. Historians must consult a wide range of sources for a balanced picture of the past.

Paintings and drawings from the pre-industrial era occasionally depict the interiors of homes. But art purchased by the wealthy provides little tangible evidence about daily lives of average households. In the seventeenth century, a new style of art appeared depicting lives of average people—genre painting. Genre paintings contrasted with previous styles

Figure 2.6. Genre paintings provide a glimpse into everyday life in the past. But the scenes often combine realistic, romanticized, imagined, and symbolic elements. Paintings of seventeenth-century Dutch homes have been compared with estate inventories from the same period, revealing that while the bed and mirror would have been in the main room of middle class homes, other elements were omitted or added by the artist.
Painting, *Interior with a Woman at the Virginals*, Emanuel de Witt, c. 1665-1670. (Courtesy of Wikimedia Commons)

of art—paintings of historic or mythical scenes and portraits of the wealthy with heroic, noble, or dramatic elements. Instead, genre painting depicted scenes of daily activities inside homes or in public places such as markets, inns, taverns, or fairs.

Genre painting first became popular in the seventeenth-century Dutch Republic where international trade and innovations in banking and corporate finance first created a large, affluent, urban middle class. This new group of patrons preferred paintings of landscapes, scenes from everyday life, and still life compositions of household objects and food. The popularity of genre painting spread to France, England, and the United States in the following centuries. As printing technology improved, inexpensive prints made from engravings of these images were affordable and especially popular with the middle class.

Genre paintings and prints provide a glimpse into homes before the invention of the camera, but historians must beware. The scenes in genre paintings are combinations of realistic, romanticized, imagined, and symbolic elements, just like many modern photograph and film images depicting contemporary homes. The historian must ask what is real, what is ideal, and what is missing that would have been a part of daily life, as well as consult additional sources.

Figure 2.6 is an example of a seventeenth-century Dutch genre painting. Several elements in this scene from the main room in middle class urban home are historically accurate. Decorative mirrors on the wall were popular. The large curtained bed of the homeowners would have been prominently located in the main room in which guests were greeted. In the wet, cool Dutch climate, the woman would have worn several layers of clothing indoors.

But other elements in the painting are not literal depictions of life during this era. Most urban Dutch homes were attached with windows at the front and back of the house or along one side, but not on both sides. Yet in this painting, the artist depicted light coming into the rooms from both sides of the house for a dramatic effect. A maid is sweeping the floor in the back room. But fewer than 20 percent of Dutch homes of the era employed servants.

To ascertain what was real and what was not, historians compare genre paintings to information from house inventories of the same era, in this case the Dutch Republic from 1665 to 1670. Since the Middle Ages, European and later, American, church, or secular authorities appointed appraisers to make probate inventories that were used to divide possessions of the deceased. In some cases, these appraisals listed items room-by-room, providing clues about the functions of various rooms, the activities that took place in different areas of the house and its outbuildings, and how the names of rooms and their contents changed over time.[46] For example, spitting in public, to clear phlegm from the throat or when chewing tobacco, was an acceptable part of daily life until the early twentieth century. European and American home inventories commonly included spittoons or cuspidors. Yet these items rarely appear in historic drawings and paintings of homes or public places.[47]

In figure 2.6, the black and white marble floors and the brass chandelier would not have been found in the middle class Dutch family homes. But both items were common in large public buildings such as courthouses. The Oriental rug on the floor in front of the bed was an expensive imported item in seventeenth-century Netherlands. If the family did own one, they would have displayed it on the table as a prized possession rather than allow it to get dirty on the floor. And only the wealthiest households owned a clavichord, a keyboard instrument similar to the modern piano.

Other items common in Dutch houses in the seventeenth century are missing: candlesticks, lamps, fireplaces, and stoves, which were regularly used for heat and lighting, are usually missing in paintings. Cupboards and chests used for storage, items used for work such as spinning wheels, everyday pewter dishes, tankards, pots, and pans are absent. Luxury goods that really were prominently displayed were often omitted by artists—porcelain dishes, patterned fabrics on walls and chairs, and paintings crowded together on the walls.

Artists chose to include or exclude items in paintings for several reasons. Adding objects that represented wealth may have appealed to buyers with aspirations to move up to a higher status. Various objects were often added or removed to create pleasing compositions and color combinations.

Furthermore, many of the objects were included because they held a symbolic meaning completely lost on the modern viewers. For example, images of children feeding cats or dogs were warnings against extravagance and waste. Warnings against sexual sins were often represented with musical instruments; mirrors symbolized vanity; maps symbolized worldly temptation. Tables loaded with food and porcelain and silver tableware may have represented wealth the owner of the painting had or hoped to have. But scenes of plenty also carried a religious warning that food and wealth were transitory but the Christian God was eternal.[48]

Genre paintings provide glimpses of daily life as well as political, economic, and social circumstances. This type of painting was especially popular during periods of technological, economic, social, or political change such as the Dutch Republic or the United States in the first half of the nineteenth century. American genre art flourished from 1830 to 1850 when Americans were seeking to define a new political system, understand the shift from an agricultural to urban economy, reinterpret regional differences as Americans moved westward, and sort out a new social hierarchy.

William Sidney Mount, John Lewis Krimmel, George Caleb Bingham, Eastman Johnson, and Lilly Martin Spencer are a few examples of popular artists of this era (figures 2.4 and 2.7). Their paintings and others with similar themes were reproduced as inexpensive lithograph prints to decorate the homes of average Americans. The items in homes and the people portrayed in these works were glimpse into homes, but also symbolic of how Americans thought of urban and rural Americans of different social status.[49]

In the Classroom

Students come from different cultures, social classes, and households and may not want to share personal details in a school setting. Care should be taken to respect the dignity of all students. Therefore, the following activities require teachers to gather resources representing the range of homes and families in their students' communities rather than asking students to make comparisons to their own homes. Students may choose to volunteer examples from their lives

Figure 2.7. This 1856 genre painting depicts an upper middle class woman preparing food. But she is not at a hot stove in the kitchen. Instead, picturesque baskets of fruit are arranged on a table in a room with a carpeted floor. It was much more likely a cook and maid were preparing and serving food in a house of this status. The artist, Lilly Martin Spencer, was sending mixed messages about the role of the ideal housewife. On one hand, the image represents the nineteenth-century woman's sphere in the home. But the woman does not conform to the ideal in her flirtation with the viewer and saucy statement "if you try to kiss me, you'll really get a spoon full of molasses."

Painting, *Kiss Me and You'll Kiss the 'Lasses*, Lilly Martin Spencer, 1856. (Courtesy of Brooklyn Museum and Internet Archive)

and these contributions will certainly make the lesson richer, but teachers should mediate these discussions so that respect is given to all.

Essential Question

How did daily home life of pre-industrial families differ from life today?

The following activity can be incorporated into any unit of study from the ancient world to colonial America or a longer, interdisciplinary, thematic approach to family, food, and housing.

Before students arrive, measure and mark a space approximately 16 × 20 feet using masking tape to resemble a floor plan of a pre-industrial home. Divide the space into two rooms labeled hall and parlor. Later in the activity, students will explore this pre-industrial dwelling.

After students arrive, ask students, in small groups, to list the names of the rooms and spaces inside and outside a dwelling of a twenty-first-century family in their community. Do this prior to calling students' attention to the area marked with masking tape. Ask students to list the activities that take typically take place in each room, the most common appliances and furniture and if rooms are used primarily by males or females, adults or children.

Alternatively, to save time, the teacher can compile a list of rooms and spaces, assign a room to each group, and ask students to list the activities and objects in an assigned room. Lists of modern rooms and spaces might include kitchen, living or family room, dining room, bedroom, bathroom, basement, indoor or outdoor storages spaces such as garages or attics, porches, yards, or gardens as well as specialized spaces such as home offices, craft or hobby rooms, play or game rooms, laundry rooms, or man caves.

After students have considered the functions of modern dwellings, ask them to "step inside a two-room pre-industrial house" marked on the floor and imagine the daily life of a household of six people, the average household size of free Americans between 1790 and 1840.[50] Ask student groups to brainstorm what furniture might have been in the house, where it would have been located, and in what areas the daily activities such as eating, cooking, sleeping, working, or relaxing would have taken place. Ask them to consider if certain spaces and tasks in the home were primarily for men, women, or children.

At this point, the activity can be adapted in various ways to focus upon different elements of pre-industrial life, such as work, food, or family life, or the transition from pre-industrial to the modern world.

- Images and texts related to housing or households from a specific historical era can be provided by the teacher for student analysis.
- Through questioning and primary source analysis, students can analyze how technological change impacts people in a culture (pre-industrial or modern) at different rates and in different ways depending upon the social class, sex, and ethnicity of the household.
- As a follow up activity, individuals or groups can research and present how various household tasks were accomplished in a specific pre-industrial era, such as the layout and construction of dwellings, heating or cooling the home, how water was obtained and sewage disposed of, food production, preservation, and preparation, clothing production, cleaning, and laundry, the work that supported the household, and entertainment. Be sure to create an assignment requiring students go beyond just reporting or copy/pasting facts. Research projects should focus on larger essential questions such as those at the beginning of this chapter.

To illustrate how the transition from the pre-industrial to industrial economy and how it impacted household work, the following activities can be included.

- Describe how the pre-industrial dwelling was not just the home of a family, but also the workplace of the household. Ask students to imagine how this would impact how space was used in the dwelling and relationships between family members. Compare this to work in the modern era. In 2015, according to the Bureau of Labor Statistics, only 24 percent of employed people did all or some of their work at home.[51]
- Ask students what items in modern homes are handmade by the family without electric or power tools, thus excluding all factory-made items purchased in stores. With only a very few exceptions, students will struggle. They may mention antiques, but upon closer examination realize most are not used for their original purpose. The teacher may need to provide examples or show images of completely handmade pre-industrial household objects such as handmade furniture, fabrics, or household tools.

Essential Question

How do historical sources affect interpretations of houses and homes?

In the following activity, students interpret images of modern dwellings as symbols of social class and status and sources of information for daily living and cultural conceptions of home. It is also an excellent opportunity to introduce the meaning of enculturation, cultural construct, and the distinction between social class as determined by income, and social status demonstrated by lifestyle and manners.

Collect modern images of the inside and outside of dwellings representing upper, middle, and lower social class and status. Be sure to include idealized images from sources such as decorating magazines or websites, as well as photographs depicting actual dwellings. Provide sets of images to students and ask them to categorize the images by social class or status, identifying specific details leading to each decision. The teacher may want to provide distinctions between class and status to the students before the activity or explore the meanings afterward. Direct students to discuss and determine names of the social class and status categories used for categorization.

As student groups work, the teacher may need to provide hints or ask questions prompting students to consider what items are not present. For example, are dirty dishes, electrical extension cords, unemptied trash cans, and junk mail visible?

After students have categorized the images, through inquiry-style questioning, ask students to carefully examine *why* certain visual clues symbolize or represent social class or status. Encourage students to consider the source of this knowledge. Did they learn it from direct experience or from family, friends, or media (enculturation)? Students should also be asked to consider if a person from another country or historical era would make the same conclusions about class and status. What mistaken assumptions might be made (cultural construct)?

Next, ask the students to rate, on a scale of 1–5, whether various images represent an ideal home or one in which people really lived. Discuss and explain the visual cues that led them to assign the rating. Finally, ask students to consider the purpose of the creators of the images.

- Are the creators seeking to sell products, start a new household habit or routine, or convey messages about how individuals and families ought to act in their home?
- Is the creator seeking to make money, inspire reform, advocating a moral or religious belief, recommending ways to adapt to new conditions or technology?
- Do these types of ideal or prescriptive images really cause people to change how they think about their home and family?
- What is the long-term effect on individuals and a society of many different images with the same message? For example, if advertising for kitchen appliances and furnishings or craft rooms always feature women, how might this influence people viewing these advertisements? Or if images and advertising feature outdoor grills or lawn equipment always feature men, what might one conclude?

Essential Question

How do we separate the reality of daily life in the past from idealized depictions?

Home sweet home. What does the phrase really mean? The first documented use of the phrase "home sweet home" printed in English was in a collection of poems published in 1749. "Home sweet home" became the theme of songs, poems, stories, art, and chromolithography prints, inexpensive color images. A similar phrase "home is where the heart is" was first used in a poem published in an American newspaper in 1829 and several versions of songs with the phrase became popular in the 1840s.[52] Both phrases embody the nineteenth-century middle class glorification of home and family as well as a nostalgia for an idealized rural past.

The purpose of this activity is to explore the concept of place, discussed in more depth in chapter 6. Begin by asking students to describe, in writing, their own interpretation of the phrases "home sweet home" and "home is where the heart is." Ask volunteers to share all or part of their answers and discuss similarities and differences in interpretations.

Next, provide students, individually or in groups, the text of the following song and poem as well as artists' interpretations of "home sweet home." Many different recordings of the nineteenth-century song are available on the internet and can be played for students. Searching for the phrase "home sweet home" in Library of Congress's photos, prints, and drawings will provide dozens of nineteenth-century images contemporary to the poem and lyrics below. The 1985 version "Home Sweet Home" by the rock band Mötley Crüe and modern imagery for the phrase can also be provided for comparison.

The following questions can be used to focus student inquiry.

- According to the source, what type of house is the best?
- What people can be found in that house?
- What feelings and emotions are associated with home?
- What characteristics of home are supposed to draw the reader toward home?
- Is home located in the city or the country? What is the location appealing?
- What type of physical structure is home? Does that structure represent the experiences of all people? What groups are included? What groups are excluded?
- Does the source suggest the best home represents a specific social class? If so, identify these words or phrases. What social class is believed to be the best? Is a different social class criticized directly or indirectly?
- Do these depictions of home describe the experiences of everyone? Describe a different interpretation of home.
- Explain how these sources are representative of the concept of nostalgia.

In Song—"Home, Sweet Home"

These lyrics were written by American John Howard Payne and the melody composed by an Englishman Henry Bishop in the 1820s. The song was performed in musicals in London, Ireland, and New York City and quickly became a hit.[53]

Mid pleasures and palaces though we may roam
Be it ever so humble, there's no place like home
A charm from the skies seems to hallow us there
Which seek thro' the world, is ne'er met elsewhere

CHORUS: Home! Home!
Sweet, sweet home!
There's no place like home
There's no place like home!

An exile from home splendor dazzles in vain
Oh give me my lowly thatched cottage again
The birds singing gaily that came at my call
And gave me the peace of mind dearer than al
CHORUS
How sweet 'tis to sit 'neath a fond father's smile,
And the cares of a mother to soothe and beguile.
Let others delight 'mid new pleasures to roam,
But give me, oh give me the pleasures of home.
CHORUS

―――――◆―――――

In Poetry—*Home* by George Horton, 1893[54]

The prince rides up to palace gates,
And his eyes with tears are dim,
For he thinks of the beggar maiden sweet
Who may never wed with him.
    For home is where the heart is,
    In dwelling great and small
    And there's many a splendid palace
    That's never a home at all.
The yeoman comes to his little cot(tage)
With a song when day is done,
For his dearie is standing in the door
And his children to meet him run.
    For home is where the heart is,
    In dwelling great and small
    And there's many a splendid palace
    That's never a home at all.
Could I but live with my own sweetheart
In a hut with a sanded floor,
I'd be richer far than a loveless man
With fame and a golden store.
    For home is where the heart is,
    In dwelling great and small
    And a cottage lighted by lovelight
    Is the dearest home of all.

Historic Housing in Your Community

The database of the National Historic Register is a helpful tool for locating historical buildings and neighborhoods in your community. Created in 1966, the National Register of Historic Places and corresponding state historical preservation offices gather information and officially list buildings, sites, and neighborhoods worthy of historic preservation. The sites listed on the Register may or may not have been restored and many are not open to tourists, but the listing can help students learn about the history of their own community. Extensive research and documentation must be gathered to place a property on the National Historic Register, a project that is not beyond the abilities of many students.

The Historical American Buildings Survey is a collection of more than a half a million drawings, photographs, and histories of 38,600 of historic structures and sites, accessible online through the Library of Congress. Teachers and students can easily search for examples of buildings in their own communities and states. The collection is a part of the National Park Service's Heritage Documentation Programs that document the nation's important historic structures and landscapes.

Answering Essential Questions with Primary Sources

The following primary source excerpts, spanning American history from the late eighteenth to the mid twentieth centuries, can be used together or individually to illustrate several themes.

- The concept that dwellings, household furnishings, and daily routines change at different rates among different groups of people.
- How dwellings, furnishings, and customs are used to judge the social class and status of families.
- The wide range of primary sources used by historians to reconstruct information about dwellings and daily routines.
- Often accounts by tourists or outsiders can provide insight into daily life of the places they visit. Daily habits become invisible to a native of a culture or country because they are so familiar. Outsiders describe and comment upon local customs by making comparisons to their own, different experiences. But outsiders can also misinterpret the reasons for the local customs they observe. For example, in Source 6, "The Hillbillies Invade Chicago," the author fails to recognize the housing choices of Appalachians in Chicago are a result of economic limitations, not lazy lifestyle choices.

SOURCE 1

Excerpt from *Travels of a Frenchman in Maryland and Virginia* (1791) by Ferdinand-M. Bayard[55]

Description of slave quarters

A box-like frame made of boards hardly roughed down, upheld by stakes, was the family home. Some wheat straw and cornstalks, on which was spread a thin woolen blanket that was burned in several places, completed the wretched pallet of the enslaved couple... An old pot, tilted on some pieces of brick, was still white with *hominy*. A few rags... were hanging in one of the corners of the fireplace. An old pipe, very short, and a knife blade, which were sticking in the wall, were the only other items I found in this dwelling.

hominy—a dish made of corn.

SOURCE 2

Estate Inventory, Kentucky, 1802[56]

The following is an appraisal, or estate inventory, recorded in Kentucky in 1802. Moses Hiatt was born between 1775 and 1780, married in 1796, and died in his twenties in 1802. Hiatt lived in Garrard County, Kentucky, an area of the state first settled in the 1770s before the Revolutionary War. Kentucky became the fifteenth state in 1792, ten years before Hiatt's death.

The complete set of surviving appraisal documents for his estate includes a record of the sale of each item and the person to which it was sold. His widow, Isabella, purchased the largest part of the items listed in the appraisal. When compared to the appraisals of other estates in same area, the estate of Moses Hiatt was modest. But Moses Hiatt died in his twenties and likely would have accumulated more belongings over a lifetime. On the frontier, the challenges of long distance travel meant families of average means had few manufactured items that were available and affordable in cities and ports.

In appraisement of Moses Hiatt deceased estate

	£	s	d
One feather bed and furniture			12
Pewter (six plates and a dish), 2 pots, one skillet		3	17
Tin cups and crocks			
Two piggans, one bottle, one set knives and forks		11	6
One spinning wheel		12	
One pair cotton bands and one chain		8	
One chain and pothooks		8	
One ax and hoe			18
One plow, single trees and clevaces	1	20	
Two cows and calves and one heifer	6		
One cow and calf and one heifer	4	4	
Two heifers and one steer	5	8	
One cow and calf and yearling heifer	4		
Two pair harness (traces and collars) and one bell		13	
One mare and colt and one yearling colt		26	
One man's saddle and bridle and one steel trap		1	10
One pack saddle and washing tub		10	
Powder horn, shot bag and knife		5	
One hatchet		3	
Total	69	0	6

- £, s, d were the abbreviations for pounds, shillings, and pence, the British currency used in colonial America. There are 12 pence in a shilling and 20 shillings, or 240 pence, in a pound
- A piggan, usually spelled piggin, was a small wooden pail
- Chain and pothooks were used for cooking on a hearth
- Single trees and clevaces were equipment used to harness a plow to a horse
- Heifer—a young, female cow
- Steer—a young castrated bull that will become an ox used to pull wagons or plows

---

SOURCE 3

Excerpt from *Domestic Manners of the Americans* (1832) by Fanny Trollope[57]

Frances Milton Trollope (1779–1863) was an English novelist and writer who published an account of her travels through the United States. She lived briefly in Cincinnati, Ohio, which was a frontier town in the early 1800s.

The class of people [in Maryland] the most completely unlike any existing in England, are those who, farming their own freehold estates, and often possessing several slaves, yet live with as few of the refinements . . . the comforts of life as the very poorest English peasant. When in Maryland, I went into the houses of several of these small proprietors, and remained long enough, and looked and listened sufficiently, to obtain a tolerably correct idea of their manner of living.

One of these families consisted of a young man, his wife, two children, a female slave, and two young slave boys. The farm belonged to the wife, and, I was told, consisted of about three hundred acres of cleared land. The house was built of wood, and looked as if the three slaves might have overturned it, had they pushed hard against the gable end. It contained one room, of about twelve feet square, and another adjoining it, hardly larger than a closet; this second chamber was the lodging-room of the white part of the family. Above these rooms was a loft, without windows, where I was told the "staying company" who visited them, were lodged. Near this mansion was a "shanty," a black hole, without any window, which served as kitchen . . . and also as the lodging of the blacks.

We were invited to take tea with this family, and readily consented to do so. The furniture of the room was one heavy huge table and about six wooden chairs. When we arrived the lady was in rather a *dusky dishabille*, but she vehemently urged us to be seated, and then retired into the closet-chamber above mentioned. She continued to talk to us from behind the door, all kinds of "genteel country visiting talk," and at length emerged upon us in a smart new dress.

dusky dishabille—A loose, somewhat dirty, work dress.

SOURCE 4

Excerpt from *My Bondage and Freedom* (1855) by Frederick Douglass[58]

In the summer of 1843, I was traveling and lecturing, in company with William A. White, Esq., through the state of Indiana. Anti-slavery friends were not very abundant in Indiana, at that time, and beds were not more plentiful than friends. We often slept out [doors], in preference to sleeping in the houses, at some points. At the close of one of our meetings, we were invited home with a kindly-disposed old farmer, who, in the generous enthusiasm of the moment, seemed to have forgotten that he had but one spare bed, and that his guests were an ill-matched pair.

All went on pretty well, till near bed time, when signs of uneasiness began to show themselves, among the unsophisticated sons and daughters. White is remarkably fine looking, and very evidently a born gentleman; the idea of putting us in the same bed was hardly to be tolerated; and yet, there we were, and but the one bed for us, and that, by the way, was in the same room occupied by the other members of the family. White, as well as I, perceived the difficulty, for yonder slept the old folks, there the sons, and a little farther along slept the daughters; and but one other bed remained. Who should have this bed, was the puzzling question. There was some whispering between the old folks, some confused looks among the young, as the time for going to bed approached.

After witnessing the confusion as long as I liked, I relieved the kindly-disposed family by playfully saying, "Friend White, having got entirely rid of my prejudice against color, I think, as a proof of it, I must allow you to sleep with me to-night." White kept up the joke, by seeming to esteem himself the favored party, and thus the difficulty was removed. If we went to a hotel, and called for dinner, the landlord was sure to set one table for White and another for me, always taking him to be master, and me the servant. Large eyes were generally made when the order was given to remove the dishes from my table to that of White's. In those days, it was thought strange that a white man and a colored man could dine peaceably at the same table, and in some parts the strangeness of such a sight has not entirely subsided.

SOURCE 5

Excerpt from "Curious Kentuckians," *New York Times*, August 7, 1886.[59]

Kentucky Congressman Taulbee tells how his constituents live.

The ordinary house is a log one, consisting of two rooms, with boards shaved smooth with a draw knife, or slip, nailed over the cracks between the logs. One of the rooms is used for a sleeping room, and the other is the living room, dining room, kitchen, and parlor, all in one, in which the family stay during the daytime. There is but one sleeping room for a whole family, and when they have a guest visiting them the guests turn in and sleep in the same room. There are a number of beds used, and a stranger always gets the best bed. They are very modest with it all. They turn their backs if you are up, while the others of the family are undressing.

SOURCE 6

Excerpt from "The Hillbillies Invade Chicago" by Albert N. Votaw in *Harper's Magazine*, February 1958[60]

The city's toughest integration problem has nothing to do with Negroes. . . . The problem involves a small army of white, Protestant, Early American migrants from the South—who are usually proud, poor, primitive, and fast with a knife. . . . But the most conspicuous reason why the Southerners look all wrong in the city setting is the domestic habits they bring from small backwoods communities. Settling in deteriorating neighborhoods where they can stick with their own kind, they live as much as they can the way they lived back home. Often removing window screens, they sit half-dressed where it is cooler, and dispose of garbage the quickest way. . . . Their housekeeping is easy to the point of disorder, and they congregate in the evening on front porches and steps, where they find time for the sort of motionless relaxation that infuriates bustling city people. Their children play freely anywhere, without supervision. Fences and hedges break down; lawns go back to dirt.

Notes

1. *Oxford English Dictionary Online*, s.v. "house, n.1 and int.," June 2016, http://www.oed.com/view/Entry/88886.
2. *Oxford English Dictionary Online*, s.v. "home, n.1 and adj.," March 2017, http://www.oed.com/view/Entry/87869?redirectedFrom=home+sweet+home.
3. Paul Oliver, *Dwellings, The Vernacular House World Wide* (London: Phaidon Press Limited, 2003), 15.
4. Clay Lancaster, *The American Bungalow in Common Places: Readings in American Vernacular Architecture*, eds. Dell Upton and John Michael Vlach (Athens: University of Georgia Press, 1986), 79–106; Scott Erbes, "Manufacturing and Marketing the American Bungalow, The Aladdin Company, 1906–20," in *The American Home, Material Culture, Domestic Space, and Family Life*, ed. Eleanor Thompson (Winterthur, DE: Henry Francis Du Pont Winterthur Museum, 1998), 45–69.
5. U.S. Census Bureau, "American Housing Survey 2013 National Summary Tables," General Housing Data-All Housing Units, Table C-01-AH, https://www.census.gov/programs-surveys/ahs/data/2013/ahs-2013-summary-tables/national-summary-report-and-tables---ahs-2013.html, accessed October 2016.
6. Ernie Hood, "Dwelling Disparities: How Poor Housing Leads to Poor Health," *Environmental Health Perspectives* 113, no. 5 (May 2005): A310–A317, accessed October 2016, https://www.ncbi.nlm.nih.gov/pmc/articles/PMC1257572/.
7. Jack Larkin, *The Reshaping of Everyday Life: 1790–1840* (New York: HarperPerennial, 1988), 11.
8. U.S. Census Bureau, "American Housing Survey 2013 National Summary Tables," Household Demographics-All Occupied Units, Table C-08A-AO, https://www.census.gov/programs-surveys/ahs/data/2013/ahs-2013-summary-tables/national-summary-report-and-tables---ahs-2013.html, accessed October 2016.
9. U.S. Census Bureau, "Historical Households Tables," Table HH-4. Households by Size: 1960 to Present, https://www.census.gov/data/tables/time-series/demo/families/households.html, accessed October 2016.
10. U.S. Census Bureau, "Historical Census of Housing Tables," Crowding, http://www.census.gov/housing/census/data/crowding.html, accessed October 2016.
11. U.S. Census Bureau, "American Housing Survey 2013 National Summary Tables," Table C-02-AH, Rooms, Size, and Amenities—All Housing Units, http://www.census.gov/programs-surveys/ahs/data/2013/ahs-2013-summary-tables/national-summary-report-and-tables---ahs-2013.html, accessed October 2016.
12. U.S. Census Bureau, "Historical Census of Housing Tables," Plumbing Facilities, https://www.census.gov/housing/census/data/plumbing.html.
13. U.S. Census Bureau, "Series D 167-181- Labor Force and Employment by Industry: 1800–1960," Labor, Labor Face, Series D 1-682, 139. https://www2.census.gov/prod2/statcomp/documents/CT1970p1-05.pdf, accessed October 2016.
14. U.S. Census Bureau, "Geography" 2010 Census Urban Area Facts, https://www.census.gov/geo/reference/ua/uafacts.html, accessed October 2016.
15. U.S. Census Bureau, "American Housing Survey 2013 National Summary Tables," Table C-01-AH, General Housing Data—All Housing Units, http://www.census.gov/programs-surveys/ahs/data/2013/ahs-2013-summary-tables/national-summary-report-and-tables---ahs-2013.html, accessed October 2016. The remaining 37 percent of modern housing is made up of apartments, mobile homes, and other types of dwellings.
16. Richard Fry and Rakesh Kochhar, "Are You in the American Middle Class?" Pew Research Center, May 11, 2106, accessed October 2016, http://www.pewresearch.org/fact-tank/2016/05/11/are-you-in-the-american-middle-class/.
17. U.S. Census Bureau, "Historical Census of Housing Tables," Units in Structure, accessed October 2016, https://www.census.gov/hhes/www/housing/census/historic/units.html.

18. Signe Isager and Jens Erik Skydsgaard, *Ancient Greek Agriculture: An Introduction* (London: Taylor & Francis Routledge, 1992), 68–70.

19. Kim Bowes, Mariaelena Ghisleni, Cam Grey, and Emanuele Vaccaro, "Excavating the Roman Peasant," *Expedition Magazine*, 53, no. 2 (July 2011): 4–12, accessed June 2016, http://penn.museum/documents/publications/expedition/PDFs/53-2/bowes.pdf.

20. Mariaelena Ghisleni, Emanuele Vaccaro, Kim Bowes, Antonia Arnoldus, Michael MacKinnon, and Flavia Marani, "Excavating the Roman Peasant: Excavations at Pievina," *Papers of the British School at Rome* 79 (2011): 135, accessed June 2016, http://www.jstor.org/stable/41725305.

21. John Stambaugh, *The Ancient Roman City* (Baltimore: The Johns Hopkins University Press, 1988), 149, 168.

22. Ibid., 174–78.

23. Lefteris Sigalos, "Housing People in Medieval Greece," *International Journal of Historical Archaeology* 7, no. 3 (September 2003): 204–6, accessed June 2016, http://www.jstor.org/stable/20853025.

24. Christopher Dyer, *Everyday Life in Medieval England* (London: Hambledon Continuum, 2000), 134, accessed July 2016, eBook Collection EBSCOhost.

25. Sticks and twigs are interwoven to form a wall and then covered with various mixtures of clay, mud, animal dung, and straw.

26. A cow can generate enough 3,500–4,000 BTU an hour to warm an uninsulated 8 x 8 foot room to 65 degrees if the temperature outside is 30 degrees. Leifa Riis-Carstensen, "Using Cow Thermal Energy to Heat Homes in Winter," *Mother Earth News* (November/December 1982), accessed July 2016, http://www.motherearthnews.com/homesteading-and-livestock/cow-thermal-energy-to-heat-homes-zmaz82ndzgoe.

27. Robert Fossier, *Peasant Life in the Medieval West*, trans. Juliet Vale (Oxford, UK: Basil Blackwell, 1988), 67–72.

28. June A. Sheppard, "Vernacular Buildings in England and Wales: A Survey of Recent Work by Architects, Archaeologists and Social Historians," *Transactions of the Institute of British Geographers* 40 (December 1966): 21, 28–29, accessed June 2016, http://www.jstor.org/stable/621566.

29. Chris Catling, "How the Black Death Prompted a Building Boom," *Current Archaeology* 279 (June 2013): 13.

30. Dyers, *Everyday Life in Medieval England*, 140–41.

31. Fred B. Kniffen, "Folk Housing: Key to Diffusion," *Readings in American Vernacular Architecture*, eds. Dell Upton and John Michael Vlach (Athens, GA: University of Georgia Press, 1986), 13; Jan K. Gilliam, "The Evolution of the House in Early Virginia," *The American Home: Material Cultures, Domestic Space, and Family Life*, ed. Eleanor McD. Thompson (Winterthur, DE: Henry Francis du Pont Winterthur Museum, 1998), 177.

32. Virginia S. McAlester and Lee McAlester, *A Field Guide to American Houses* (New York: Alfred A. Knopf, 2006), 94–95.

33. Larkin, *The Reshaping of Everyday Life*, 186, 189.

34. Judith Flanders, *The Making of Home: The 500-Year Story of How Our Houses Became Our Homes* (New York: Thomas Dunne Books, 2014), 126–27; Larkin, *The Reshaping of Everyday Life*, chapter 3.

35. Larkin, *The Reshaping of Everyday Life*, 159–61.

36. John Stilgoe, *Common Landscape of America, 1580 to 1845* (New Haven, CT: Yale University Press, 1982), 159–64.

37. Flanders, *The Making of Home*, 55–93, 128 – 129; Larkin, *The Reshaping of Everyday Life*, 121–26, 139–48.

38. Kenneth L. Ames, *Death in the Dining Room and Other Tales of Victorian Culture* (Philadelphia: Temple University Press, 1992), chapter 1.

39. Ames, *Death in the Dining Room*, chapter 4; Clifford Edward Clark Jr., *The America Family Home, 1800–1860* (Chapel Hill: The University of North Carolina Press, 1986), chapter 2.

40. Ames, *Death in the Dining Room*, chapter 2; Clark, *The America Family Home, 1800–1860*, chapter 2.

41. John R. Stilgoe, *Borderland, Origins of the American Suburb, 1820–1939* (New Haven, CT: Yale University Press, 1988).

42. Dolores Hayden, *The Grand Domestic Revolution: A History of Feminist Designs for American Homes, Neighborhoods, and Cities* (Cambridge, MA: The MIT Press, 1981), 72.

43. John Stilgoe, *Common Landscape of America*, 321–22.

44. Andrew Jackson Downing, *The Architecture of Country Houses* (New York: D. Appleton & Company, 1851), Internet Archive, https://archive.org/details/architectureofco00down.

45. Robert A. Schweitzer and Michael W. R. Davis, *America's Favorite Homes: Mail-Order Catalogues as a Guide to Popular Early 20th Century Houses* (Detroit: Wayne State University Press, 1990).

46. Abbott Lowell Cummings, "Inside the Massachusetts House," *Readings in American Vernacular Architecture*, eds. Dell Upton and John Michael Vlach (Athens: University of Georgia Press, 1986), 219–39.

47. Flanders, *The Making of Home*, 12–15.

48. Ibid., 5–12.

49. Elizabeth Johns, *American Genre Paintings: The Politics of Everyday Life* (New Haven, CT: Yale University Press, 1991).

50. Larkin, *The Reshaping of Everyday Life*, 11.

51. Bureau of Labor Statistics, "24 percent of employed people did some or all of their work at home in 2015," July 8, 2016, accessed November 2016, https://www.bls.gov/opub/ted/2016/24-percent-of-employed-people-did-some-or-all-of-their-work-at-home-in-2015.htm.

52. *Oxford English Dictionary Online*, s.v. "home, n.1 and adj." March 2017, http://www.oed.com/view/Entry/87869?redirectedFrom=home+sweet+home.; Karl W. Petersilie and L. M. Brown, "'Tis Home Where the Heart Is," Notated Music (Philadelphia: George Willig, 1847), Library of Congress, accessed May 2017, https://www.loc.gov/item/sm1847.430850/; and "'Tis home where the heart is." Library of Congress, accessed May 2017, https://www.loc.gov/item/amss.hc00027d/.

53. Rosa Pendleton Chiles, "John Howard Payne: American Poet, Actor, Playwright, Consul and the Author of 'Home, Sweet Home,'" *Records of the Columbia Historical Society*, vol. 31/32 (Washington, DC, 1930): 251, accessed April 2017, http://www.jstor.org/stable/40067449.

54. George Horton, "Home," *Mansford's Magazine*, 37, no. 4 (April 1893): 237, accessed April 2017, Google Books.

55. Ferdinand-M. Bayard, *Travels of a Frenchman in Maryland and Virginia with a Description of Philadelphia and Baltimore, in 1791*, trans. and ed. Ben C. McCary (Williamsburg, VA: Ben C. McCary, 1950), 13, accessed April 2017, Hathi Trust Digital Library, https://babel.hathitrust.org/cgi/pt?id=mdp.39015027057820;view=1up;seq=6.

56. Estate Inventory of Moses Hiatt, 1802. Original document located in the Garrard County Court Clerk Archive, Garrard County Court House, Lancaster, Kentucky.

57. Fanny Trollope, *Domestic Manners of the Americans* (London: Whittaker, Treacher & Company; New York, 1832), 195, accessed April 2017, Internet Archive, https://archive.org/stream/domesticmannerso00troliala#page/194/mode/2up.

58. Frederick Douglass, *My Bondage and Freedom* (New York: Miller, Orton & Mulligan, 1855), 401–2, accessed April 2017, Documenting the American South, http://docsouth.unc.edu/neh/douglass55/douglass55.html.

59. "Curious Kentuckians," *New York Times*, August 7, 1886. *New York Times*, retrieved from ProQuest Historical Newspapers: New York Times.

60. Albert N. Votaw, "The Hillbillies Invade Chicago," *Harper's Magazine* (February 1958): 64–65.

CHAPTER THREE

Housework and Domestic Service

A Woman's Work Is Never Done

Essential Questions
- Who should do the chores in the home?
- Has the person responsible for the housework changed over time?
- How are social class and status of a family defined by who does household chores?
- How is housework valued by family members? By the wider society?

Today and in the past, families and houses require work. But over time, the nature of that work has changed dramatically. In the pre-industrial era, everyone in the household worked in an economic system where home and job were combined. Women, men, and children were a team who produced what was needed for survival—food, clothing, shelter, household goods, items to trade or sell. Wealthy households could afford servants or slaves to lighten the workload, but for average people, the work for survival was an unending cycle of physical labor.

Nineteenth-century industrialization dramatically changed the meaning of work—its location, the tasks defined as work, and how people were rewarded for work. Work became a location separate from the household; workers earned wages or salaries. Work and housework took on different meanings. In the new economic system, wives stayed at home and performed *housework* for free. Husbands left home and *worked* at a job for money. These earnings purchased manufactured clothing, food, shelter, household furnishings. Households evolved from producers to consumers.

Even though industrialization changed the meaning of work, one factor remained the same. Daily household chores such as cooking, cleaning, caring for the young are mostly done by women—mothers, daughters, unmarried female relatives, servants, or slaves. Even in the modern world, studies show while men and women are sharing household chores more than in the past, women are still responsible for most of the housework.[1] Over thousands of years, the daily work of women and qualities defining the feminine gender have become so intertwined that even today, the association between the two appears natural. Women's roles in the home have been idealized by many cultures and portrayed as a requirement for the proper functioning of the female, the family, society, and government.

The following chapter and primary source excerpts focus on the nineteenth- and early twentieth-century transition in the United States from a pre-industrial to an industrial economy and how those changes impacted housework and beliefs about who should perform that work. During this era, a maid became a symbol of economic success for a growing new group—the middle class. This trend impacted the design and uses of the houses as well as perceptions of social class, ethnicity, and the roles of women.

Upper class households had always been able to afford the expense of household slaves or servants. In the nineteenth century, families in the new affluent middle class could also hire help. Technology was changing household chores, but hard labor was still required. The ideologies of republican motherhood and the culture of domesticity prescribed new roles for the wife—educating moral children, creating comfortable living spaces that sheltered husband and family, and

Figure 3.1. Prang's Aids for Object Teaching—The Kitchen, c. 1874. This lithograph was one of a set of twelve used to teach elementary students about trades and occupations. Women are pictured in only three of the prints—in the kitchen, as an assistant to the male tailor, and working at the sales counter for a male baker. The other nine occupations featured only men, reinforcing the ideal of a separate sphere for men and women.
Lithograph, *Prang's Aids for Object Teaching—The Kitchen,* Boston: L. Prang & Co., c. 1874. (Courtesy Library of Congress)

doing worthy religious and charitable work. This left little time for daily chores; a maid was required if a middle class wife was to live up to these lofty goals. Hiring a maid also symbolized the charitable nature of the housewife, who in popular literature of the time was seen as a role model and teacher who turned lower-class servants into proper middle-class Americans.

Nineteenth-century domestic ideals set impossibly high and unrealistic standards for the behavior of both women and men. Many middle class women who employed servants struggled to understand why their servants did not appreciate the charity extended, failing to recognize their servants resented the low wages and difficult working conditions. Not all middle class husbands earned enough to employ domestic help, making them and their wives feel as if they were falling short of the ideal American family. Working-class husbands struggled to earn enough money so their wives could stay at home and achieve the domestic ideal. Working-class wives challenged feminine models when they entered the workforce, often working as servants in middle- and upper-class homes, instead of only serving only their family at home.

Domestic Service in America History

Today, *domestic worker* is the commonly used term for a person who cleans, cooks, or takes care of children or elderly dependents in the home. The people who provide domestic help today rarely live in the home full time, but rather work by the day or night while living in their own homes. While day workers did exist throughout history, live-in domestic servants were much more common.

Slaves, serfs, indentured servants, or hired workers, both male and female, have performed household work throughout time. Upper-class households have traditionally had the economic resources for household help and lower-class households have provided that help in one form or the other. In late medieval and early modern Europe, young men and

Figure 3.2. Domestic scenes in middle class homes were popular in nineteenth-century magazines and newspapers. This 1843 example, entitled the *Happy Family*, glorified the middle class home. The father, dressed not as a farmer but as a businessman or gentleman appears in the center, surrounded by his elegantly dressed wife and daughters. A maid appears in the background, holding the baby. The home is complete with elegant furnishings and a faithful dog. No evidence of the hard work needed to maintain the house and family is included in the image.

Print, *Happy Family*, by Engraver John Sartin for *Miss Leslie's Magazine*, 1843.

women from rural settings migrated to towns for new opportunities. Many worked as domestic servants for only short periods of time while adjusting to their new lives and saving the resources to marry or establish their own households and businesses.

In seventeenth-century America, one-third of the colonial households included domestic workers. Many of these workers were young men or women who immigrated to the colonies as indentured servants, serving for a period of years in exchange for their passage, room, and board. At the same time, it was not unusual for free young women to live and work in the households of others before marriage to earn money and learn housekeeping skills. By the time of the American Revolution, indentured servitude had declined and was replaced by slavery defined by race. In the northern colonies especially, domestic help was mostly provided by native, white, single farm girls working before marriage.[2]

Ninety percent of all servants in the nineteenth century were women, and until 1870, at least 50 percent of America's employed women were servants. Servants made up 5 to 6 percent of the total labor force during the first half of the nineteenth century; 7 percent by 1860; and 8 percent by 1870. Not until after 1890 did domestic service begin to decline as an occupation for women. From 1800 to 1920, most servants worked in cities for upper- and middle class households or in hotels and boarding houses that required waiters, porters, cooks, and chambermaids. In larger American cities in the nineteenth century, more families employed servants than in rural America.[3]

Around the middle of the nineteenth century, the ethnicity of northern domestic workers shifted. First, native farm girls began to take higher paying positions in manufacturing, such as those in Lowell, Massachusetts, textile mills. These jobs allowed for more personal freedom away from their local community. Second, increased immigration from Ireland, and German, Scandinavian, and Slavic countries provided a new source of cheap domestic labor. Domestic positions were filled by immigrant and African American women who had to work to survive and had few other employment opportunities.

These demographic changes were at the core of two different words commonly used to describe domestic workers. The words *help* and *domestic* exemplified how Americans viewed the differences in culture, ethnicity, and social class between their servants and themselves. *Help* often referred to young and usually American-born women who moved to the city to work in a household or worked in the homes of neighbors in their own rural area. These women worked for pay but chose to be employed for a period of time that met personal goals, such as saving money for their own future marriage and household. They would have likely been offended if called a servant, a term denoting a much lower social status.[4] When local, native girls were employed, the differences in culture and social status between the help and the employer were small. Women who had worked in the homes of neighbors usually went on to establish their own households of equal social class and status of their former employers.[5]

On the other hand, a *domestic*, a term that became more common in the last half of the nineteenth century, would have been expected to accept the title of servant. Domestics were often immigrants who faced barriers young native-born woman did not. Because the immigrant servants came from different cultures, spoke different languages, were of different religions or Christian denominations, and much poorer than their employers, they were perceived as ignorant, lazy, or immoral. Domestics worked because of economic necessity and the terms of their employment, hours and duties depended strictly upon the needs of their employers. Employers demanded longer hours, more discipline, and often delegated the worst household duties to domestic servants. Native-born women often avoided the work of the domestic, as the job was much more demanding and less respected.[6]

Nineteenth-century authors perceived this demographic shift toward more immigrant women as domestic workers, but framed it as the decline from reliable help of native, white hired girls to undependable foreign domestics. The struggle to hire good help for the middle- and upper class homes was referred to as *the servant problem*. Those that addressed the servant problem in articles and advice books often idealized a golden age in colonial and early nineteenth-century New England when a mistress and her help lived and worked companionably together in log cabins. This ideal past was contrasted to current problems middle- and upper class wives faced when trying to find, train, and retain good domestics.

The contrasts in nineteenth-century sources between the lack of good help and problems of undesirable domestics was often nostalgia for the rural or pre-industrial past. In reality, both types of domestic laborers existed throughout the nineteenth and into the twentieth century.[7] Nostalgia is longing for a lost time and was prevalent in the nineteenth century when the social and cultural order were shifting due to industrialization.

Longing for a previous, mythical golden age of home and family that celebrated home, Republican motherhood, and the cult of domesticity was common. The ideal home was imagined as a rural farm house, handed down from genera-

Figure 3.3. This 1909 advertisement for Campbell's soups says their fresh, convenient, and inexpensive canned soups taste good enough for the finest tables. A maid serves the soup to the stylishly dressed diners and guests. The wife appears to be receiving praise for providing a wonderful meal. At the bottom of the advertisement, in small print, the reader is encouraged to order a free copy of the Campbell's Menu Book for more ideas for canned soup. A Campbell's Kid also appears in the bottom, left corner. See Figure 1.5 for more about Campbell's Kids.

Advertisement, Campbell's Soup, *McClure's Magazine* (December 1909): 53.

tion to generation, recalling an age before change.[8] The use of these two words, *help* and *domestics*, reflected feelings of uncertainty about the socioeconomic transformations of the nineteenth century from rural and agricultural to urban and industrial.

The servant problem was frequently referenced in nineteenth- and early twentieth-century publications. What, exactly, was the problem? The answer depends upon who is asked—the employer or the servant. Employers complained about the lack of "good" servants for hire. Employers often defined the good servant as the native, white, hired girl and complained about the qualities of any who did not fit that description. Depictions of ignorant, lazy, or dishonest immigrant or black servants were common in fiction, magazines, and newspapers.

On the other hand, those working as servants complained about the low status, meager pay, hard labor, and long working hours. Many women preferred jobs in factories, shops, or offices because of the lack of freedom and other negative perceptions and realities associated with domestic service.

Irish women made up the majority of domestic servants in New York, Boston, and Philadelphia from the 1850s to 1920s. Irish servants, collectively named Bridget or Biddy, a nickname for Bridget, were portrayed as hot-tempered, domineering, masculine, and ignorant. Comedy stage performances and twenty-eight films featuring Bridget spanning from 1895 to 1917 were produced that focused on her incompetence and resistance to the ideal middle class feminine and domestic expectations.[9]

The highly publicized story of Irish-born Mary Mallon seemed to prove the stereotypes of dirty and ignorant servants. Mallon, commonly referred to as Typhoid Mary, was a carrier of typhoid who infected twenty-two people from five families while working as a cook in New York City between 1901 and 1907. The use of these and other stereotypes in middle class publications reinforced the perception that the middle class housewife was a moral educator of the home with a responsibility to reform immigrants into the American ideal women and citizen—domestic, respectful, and obedient.[10]

Domestic service and the servant problem in the South was unique from the rest of the nation. In the South, domestic service was a part of an ingrained social system based on race. Black domestic workers were subjugated by both the low status of domestic service *and* a wider social and economic system that left no opportunities for black people to advance beyond the most menial jobs. The excess labor supply in the South after the Civil War meant that wages were low in all occupations open to black men and women. Because the wages of black parents or husbands were so low, black daughters and wives also had to work for wages, and domestic service was one of the few jobs available. While many domestic servants in the north and west only worked before marriage, southern black women had to work their entire lives. Servants were rare in lower middle class or working-class families in the North, yet in the South, because black servants were so poorly paid, even lower-income families could often afford to hire a cook or a nanny.[11]

Throughout the nation, servants were often viewed as childlike, lazy, irresponsible, and dishonest. But these racial stereotypes were especially pervasive in the South. After the Civil War, white southerners romanticized the days of slavery, nostalgically recalling the faithfulness, loyalty, and competence of former house slaves. Many white employers continued to expect black servants to act as slaves.

Employers made comparisons between faithful, stereotypical Mammy or Uncle Tom slaves and servants with bad attitudes and poor skills born after the Civil War. These comparisons were similar to comparisons between help and domestics in the rest of the nation. Unlike other regions of the nation, Southern white employers made no efforts to solve the servant problem because it was so intertwined with the larger perceived "trouble with Negroes" and the refusal of African Americans to continue to act as the slaves.[12] Reform only came with the Civil Rights Movement in the 1960s.

Solving the Servant Problem

Reforming the servant was a dominant theme of servant reform literature, especially in the first half of the nineteenth century. Various authors and publications, most representing the middle class, focused upon servant reform as a moral or religious imperative. Servants were informed they should accept their station in life and their inferior social status, take pride in their work, and be loyal to their employers. Instructional booklets, moral tracts, and household manuals usually failed to address the poor working conditions and real daily problems faced by servants. Only occasionally were employers instructed to make improvements in working conditions or raise wages. The most common admonitions were employers should be tolerant, pay wages on time, and avoid excessive scolding. The tone of this advice was often very condescending and equated servants with children.[13]

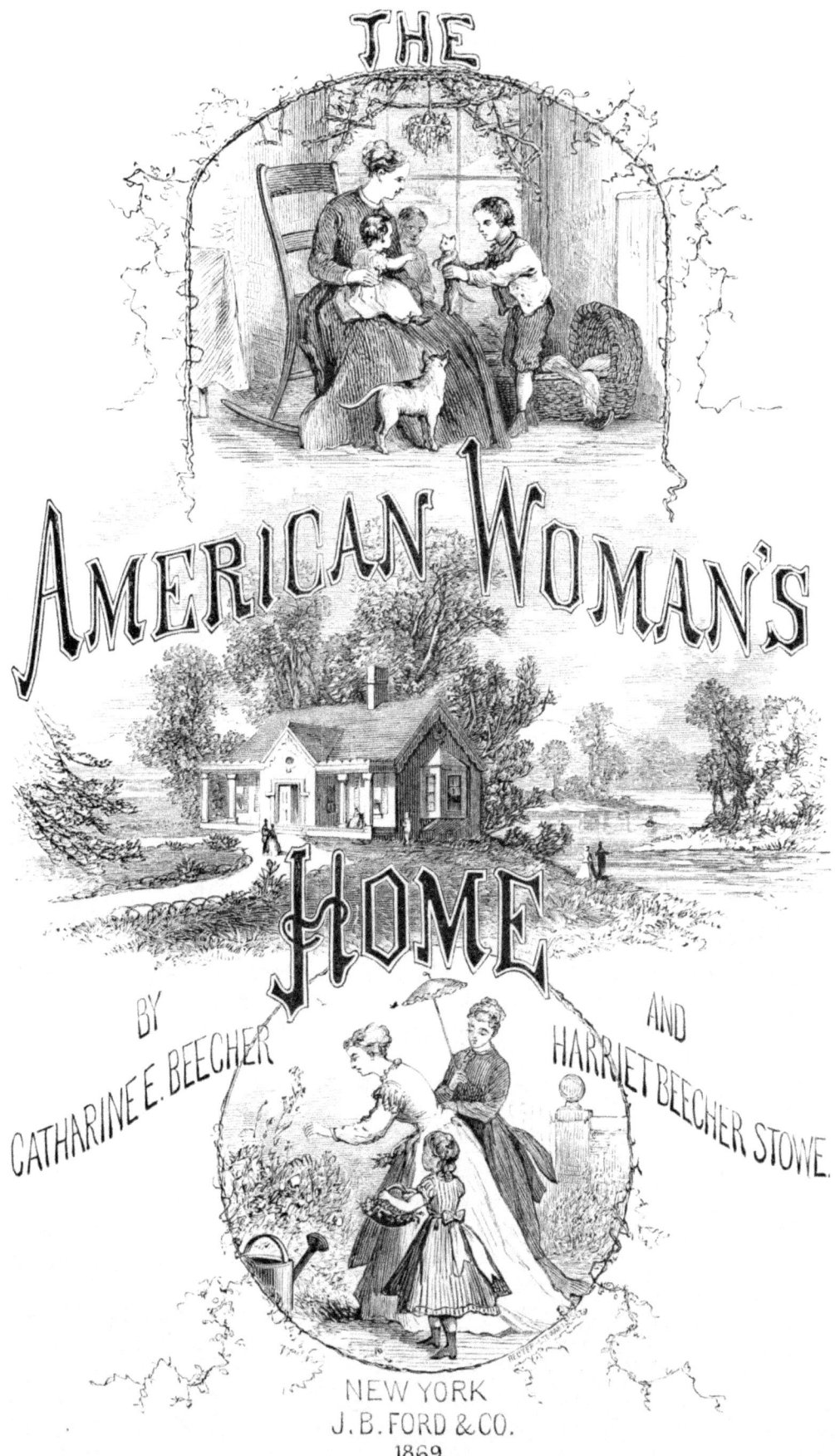

Figure 3.4. Catharine Beecher's work to improve female education, housekeeping, and women's status in the home spanned over forty-five years. Although she was a champion of women, she did not support suffrage. Beecher supported the concept of separate spheres for men and women, believing women should be the authority for morality, religion, and the family home. The title page of one of her many publications—*The American Woman's Home*, 1869—is pictured here. Domestic scenes featuring a mother and children and the ideal home are pictured. In the image at the bottom, the woman in the dark dress is probably a maid even though Beecher advised those following her advice did not need a maid.

Title Page of *The American Woman's Home* by Catharine Beecher and Harriet Beecher Stowe. New York: J. B. Ford and Company, 1869. (Courtesy of Internet Archive)

Catharine M. Sedgwick's (1789–1867) novel, *Live and Let Live; or, Domestic Service Illustrated* (1837), is about the trials of a young servant girl and illustrates the role of the middle class housewife as a sympathetic reformer of and domestic model for lower-class servants. The novel also contrasts the native white servant girl with other undesirable types of servants.

The main character is Lucy, a native-born white girl from the country who is forced to enter domestic service due to poverty caused by her father's alcoholism. In Sedgwick's novel, Lucy faces and overcomes the dangers and challenges of the city and her new role as a servant. Stereotyped descriptions of every type of undesirable servant and disagreeable employer provide contrast to Lucy's quest to be the best possible servant. Finally, Lucy finds the perfect employer, Mrs. Hyde, the ideal nineteenth-century wife and mother. With Mrs. Hyde's lessons in manners and household management, Lucy improves so she can marry the perfect husband and establish a home of her own.[14]

Several other reform movements took a different approach, seeking to redefine the work of housewives and domestic servants and therefore solve the servant problem, instead of just admonishing the servants themselves.

Catharine Beecher (1800–1878) was one of the earliest proponents of reforming the work of women so servants were not needed. Beecher and many other prominent writers and reformers of the era advocated for a variety of changes in the domestic roles of women in the home, but did not support political roles or suffrage for women. Historians label these women domestic or material feminists to distinguish them from other women's movements that demanded suffrage or opportunities for women outside of the home and family.[15]

Beecher championed the concept of separate spheres for men and women. In her writing, she encouraged women to view themselves as professionals within the home, arguing women should be the authority of morality, religion, and the business of keeping the home. Her goal was to make the profession of homemaking by women just as respected as the "honored professions of men."[16] Her work provided detailed advice on how to conduct the business of housekeeping so efficiently that servants were not even required for the average middle class home.

Catharine Beecher's incredibly popular *Treatise on Domestic Economy* was first published in 1841, revised and republished in fifteen editions and adopted as a school textbook. In 1869, she coauthored *The American Woman's Home* with her sister, Harriet Beecher Stowe. Instructions for every aspect of household management are included in the 500-page manual, a revision and expansion of her previous publications.

Although Beecher maintained servants were not needed if one followed her instructions, she did advise readers on proper servant–employer relationships for readers with very large families or upper-class households. Beecher provided architectural plans for the model single-family home and recommendations for tenement houses, settlement houses, and a Model Christian Neighborhood in which ten or twelve families could combine resources and share a laundry and bake house, further lightening the load of the housewife.

Other proposals for new types of domestic living that directly or indirectly addressed the burdens of housekeeping and the servant problem were made by reformers of all types in the late 1800s and early 1900s. Communal cooking, dining, and daycare facilities that served single family homes, urban middle- and upper-class apartments, and working-class tenements were recommended.[17]

In the Shaker, Oneida Perfectionist, and other nineteenth-century utopian communities, various communal lifestyles explored new conceptions of household and housework. Both the Shakers and the Perfectionists considered women as equals to men and lived in communal dwellings with work systems for women and men that lightened the burden of physical labor on the individual. They adopted new household and industrial technology that improved work conditions, productivity, and profits for the community.

Women such as Marie Stevens Howland proposed and participated in even more radical experiments of cooperative housekeeping. Howland (1836–1921) worked with socialists and trade unionists, participated in the Free Lover Unitary Household in New York City in the 1850s, and lived in Fourierist utopian communities in France and Mexico. Her utopian novel, *Papa's Own Girls* (1874), described an ideal community in which women had economic independence, childcare was provided, and cooking was done by a community chef.[18]

Edward Bellamy's best-selling novel *Looking Backward 2000–1887* described a future utopian world in which housekeeping was minimal, food was prepared by others, and domestic servants were no longer required. The popularity of the communal living plans and experiments waned in the Red Scare of the 1920s because they began to be viewed as un-American and an imitation of Soviet communal living.[19]

In the late 1800s, reforms for housekeeping and solutions to the servant problem promoted by Catharine Beecher and others merged with the domestic science or home economics movement that sought to apply new scientific, technological, and industrial practices in the home. The principles of industrial efficiency and scientific management of factories advocated by Frederick Taylor were applied to the kitchen and home, so the housewife could manage without servants. Home economists promoted schools for training domestics such as the Women's Educational and Industrial Union founded in Boston in 1877.[20] Ellen Richards, a leader in domestic science, opened the Boston School of Housekeeping (1897). The school was meant to solve the servant problem but it failed; domestics did not want to go to school for eight months, without wages, and employers did not want to pay to send them.[21]

Proposals made by Lucy Maynard Salmon (1853–1927) echoed many of the solutions proposed by Beecher and the home economics movement. Salmon was a professor of history at Vassar College, the first woman to be a member of the executive committee of the American Historical Association, and a social historian of everyday life long before social history became popular. Her pioneering *Domestic Service* (1897), the first scholarly work on the servant problem, was based upon questionnaires completed by domestic servants and their employers. She examined the historical aspects of domestic service and proposed reforms such as creating explicit employment contracts, allowing domestic workers to live in their own homes, and establishing commercial laundries, bakeries, and other businesses from which housewives could purchase services and goods.[22]

Women willing to work as a live-in domestic became harder and harder to find in the early twentieth century. Immigration restrictions in the 1920s cut the supply of poor immigrants willing to work as domestics. African American women migrated from the South to find opportunity in northern cities and filled many domestic positions. But they tended to live in their own homes, usually because they continued to work after marriage. Young women who had formerly served as domestic servants before marriage were more likely to attend high school or prefer one of the many other jobs in offices or stores opening to women in the early decades of the twentieth century.[23]

Ultimately, the solution to the servant problem came not from reform, but changes caused by industrialization that made it easier to manage a home without a servant. New products and electric or gas appliances changed the nature of work in the home. Ready-to-use laundry detergents and washing machines reduced the need to make soap and wash clothing by hand. Convenience foods such as canned foods, bakery bread, or products like Knox and Jell-O gelatin saved time in the kitchen.

Apartment living became more common in urban areas. Apartments and new houses were smaller with built-in plumbing, electricity, and mechanical heat systems, ending the chores of carrying fuel and water, stoking fires, and cleaning lamps. The etiquette for dining and entertaining became less formal, decreasing the need for servants to cook and serve. By the 1920s, for those who required or could afford domestic help, day workers replaced live-in domestic servants. In the South, the scarcity of domestic help did not occur until the 1940s and 1950s when large numbers of African Americans migrated to northern cities in search of better opportunity.[24]

Female domestic workers and the women who employed them were both expected to conform to sex, race, and social class expectations. But the efforts of these women to conform to or resist societal expectations are often invisible to historians. The words of domestic workers throughout most of history were not recorded, but several oral histories record the experiences of black domestic workers in the twentieth century and can provide insight.

The novel *The Help* (2009) and the 2011 film based on the novel demonstrate the range of attitudes and actions taken by African American maids to maintain their dignity in the early 1960s. For example, domestic workers had little power to change working conditions, but they frequently changed employers hoping for improvements. African Americans were actively recruited by employment agencies and black newspapers for domestic service jobs in the North and West and many chose to leave the South for better opportunities.

Domestic workers appear to have little power, or agency. But upon closer examination, they do have agency in how their jobs are performed. For example, African American servants in the South may have reduced the demands of their employers by choosing to do work slowly or poorly, a habit their white employers attributed to them anyway whether it was true or not.[25] In *The Maid Narratives: Black Domestics and White Families in the Jim Crow South*, seventeen African American women were interviewed about their experiences as domestic workers. Annie Victoria Johnson (born 1925) shared a story in which her sister, while working as a maid, was paid by her employer at the beginning of the work day. But during the day as she worked, her employer stole the money back from her purse. Johnson described her sister's reaction to this discovery:

> She (*Johnson's sister*) said, "When I cleaned the bathroom, I took the toothbrush and cleaned the toilet and stuck it back in the holder." She said, "I took one of my socks and buttered that turkey! [laughing]. And she went to her (*employer's*) drawer

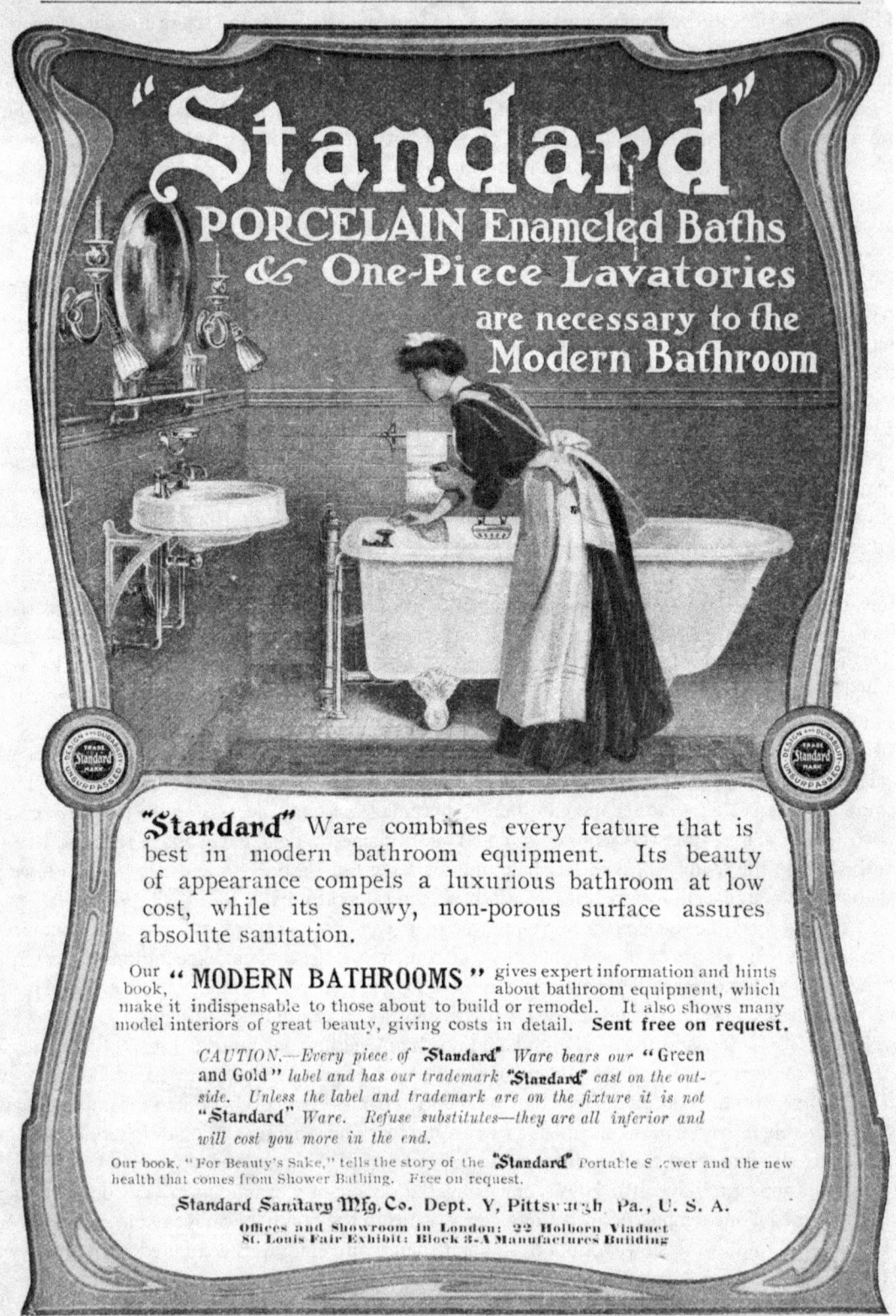

Figure 3.5. A maid is featured in this 1904 advertisement for porcelain bathroom fixtures. The text stresses Standard fixtures are modern and assure absolute sanitation, addressing concerns of domestic scientists about cleanliness and hygiene in the home. This ad also represents the shift to indoor plumbing and electric or gas power occurring in the late nineteenth and early twentieth centuries. New rooms called bathrooms were replacing privies and outhouses.

Advertisement for Standard bathroom fixtures, *Munsey's Magazine*, Vol. 31, no. 3 (June 1904), Advertising Section.

and got a pair of socks and put them on and took the train!" She said, "When they do you dirty, I got some tricks to get it back!" [laughing].[26]

Assumptions about status, class, gender, and ethnicity are still present in modern discussion concerning domestic work and domestic workers. In *Nickel and Dimed: On (Not) Getting By in America* (1996), author Barbara Ehrenreich lived the life of four low-wage female workers, including that of a domestic worker. Her experience was not far from that of turn-of-the-century female investigative reporters Lillian Pettengill and Bessie Van Vorst. A long history of assuming a women's place is in the home and the work within the home has little or no monetary value is still influencing how we view and reward those who perform those chores today.

In the Classroom

The following primary sources demonstrate the themes of status, class, race, and ethnicity that were an inherent part of domestic service and the servant problem. The sources, representing the views of both employers and domestic workers, are arranged in sets that focus upon key issues. The sources can be used independently or in sets in lessons or instructional units. As always, focus student attention on the essential questions chapter to make connections to wider issues. *Warning:* several references to race and ethnicity will be shocking to modern readers and may not be appropriate for all students.

Set A—The American Servant Problem as Viewed by Europeans

SOURCE 1

Excerpt from *Domestic Manners of the Americans* (1832) by Frances Trollope[27]

Frances Milton Trollope (1779–1863) was an English novelist and writer who published an account of her travels through the United States. She lived briefly in Cincinnati, Ohio, which was a frontier town in the early 1800s.

The greatest difficulty in organizing a family establishment in Ohio, is getting servants, or, as it is there called, "getting help," for it is more than petty treason to the republic to call a free citizen a servant. The whole class of young women, whose bread depends upon their labor, are taught to believe that the most abject poverty is preferable to domestic service. Hundreds of half-naked girls work in the paper-mills, or in any other manufactory, for less than half the wages they would receive in service. But they think their equality is compromised by domestic service and nothing but the wish to obtain some particular article of finery will ever induce them to submit to it. A kind friend helped me and tall stately lass soon presented herself, saying, "I be come to help you." I welcomed the girl in the most gracious manner possible, and asked what I should give pay her for a year's work. "Oh gimini!" exclaimed the damsel, with a loud laugh, "you be a downright Englisher, sure enough. I should like to see a young lady engage by the year in America! I hope I shall get a husband before many months, or I expect I shall be an outright old maid, for I be 'most seventeen already; besides, mayhap I may want to go to school. You must just give me a dollar and half a week, and mother's slave, Phillis, must come over once a week, I expect, from t'other side the river, to help me clean."

I agreed to the bargain, of course, with all dutiful submission; and seeing she was preparing to set to work in a yellow dress with red roses, I gently hinted that I thought it was a pity to spoil so fine a gown, and that she had better change it.

"Tis just my best and my worst," she answered, "for I've got no other." And in truth I found that this young lady had left her home with no more clothes of any kind than what she had on. I immediately gave her money to purchase what was necessary for cleanliness and decency, and set to work with my daughters to make her a gown. She grinned applause when our labor was completed, but never uttered the slightest expressions of gratitude for that, or anything else we could do for her. She was constantly asking us to lend her different articles of dress, and when we declined it, she said, "Well, I never seed such grumpy folks as you be; there is several young ladies of my acquaintance what goes to live out now and then with the old women about the town, and they and their gurls always lends them what they ask for. I guess you Inglish thinks we should poison your things, just as bad as if we was Negurs." And here I beg to assure the reader, that whenever I give conversations they were written down immediately after they occurred, with all the verbal fidelity my memory permitted.

This young lady left me at the end of two months, because I refused to lend her money enough to buy a silk dress to go to a ball, saying, "Then 'tis not worth my while to stay any longer." . . .

I might occupy a hundred pages on the subject [*of domestics*], and yet fail to give an adequate idea of the sore, angry, ever wakeful pride that seemed to torment these poor wretches.

[*Mrs. Trollope describes another girl who worked for her.*] One of these was a pretty girl, whose natural disposition must have been gentle and kind; but her good feelings were soured, and her gentleness turned to morbid sensitiveness, by having heard a thousand and a thousand times that she was as good as any other lady, that all men were equal, and women too, and that it was a sin and a shame for a free-born American to be treated like a servant.

When she found she was to dine in the kitchen, she turned up her pretty lip, and said, "I guess that's 'cause you don't think I'm good enough to eat with you. You'll find that won't do here." I found afterward that she rarely ate any dinner at all, and generally passed the time in tears. I did everything in my power to conciliate and make her happy, but I am sure she hated me.

SOURCE 2

Excerpt from *The Americans, In Their Moral, Social, and Political Relations* (1837) by Francis Joseph Grund[28]

Francis Joseph Grund (1805–1863) was a German-born American journalist and author. Note that he makes a response to Frances Trollope's comments about American servants.

Nothing but the love of independence could induce those sturdy settlers [Americans] to make the wilderness their home. If settlers wanted an easier life, they might become servants in the cities or cultivated districts . . . The willingness of the rich to work, and the disposition of the poor to prefer hard independent labor to easy, well-paid servitude, are the principal causes of the increasing prosperity of the United States.

The unwillingness of the poorer classes of Americans to hire themselves out as servants, and the little satisfaction with their lot when circumstances compel them to do it, furnish a subject of incessant complaint with the wealthier, and more aristocratic families. The theme is too fertile for European tourists not to profit by it, and, accordingly, their works are adorned with copious descriptions of the ludicrous pretensions of American servants . . .

As to female servants, few complaints, I believe, are made of their want of fidelity or submission, though they require a treatment very different from that to which the same class are accustomed in Europe. Despite of Mrs. Trollope's masterly sketches of American domestics, she could find nothing to impeach either their honesty or morality ; (which, no doubt, the fair author would have been glad to do if it had been in her power; and one instance, in particular, which she gives of the pride of a young girl, in her own service, who would rather starve than eat in the kitchen, and whom she always found obedient yet bathed in tears, exhibits a nobility of sentiment, of which certainly not a trace is to be found in her lady's writings.

Set B—Who Should Do the Household Chores? Women? Servants? Or Machines?

SOURCE 3

Excerpt from "Help on the Farm" by Mrs. H. P. Tucker, 1873 essay in a publication of the Wisconsin State Agricultural Society[29]

Woman's life upon a farm is not always a pleasant one. It is too often surrounded with grievous cares, and burdens heavy to be borne. We find her at work early and late, verifying the old rhyme—that "Man must work from sun to sun, but woman's work is never done." Reviewing her duties, you are led to conclude that there is not rest for her this side of a life somewhere else, and that her life is as devoid of flowers and as full of weeds as a farmer's garden.

We find in every well regulated farmer's home little ones dependent upon the mother for more than their daily bread . . . and how can she, wearied with the labor which is only a necessity, gather her children around her, and give them the intellectual care, which it is more necessary she should give them on a farm than in the town . . .

Help in a farmer's kitchen is not a luxury that may be dispensed with at pleasure. It is a necessity of the life and happiness of every member of the household. But, says one, we can't get the help. Why? Girls do not like to live on farms, there is so much to do. Oh, no, I guess not; there need be no more done there than in the city. Look over the labor of keeping house in the city; its restraints and meaningless formalities and compare it with the farmhouse . . . You will hear the farmer's daughter decidedly say she will never marry a farmer, no, not she, and with a careworn, overworked mother ever before her, she is not likely to change her mind.

SOURCE 4

"How to Redeem Woman's Profession from Dishonor" by Catharine Beecher, *Harper's New Monthly Magazine*, 1865[30]

Woman, as well as man, was made to work, and her Maker has adapted her body to its appropriate labor. The tending of children and doing house-work exercise those very muscles which are most important to womanhood; while neglecting to exercise the arms and trunk causes dangerous debility in most delicate organs. Our early mothers worked and trained their daughters to work, and thus became healthy, energetic, and cheerful. But in these days, young girls, in the wealthy classes, do not use the muscles of their body and arms in domestic labor or in any other way. Instead of this, study and reading stimulate the brain and nerves to debility by excess, while the muscles grow weak for want of exercise. Thus the whole constitution is weakened.

[*Beecher argues for professional training for domestic work in schools for women of all classes.*]

When, therefore, the attempt is made to introduce industrial training into our schools, we are simply aiming to carry out practically the true democratic principle. But there is a still higher aim. It will be found that the democratic principle is no other than the grand law of Christianity, which requires work and self-sacrifice for the public good, to which all private interests are to be subordinate.

Children are to be trained to live not for themselves but for others; not to be waited on and taken care of, but to wait on and take care of others; to work for the good of others as the first thing, and amusement and self-enjoyment as necessary but subordinate to the highest public good. The family is the first commonwealth where this training is to be carried on, and only as a preparation for a more enlarged sphere of action.

[*Beecher describes the model house.*]

The goal is to make the woman's profession [*in the home*] so honorable that women of the highest position and culture will seek it, as men seek their most honored professions. There must still be servants . . . where large fortunes abound . . . A woman who prefers a style of living demanding servants should be trained herself [*in housekeeping*] as not to be dependent on hirelings at the sacrifice of self-respect. On the other hand, a woman who chooses . . . to work herself and train her children to work, can do so without fear of losing any social advantages. Or, in case more helpers are needed, she can secure highly cultivated and refined friends to share all her family enjoyments, instead of depending on a class inferior in cultivation and less qualified to form the habits and tastes of her children.

SOURCE 5

Excerpt from "The Princess Biddy" by Louise Palmer Smith, in *Putnam's Monthly Magazine of American Literature, Science and Art* (1870)[31]

My knowledge of housework has stood me in right good stead; but it has not dethroned Biddy, and it never will. I can make individuals of her line abdicate my kitchen when they become unbearable; but as American housework is now organized, nothing can take from the race [*Irish*] their mission to deface and destroy, to break and to blunder. . . . [*The author continues by advocating for the manufacture of bread and other foods and commercial laundries for washing and ironing clothing.*]

May the day hasten when housekeepers, young and old, will be convinced that we are hampering and wasting our domestic peace by persisting in labors [*baking and laundry*] which do not belong to the home, but should be outside callings exclusively.

THE IRISH DECLARATION OF INDEPENDENCE THAT WE ARE ALL FAMILIAR WITH.

Figure 3.6. An Irish maid is the subject of ridicule on this 1883 *Puck Magazine* cover. The large, masculine Irish maid intimidates her delicate, feminine middle class employer, even though the maid has broken a dish, burned the food, and allowed the pot to boil over. Images and articles about the servant problem were common in the late nineteenth and early twentieth centuries and frequently used racial and ethnic stereotypes that are shocking by today's standards.
Magazine cover/cartoon by Frederick Burr Opper. *Puck Magazine* (May 9, 1883), Published by Keppler & Schwarzmann. (Courtesy of Library of Congress)

Excellent must be the results of increase of our own culinary lore, excellent (let us hope) the incoming of the Chinese; and both will help bring in the golden years of peace. But never till our homes cease to be workshops chafed by the friction of endless toil, will they rise perfectly to their true end of nurseries of a Christian nation, and the zest and delight of the land.

SOURCE 6

Excerpt from *Looking Backward: 2000–1887* (published in 1888) by Edward Bellamy[32]

Bellamy's novel Looking Backward: 2000–1887 *described a socialist utopian future. The book was a best-seller and inspired Bellamy Clubs that wanted to make his vision a reality.*

"You spoke of paying for service to take care of your houses," said I; "that suggests a question I have several times been on the point of asking. How have you disposed of the problem of domestic service? Who are willing to be domestic servants in a community where all are social equals? Our ladies found it hard enough to find such even when there was little pretense of social equality."

"It is precisely because we are all social equals whose equality nothing can compromise, and because service is honorable, in a society whose fundamental principle is that all in turn shall serve the rest, that we could easily provide a corps of domestic servants such as you never dreamed of, if we needed them," replied Dr. Leete. "But we do not need them."

"Who does your house-work, then?" I asked.

"There is none to do," said Mrs. Leete, to whom I had addressed this question. "Our washing is all done at public laundries at excessively cheap rates, and our cooking at public kitchens. The making and repairing of all we wear are done outside in public shops. Electricity, of course, takes the place of all fires and lighting. We choose houses no larger than we need, and furnish them so as to involve the minimum of trouble to keep them in order. We have no use for domestic servants."

"The fact," said Dr. Leete, "that you had in the poorer classes a boundless supply of serfs on whom you could impose all sorts of painful and disagreeable tasks, made you indifferent to devices to avoid the necessity for them. But now that we all have to do in turn whatever work is done for society, every individual in the nation has the same interest, and a personal one, in devices for lightening the burden. This fact has given a prodigious impulse to labor-saving inventions in all sorts of industry, of which the combination of the maximum of comfort and minimum of trouble in household arrangements was one of the earliest results."

Set C—Solutions for the Servant Problem

SOURCE 7

Excerpt from "Domestic Service" by Louise Clarence, published in *Far and Near*, 1891[33]

Far and Near was a monthly journal published from 1890–1894 for the Working Girls' Societies of America, social and educational clubs of unmarried women working factories, offices, and stores. Articles were written by upper-class women interested in social reform as well as club members.[34]

The foreign element, coming to our shores ignorant of our customs and household ways, yet almost invariably drifting into household service, comprises an appreciable part of incapable servants. These, however, particularly among the Germans and Swedes, prove very *tractable* under proper training, and accustomed in their own countries to hard toil, often develop into the most trustworthy and efficient help. We are now looking hopefully to cooking schools for help in this matter. It is a great movement in the right direction . . . There should be an established curriculum and standard of proficiency, as in any school, and it should be esteemed as honorable to receive a diploma . . . as from any of the schools whose course of study leads to some trade or profession . . . With a thorough understanding of this work, women undertaking it will have a great respect for their work and for themselves, and mutual respect of employer and employee will result.

tractable—easy to control or influence

SOURCE 8

Excerpt from *Household Economics* (1896) by Helen Campbell[35]

Helen Stuart Campbell (1839–1918) was one of the prominent leaders of the home economics movement.

In the situation as a whole, the objections from those "who had tried it," and those "who had been urged to try it," were practically the same. Kind as mistresses might be, there was still the loss of personal liberty and the social ostracism which goes side by side with it, and no training school on earth is likely to alter these facts, or make the self-respecting American girl accept the form of labor which bears, in spite of our best endeavors, the stamp of degradation. Certain stipulations were made by all, some laying stress upon one point, some upon another, but the general average uniting in those that follow:

1. A definition of what a day's work means, payment for all over-time required, or certain hours of absolute freedom guaranteed, especially where the position is that of child's nurse.
2. A comfortably warmed and decently furnished room, with separate beds if two occupy it, and both decent place and appointments for meals.
3. The heaviest work, such as carrying coal, scrubbing pavements, washing, etc., to be arranged for if this is asked . . .
4. No *livery* if there is feeling against it.
5. The privilege of seeing friends in a better part of the house than the kitchen, and security from espionage during such time, whether the visitors are male or female. This to be accompanied by reasonable restrictions as to hours, and with the condition that work is not be neglected.
6. Such a manner of speaking to and of the server as shall show that there is no contempt for housework, and that it is actually as respectable as other occupations.

livery—a special uniform associated with servants in the homes of the very wealthy or with domestic service in Europe

SOURCE 9

Excerpt from *Domestic Service* (1897) by Lucy Maynard Salmon[36]

Lucy Maynard Salmon (1853–1927) was a professor of history at Vassar College. Her pioneering study Domestic Service *was the first scholarly work on the servant problem.*

Other housekeepers seriously advocate abolishing the public schools above the primary grade on the ground that girls are educated above their station, and they follow the plan of one who says, "I do not engage women who have been beyond the third reader and the multiplication table." The quality of service obtained by such a policy is indicated by the remark of the father of a remarkably stupid girl, "She ain't good for much; I guess she'll have to live out." No statement can be more fallacious than that girls are educated above their station. There can be no so-called "station" in a democratic country. We have given the reins to our democratic views politically, and we must abide by the industrial and social results.

Still other housekeepers advocate the introduction of housework into all the public schools, and thus securing well-informed "help." But both this proposition and its converse overlook the fact that it is the function of the public school to educate, not to supply information on technical subjects.

Set D—Which Job Is Better, Domestic or Factory Girl?

SOURCE 10

Excerpt from *Toilers of the Home: The Record of a College Woman's Experience as a Domestic Servant* (1903) by Lillian Pettengill[37]

Lillian Pettengill lived undercover as a domestic servant after graduating from college. Her experiences were first published in Everybody's Magazine *in 1902 and later as a book.*[38] *In this excerpt, Pettengill is describing a set of rules for women who employ domestic workers.*

Does not domestic work of itself develop the individual mentality as factory work cannot? Or is it that the field of observation is wider, and that more chance is given for contact with people of different sorts? Compare the unending punching of eyelets among the same class of workers, and its probable contribution to individual development. Yet would an *eyelet-puncher* consider domestic employ? Her friends might look down upon her . . . a wide social gap exists between a housemaid and a *label paster*, a housemaid and a girl who tends store, a housemaid and a seamstress, is like that between the housemaid and her employer . . . It would be comic if it were not so pathetic . . .

As a house-keeper, then, coping with present conditions, there would be framed in my constitution several inalterable rules: . . .

2. Shall I ever fail to remember that the employee is as worthy consideration and fairness as her employer ought to be? I trust I shall remember, the days of slavery being passed, that my girl, cook or other maid is not my property, and that she is entirely free to leave my employ for that of any other housekeeper who shall make it worth her while . . .

3. Keeping house with a hired helper is the conduct of important business. All understandings and plans should be on a business basis from the start. The cooperative and profit-sharing scheme proposed by Professor Lucy M. Salmon and tried so satisfactorily by many housekeepers commends itself . . .

4. I do not take kindly to the idea of educating any possible employees from the kindergarten up, though I should expect to teach them my peculiar preferences with patience and firmness. But especially if there is more than one maid, none but experienced and competent cooks need apply. And again, especially, I shall not any more look for domestic excellence in a factory-bred American. The second generation of factory workers is said to be inferior physically and mentally, if not morally; and the third generation the last. How can a woman, working ten or eleven hours in the stifle and whirr, as her mother worked before her, practice, teach, or know aught of practical home-making?

5. I shall ask my employees what they would like me to call them . . . one may sometimes say "waitress" for short, as one says "doctor" or "nurse."

I like a uniform for indoor wear on the ground of neatness and convenience. I do not like a *livery*.

Personal service is demoralizing; save upon old age, illness, and infancy there shall be no such demand in my house. When I cook messes in the kitchen, I shall do so only on the cook's afternoon out, and the chambermaid will come down only in time to serve the dinner. And in general, having satisfied myself of the general character and orderliness of the worker in her workroom, I shall keep out of the kitchen . . .

6. And finally. When I begin to have the fidgets and much anxiety over my employees, when I perceive in myself an inclination to fret and nag, or explode, it shall be a clear sign that I need to retire from business—a housekeeper, a term of boarding, or travel, or sanitarium or the simplifying of my way of living by doing myself what cannot be done away with altogether.

eyelet-puncher—an eyelet is a small round hole in leather cloth. An eyelet puncher was job in a factory.

label paster—person who glues labels to bottles or cans.

livery—a special uniform associated with servants in the homes of the very wealthy or with domestic service in Europe.

SOURCE 11

Excerpt from *The Woman of the People*, by Mrs. John (Bessie) Van Vorst published in *Harpers*, 1903[39]

Bessie van Vorst and her sister-in-law, Maria van Vorst, worked undercover in several different factories and published their experiences in Everybody's Magazine *in 1902 and later in book form.*[40] *In this excerpt, Van Vorst summarizes her experiences.*

The working-women of the people in America I divide into four categories, considering in turn the problems of each and the circumstances that have determined their position. These four categories are the servant, the *charwoman*, the woman of a generation ago, and the factory girl. Generally speaking, the industrial aristocrat is the factory girl; the older woman has a role in the home only; and the units of a second order are the charwoman and the servant.

From my own experience as a kitchen maid [*she worked a day as a maid in the factory's dining hall*], I resume in a word my conclusions regarding the servant class. In America, where freedom is any man's to claim, the servant must of necessity be an inferior human being. Added to the futile nature of the servant's duties, there is a complete sacrifice of independence to which only the inferior will submit. No law regulates the number of hours a servant shall work; the will of a master passes before any requirements for existence as an individual. The servant belongs in the category with those who have abandoned or who ignore an ideal, who prefer relative material ease to relative moral freedom.

charwoman—a servant does general cleaning and usually does not live in the home of her employer.

Set E—Who Makes the Best Servant?

SOURCE 12

Excerpt from "Servants," *New York Times*, September 20, 1874[41]

Many of our ladies do not understand the proper mode of managing a European peasant, who, in nine cases out of ten, is the "help." The Irish peasantry make capital servants, but they are to be treated, not as equals, nor again as slaves or animals, but rather as children. An Irish peasant girl . . . is glad to learn; she entrusts her money and interests to the mistress' care; she enters into the affairs of the family, for the Irish peasant has the old Keltic clan-feeling of attachment to the person of the leader or lady; she will be indefatigable in sickness and full of sympathy in trouble; and above all, the Irish domestic is honest as to money matters.

SOURCE 13

Excerpt from "How to Sweep a Room," from *Scribner's Monthly*, 1874[42]

"How to Sweep a Room."

An uninstructed Bridget, armed with a broom is about as charming an occupant of a parlor, or a library well-stocked with the pretty little knickknacks which cultivated people like to have about them, as the celebrated bull in the china shop. Before Bridget's entrance, all fragile movables should be stored by careful hands in some neighboring closet; and the furniture, as far as possible, protected by covers and slight drapers, kept for the purpose. Then, after doors have been closed, and windows opened, Bridget may be called in and instructed.

SOURCE 14

Excerpt from *The Philadelphia Negro: A Social Study (1899)*, by W. E. B. Dubois[43]

This work was the first sociological study of an African American community done in the United States.

The question of the general bearing and manners of colored domestics was discussed by many of their employers. The general opinion of the employers is that they are "more willing and obliging" than white servants. As one employer says: "The Germans drink and the Irish order you out of the house, but the colored people are more respectful and anxious to please." "They are more agreeable and obliging and have nicer manners," says another employer, and adds; "When my sister was ill, the Irish maid I had at the time refused to carry up the breakfast tray, because, she said, 'it was not her business to do nursing, and she wouldn't do it for ten dollars.'" So the employer herself prepared and carried up the trays until the colored girl, who came soon after, volunteered her services with: "Let me take up the breakfast tray, Mrs. W__. You look ready to drop," and since she came, Mrs. W__ has never had a white girl in the house.

That the colored people are more willing and obliging in manner is attested by twenty employers and denied by no one, while one employer, who is connected with the University, and has had years of experience, both with white and colored servants, says of the colored people: "Whether they are better or worse than the whites may depend upon what whites you have. We had white servants for seven winters, and always employed the best Irish servants we could get; but they were so unsatisfactory that we gave them up and tried colored servants. Our experience of them is that they are infinitely cleaner than the white Irish, both in their work and personally; they are more self-respecting and better mannered more agreeable in manners; indeed, I have found them capable of the very highest cultivation of manner. One of our men has the education of a gentleman and is improving himself constantly; the other is ignorant, but is exceedingly refined and modest in manner. Of course they have faults; they are fickle, changing from place to place, even when they are fond of their employers, and they have quick tempers, but they are truthful and honest; we have never lost a thing by them. We keep them by preference, and shall continue to do so."

Several employers agree in regard to this instinct of the colored people for good manners. One who constantly employs nine servants, and in the last twenty-five or thirty years has had only one set of white servants says: "There is much more to them than people think; our first man servant has as many of the instincts of a gentleman as anyone I ever saw." This is high praise. "They have a native, deep-seated refinement and very lovely manners," says another who has employed them for fifteen years.

A judgment which was frequently encountered and always among those employers who had had experience of both white and colored servants was that colored servants are "just like other people of their own class." One employer says on this point: "I don't find a bit of difference; some are very neat and some are very untidy; it depends entirely on the girl." Another says: "There are good ones and poor ones among both; it varies with the individual, not with the race."

SOURCE 15

Excerpt from "The Biography of a Chinaman" by Lee Chew published in *The Independent*, 1903[44]

When I went to work for the American family [*in California*] I could not speak a word of English, and I did not know anything about housework . . . I did not know how to do anything and I did not understand what the lady said to me, but she showed me how to cook, wash, iron, sweep, dust, make beds, wash dishes, clean windows, paint and brass, polish the knives and forks, etc., by doing the things herself and then overseeing my efforts . . . She and her husband and children laughed at me a great deal, but it was all good natured. I was not confined to the house in the way servants are confined here [*in New York*] but when my work was done in the morning I was allowed to go out till lunch time . . .

Irish fill the almshouses and prisons and orphan asylums, Italians are among the most dangerous of men, Jews are unclean and ignorant. Yet they are all let in [*to the United States*], while Chinese, who are sober, or duly law abiding, clean, educated and industrious, are shut out. There are few Chinamen in jails and none in poor houses.

Notes

1. Claudia Geist and Philip N. Cohen, "Headed Toward Equality? Housework Change in Comparative Perspective," *Journal of Marriage & Family* 73, no. 4 (2011): 832–44, accessed August 27, 2016, EBSCOhost; Liana C. Sayer, "Gender, Time and Inequality: Trends in Women's and Men's Paid Work, Unpaid Work and Free Time," *Social Forces* 84, no. 1 (2005): 285–303, accessed August 2016, EBSCOhost.

2. Judith Babbitts, "Household Labor," in *Encyclopedia of American Social History*, vol. 2, eds. Mary Kupiec Cayton, Elliott J. Gorn, and Peter W. Williams (New York: Charles Scribner's Sons, 1993), 1425–26.

3. Daniel E. Sutherland, *Americans and Their Servants: Domestic Service in the United States from 1800s to 1920* (Baton Rouge: Louisiana State University Press, 1981), 45–46.

4. Faye E. Dudden, *Serving Women: Household Service in Nineteenth-Century America* (Middletown, CT: Wesleyan University Press, 1983), 6–9.

5. Babbitts, "Household Labor," 1425–26.

6. Dudden, *Serving Women*, 6–9.

7. Ibid., 5.

8. Susan J. Matt, "You Can't Go Home Again: Homesickness and Nostalgia in U.S. History," *The Journal of American History* 94, no. 2 (September 2007): 479–82, accessed March 2017, http://www.jstor.org/stable/25094961.

9. Peter Flynn, "How Bridget Was Framed: The Irish Domestic in Early American Cinema, 1895–1917," *Cinema Journal* 50, no. 2 (Winter 2011): 10.

10. Andrew Urban, "Irish Domestic Servants, 'Biddy' and Rebellion in the American Home, 1850–1900," *Gender & History* 21, no. 2 (August 2009): 264–265.

11. David M. Katzman, *Seven Days a Week: Women and Domestic Service in Industrializing America* (New York: Oxford University Press, 1978), 185–222.

12. Ibid., 185–222.

13. Sutherland, *Americans and Their Servants*, 147–61.

14. Catharine Maria Sedgwick, *Live and Let Live, or Domestic Service Illustrated* (New York: Harper and Brothers, 1837), Internet Archive, https://archive.org/details/liveandletliveo00sedggoog.

15. Dolores Hayden, *The Grand Domestic Revolution: A History of Feminist Designs for American Homes, Neighborhoods, and Cities* (Cambridge, MA: The MIT Press, 1981), 28–29; Susan Strasser, *Never Done: A History of American Housework* (New York: Pantheon Books, 1982), xi.

16. Catharine Beecher and Harriet Beecher Stowe, *The American Woman's Home* (New York: J.B. Ford and Company; Boston: H.A. Brown & Co. 1869), 13. https://archive.org/details/americanwomansho00beecrich.

17. Hayden, *The Grand Domestic Revolution*, 3–5.

18. Ibid., 91–100.

19. Ibid., 285.

20. Glenna Matthews, *"Just a Housewife": The Rise & Fall of Domesticity in America* (New York: Oxford University Press, 1987), 97–99, 145–55.

21. Sarah Stage, "Ellen Richards and the Social Significance of the Home Economics Movement," in *Rethinking Home Economics, Women and the History of the Profession*, eds. Sarah Stage and Virginia B. Vincenti (Ithaca, NY: Cornell University Press, 1997), 23–24.

22. Lucy Maynard Salmon, *Domestic Service* (New York: The Macmillan Company, 1897), Internet Archive, https://archive.org/details/domesticservice01salmgoog.

23. Sutherland, *Americans and Their Servants*, 187–90; Judith Babbitts, "Household Labor," 1426.

24. Ibid.

25. Katzman, *Seven Days a Week*, 185–222.

26. Katherine S. Van Wormer, Charletta Sudduth, and David W. Jackson, *The Maid Narratives: Black Domestics and White Families in the Jim Crow South* (Baton Rouge: Louisiana State University Press, 2012), 102, accessed July 2016, eBook Collection, EBSCOhost.

27. Frances Trollope, *Domestic Manners of the Americans* (London: Whittaker, Treacher & Company; New York, 1832), 61–63, Internet Archive, https://archive.org/details/domesticmannerso00troliala.

28. Francis Joseph Grund, *The Americans, In Their Moral, Social, and Political Relations* (Boston: Marsh, Capen and Lyon 1837), 235–36, Internet Archive, https://archive.org/stream/americansintheir00grun#page/236/mode/2up.

29. Mrs. H. P. Tucker, "Help on the Farm," *Transactions of the Wisconsin State Agricultural Society, including a full report of the state agricultural convention, held in February 1873, and numerous practical papers and communications*. Wisconsin State Agricultural Society, XI (1872–1873): 432, accessed July 2016, http://digicoll.library.wisc.edu/cgi-bin/WI/WI-idx?type=turn&entity=WI.WSASv11.p0437&id=WI.WSASv11&isize=M.

30. Catharine Beecher, "How to Redeem Woman's Profession from Dishonor," *Harper's New Monthly Magazine* 31 (November 1865): 710–16.

31. Louise Palmer Smith, "The Princess Biddy," *Putnam's Monthly Magazine of American Literature, Science and Art* 15, no. 25 (January 1870): 114–17, accessed July 2016, http://ebooks.library.cornell.edu/cgi/t/text/pageviewer-idx?c=putn;cc=putn;rgn=full%20text;idno=putn0015-1;didno=putn0015-1;view=image;seq=116;node=putn0015-1%3A1;page=root;size=100.

32. Edward Bellamy, *Looking Backward: 2000–1887* (1888), 94, accessed July 2016, Project Gutenberg Ebook, http://www.gutenberg.org/ebooks/624.

33. Louise Clarence, "Domestic Service," *Far and Near* (1891): 24–26.

34. Kathleen L. Endres and Therese Lueck, eds. *Women's Periodicals in the United States: Social and Political Issues*, Historical Guides to the World's Periodicals and Newspapers (Westport, CT: Greenwood Press, 1996), 78.

35. Helen Stuart Campbell, *Household Economics: A Course of Lectures in the School of Economics of the University of Wisconsin* (New York: G.P. Putnam's Sons, 1896), 223–23, Internet Archive, https://archive.org/stream/householdeconomi00camp#page/222/mode/2up.

36. Lucy Maynard Salmon, *Domestic Service* (New York: The Macmillan Company, 1897), 179, Internet Archive, https://archive.org/details/domesticservice01salmgoog.

37. Lillian Pettengill, *Toilers of the Home: The Record of a College Woman's Experience as a Domestic Servant* (New York: Doubleday, Page & Company, 1903), 380, 394, 397, Internet Archive, https://archive.org/details/toilershomereco00pettgoog.

38. "*Toilers of the Home*—Lillian Pettengill—*Everybody's*," Undercover Reporting, Deception for Journalism's Sake: A Database, accessed July 2016, http://sites.dlib.nyu.edu/undercover/toilers-home-lillian-pettengill-everybodys.

39. Mrs. John (Bessie) Van Vorst, *The Woman of the People, Harpers* (May 1903): 871–75, accessed July 2017, Harpers Archive Online.

40. "*The Woman Who Toils*—Bessie and Marie van Vorst—*Everybody's*," Undercover Reporting, Deception for Journalism's Sake: A Database, accessed July 2016, http://sites.dlib.nyu.edu/undercover/woman-who-toils-bessie-and-marie-van-vorst-everybodys.

41. "Servants," *New York Times* (September 20, 1874), retrieved from ProQuest Historical Newspapers: New York Times.

42. "How to Sweep a Room," *Scribner's Monthly* 9, no. 1 (November, 1874): 118–19, accessed July 2016, http://ebooks.library.cornell.edu/cgi/t/text/pageviewer-idx?c=scmo;cc=scmo;rgn=full%20text;idno=scmo0009-1;didno=scmo0009-1;view=image;seq=124;node=scmo0009-1%3A18;page=root;size=100.

43. W. E. B. Dubois, *The Philadelphia Negro: A Social Study* (New York: Schocken Books, 1899), 487–88m, Internet Archive, https://archive.org/details/philadelphianegr001901mbp.

44. Lee Chew "The Biography of a Chinaman," *The Independent* 55, no. 2829 (February 19, 1903): 417–23, HathiTrust Digital Library, https://babel.hathitrust.org/cgi/pt?id=inu.32000000688715;view=1up;seq=463.

CHAPTER FOUR

Food

We Are What We Eat

Essential Questions
- What influences our food choices?
  - Personal tastes; family or cultural traditions; geographic location; sex or gender; social class; government; advertising; government policies?
  - What influenced food choices of people in the past?
- What do table manners communicate about an individual? About a culture? About a historical era?

Food is a hot topic in modern America. A countless number of magazines, books, websites, and television shows explore growing, cooking, serving, and eating food. We are bombarded with information on the newest diets and ingredients, the best restaurants, and most popular chefs. New foods are introduced; old foods disappear or are reinvented. Conflicting adjectives categorize food as healthy or unhealthy; pure, clean, and natural or processed, prepackaged, and junk; fast food or slow; traditional and comfort or fusion or haute cuisine—each word or phrase reflecting assumptions about food. The common phrase "we are what we eat" can be interpreted on many levels—nutritional, political, economic, historic, scientific, or cultural; by individuals, groups, or society.

Food is studied in every discipline. Psychologists and sociologists explore how individuals and cultures decide what to eat, how to prepare it, and how to consume it. Anthropologists explore the meaning and symbolism of food in a culture or how food relates to social class, sex, gender, or ethnicity. Economists study the production, distribution, marketing, sales, trade, and prices of food. Political scientists examine the government food policies such as taxation, regulation, and debate the government's role in feeding its citizens. Scientists from the fields of nutrition, medicine, chemistry, biology, and agriculture study every aspect of food, from diet, health, and nutrition to chemical composition, production, and preservation.

But food was not a popular topic among historians until recent decades. Prior to the 1980s, the study of food and cooking was usually dismissed by political, intellectual, or economic historians as a trivial topic related to the uneventful lives of women. Occasionally written accounts of great banquets and celebrations and recipe manuscripts were analyzed, but these studies focused mostly upon the wealthy elite. Little attention was paid to food in the daily lives of average people.

Independent historians, sometimes referred to as culinary historians, had studied historical cooking methods and kitchen equipment, but their work was often dismissed as the work of antiquarians. Technically, an antiquarian studies objects from the past such artifacts or historical sites, rather than documents. But the term is also used to imply antiquarians' work as too local, narrow, or amateur to qualify as legitimate historical scholarship.[1]

In recent decades, new approaches incorporating a wider range of primary sources, archeological and scientific discoveries, and computer analyses are providing insights into the history of food in the lives of average people. For example, medieval historians, using statistical methods, have examined the surviving records of great estates to assess agricultural production to make conclusions about living standards, prices, wages, and nutrition. Nutritionists analyze historical records to study the nutritional value of foods to determine what deficiencies in quantity and quality existed. Zooarchaeologists and archaeobotanists evaluate material from archaeological digs, human skeletons, plant and animal remains, pot shards, and other historical remains from trash pits and latrines for information about diet and diet-related diseases.

In the 1980s and 1990s, new interdisciplinary histories of food began to be published examining the social, economic, and political history of a food or agricultural products. One of the first, Sidney Mintz's *Sweetness and Power: The Place of Sugar in Modern History* (1985) traced the evolution of sugar as a food for the rich in the pre-industrial era to one that eventually was consumed by the poor in the industrial age.[2] Food historians use interdisciplinary approaches that relate continuity and change in diet to social class, religious practice, immigration, urbanization, technological change, the growth of the food industry, counterculture movements, and government policy.

In the 1990s, several histories of food and household work were published with a focus upon the lives and issues faced by women as a whole as well as women of different ethnicities and social classes. Because there are fewer sources documenting the lives of women, historians turned to items previously ignored. Cookbooks, manuscript recipe collections, scrapbooks, and other domestic or household literature, produced largely by women and for women, came to be recognized as valuable primary sources. These sources document perceptions and reality of daily life for women and families as well as wider technological, cultural, and political changes.

Because food is such a broad theme, the focus of what follows must be narrowed. First, the diet of the medieval peasant is featured as an example of a pre-industrial diet. While the foods eaten by pre-industrial people varied by culture and climate, two factors were common worldwide for average households. Food choices were limited and hunger was not unusual. Second, social class differences in dining and table manners are examined from the Middle Ages to the twentieth century. The attention is on Western Europe and the United States, but similar patterns are common in all cultures.

Pre-Industrial Diet of the Medieval Peasant

Most humans throughout history struggled to get enough food or required nutrients to meet the dietary requirements for good health. Average people in the pre-industrial era had limited food choices and faced seasonal food shortages. Short-term regional shortages and widespread and long-term famines caused by war, government policies, or crop failures caused by natural or man-made disasters, while not unheard of today in some parts of the world, were common in the past. On the other hand, the elite and wealthy were more likely to be well-fed, less likely to suffer from food shortages and famines, and had access to a much wider range of foods.

Food in the pre-industrial world was local. The diet of households in the ancient and medieval world depended upon what they could produce and preserve themselves, a system referred to as subsistence agriculture. When pre-industrial farming households did manage to produce surplus food, it paid taxes or was sold and traded in nearby villages and towns. For example, in medieval England, the housewife usually brewed the ale. She sold or traded what the household did not consume for items they could not produce themselves, such as metal tools; buckets, barrels, or pots for storage or cooking; or materials and labor required to build houses or barns. The medieval household might sell or trade extra eggs, poultry, fruit, vegetables, honey, or beeswax, or gather additional wood or peat to sell for fuel. Those living in towns could grow some food in urban gardens, or keep a few animals, but usually food had to be purchased or obtained through trade from local farmers.[3]

Perishable foods were difficult to transport over long distances in large quantities, especially overland. For example, Asian spices such as cinnamon and cloves and tropical cane sugar were expensive luxury goods in Western Europe prior to the Age of Exploration because of the long distances and expense involved. In a few instances, long-distance trade in large quantities of food did exist in the ancient and medieval world. For example, the government in ancient Rome supervised the transport and importation of huge quantities of grain on ships from Egypt and North Africa. Long distance trade in salted herring took place in the Middle Ages. But those are exceptions in the pre-industrial world. The majority of average people produced what they ate before the era of industrialization.

In the one-thousand-year span of the European Middle Ages, change in diet occurred slowly. But over time, diet gradually improved for average people due to improvements in transportation, innovations in technology and trade, increased land cultivation, and government centralization. Improved harnesses for horses to pull plows, innovations

Figure 4.1. A wealthy couple, with their maid, visit a peasant farm in this seventeenth-century Flemish painting. Everyday activities are taking place in the main room—eating, churning butter, caring for children. In this pre-industrial home, household items are stored around the edges of the room in a cupboard, barrels, and baskets. A staircase in the rear goes to an upper chamber or loft. The food on the table is served in bowls. There is only one spoon on the table and a man is eating directly from the bowl. Even though chimneys providing smoke ventilation were used in the seventeenth century, this painting depicts a hearth in the center of the room with food cooking in a large pot hanging from a hook.
Painting, *The Visit to the Farm*, Pieter Brueghel the Younger, 1622. (Courtesy of Wikimedia Commons)

in plowing equipment, new systems of field rotation, and water-powered mills for grinding grain were adopted.[4] These improvements supported higher agricultural yields. By the fifteenth century, the growth of a market economy made imported foods more widely available to those who could afford them. Non-local fish, spices, dried and exotic fruits, and imported alcohol such as wine in England were in larger supply. But the diet of peasants was still typically local or regional.[5]

Population density and increases or decreases in population over time also impacted the diet of peasants. As the population increased between the eleventh and end of the thirteenth centuries, more agricultural land was used for grain production and the quantities of livestock declined. Therefore, the diet of both peasants and the urban worker depended more and more on grains. As livestock production declined, so did the amount of two essential nutrients, protein and fat, provided by dairy products and meat.

The increase in grain production over time slowly reduced the fertility of the soil. Modern chemical fertilizers were unknown in the Middle Ages, and the main source of fertilizer, animal manure, was not sufficient in the amounts needed to replenish depleted soils. As result, famine and starvation occurred in some areas. Overall population was declining by the early fourteenth century, even before the Black Death. By the late fourteenth century, after the dramatic decline in population caused by the Black Death, diet began to improve and consumption of meat and dairy products began to increase.[6]

Despite the variations over time and region, several generalizations can be made about the diet of medieval peasants from around 1000 to 1500 that are a marked contrast to modern American diets. First, the majority of calories consumed were carbohydrates in the form of whole grains, not from refined carbohydrates and sugars. Second, fat was limited in the peasant's diet. And finally, protein was much less likely to come from eating meat.

The mainstay of the medieval peasant's diet was grains—primarily wheat, barley, rye, and oats—creating a diet high in complex carbohydrates and fiber. These grains could be ground into flour and made into bread, boiled to make gruels, soups, or stews, or brewed into ale or beer. In the Middle Ages, as in other cultures, grains used and the color and texture of bread fell on a spectrum with the lightest wheat breads for the wealthiest and the darker, courser breads of cheaper grains or the low-quality wheat for the poor. Medieval loaves of bread were not the light, white, sliced breads baked in industrial factories and consumed in the modern world.[7]

Bread was baked by the village baker because peasant households only had a hearth and open fire for cooking. Only great households could afford the expense of baking ovens and the fuel to heat them. The businesses of the miller who ground grain into flour and the baker were regulated to ensure the quality of the products and both were taxed by the lord or town government. Because bread was such an important part of the diet, medieval laws often regulated the quality and price that could be charged by bakers. The assize (laws) governing the quality and price of bread in medieval England were the most widely enforced statutes. These laws specified prices for loaves made of different grains, but the weight of the loaf could vary depending upon the price of grain.[8]

Ale and beer were also an important part of the medieval diet. These beverages were as important to daily nutrition as eating bread or stews made of grains. Medieval ale and beer had very low levels of alcohol compared to modern beers and were consumed daily by all members of the family, men, women, and children. Estimates from the late Middle Ages indicate that drinking a gallon of ale over the span of a day was not unusual. Other low-alcohol, fermented beverages, mead made from honey, cider from apples, and perry from pears, were also consumed in some regions. Milk was consumed primarily by children. Whey, the liquid byproduct from milk leftover from cheese-making, was also a part of the peasant diet.[9]

Modern conceptions of beer and alcohol consumption as dangerous to health and morality were not a part of the medieval experience. In the Middle Ages, alcohol was considered a normal part of life and daily diet and required for social occasions. The medieval Catholic Church did not condemn normal daily consumption of beer or wine; only overindulgence was considered sinful. Condemnation of *all* consumption of alcoholic beverages as inherently sinful or unhealthful was a product of nineteenth-century temperance movements.[10]

Fats provided essential calories for energy, and the medieval peasant usually consumed fat in the form of cheese, butter, nuts, and eggs. Small amounts of beef, pork, and sheep fats were used in cooking, but were not often available to peasants. Vegetable oils were not easily obtained in Europe except for olive oil for those living in warm, Mediterranean regions. Walnuts, hazelnuts, pine nuts, chestnuts, and even acorns also provided fat in the diet and were cultivated or gathered from forests.

Most of the protein in the peasant diet was provided from legumes such as beans, peas, or lentils. Protein from the meat of domestic stock, wild game, or fish was possible, but in general, meat consumption among peasants was very low, especially compared to the modern American diet. Medieval records show the most common domesticated animals were cattle, swine, sheep, goats, and poultry. While the consumption of meat also varied somewhat over time and by region, several factors contributed to its low consumption by medieval peasants.

Cattle and sheep require access to a substantial amount of land for grazing and from which to make hay to feed the animals in the winter. Many peasant households did not have access to enough land for these animals. On the other hand, pigs, goats, and poultry were foragers that could survive on much more limited resources. Fish also provided protein for peasant households located near rivers, streams, lakes, or the coast, but because fish bones decompose more quickly, archaeologists find it difficult to determine consumption patterns.[11]

Domestic animals were often more valuable to the peasant households when they did not become meat on the table. For example, sheep were valuable for wool, chickens for eggs, cattle and goats for milk. These products were consumed by the family and could be sold or traded for cash or other needed supplies. Pigs, chickens, ducks, or geese could be used to pay taxes to the landlords or sold or traded to the wealthy or urban workers in nearby towns, providing more for the family than if used as simply food for the household. Archaeologists' examinations of animal bones from trash pits of the period show that animals eaten were old, indicating they had been kept for other purposes for as long as possible and slaughtered for the table at the end of their productive lives.[12]

Figure 4.2. Everyone in a pre-industrial household worked for the family's survival. In this fourteenth-century image, cheese is being made. The woman warms the milk in a large pot on the outdoor fire. The man holds a molded cheese, and the seated boy eats the curds or whey. On the table are simple tools, a bowl, the cheese mold, a knife, and a large spoon.
Image from *Tacuinum Sanitatis* (*Health Handbook*) fourteenth-century text. (Courtesy of Wikimedia Commons)

Seasonal vegetables and fruits provided additional essential nutrients, but did not provide large amounts of calories in the daily diet. Cabbages and root vegetables such as beets, carrots, turnips, parsnips, radishes, garlic, onions, and leeks could be stored for long periods and used as needed. Cold-tolerant greens such as lettuce, cress, arugula, parsley, or endive would grow through mild winters. Fruits included pears, apples, plums, cherries, mulberries, all of which could be dried, pickled in vinegar, or turned into fermented beverages. Wild plants such as mushrooms, greens, wild strawberries, raspberries, and blackberries were also consumed.

Sweeteners and seasonings were limited to honey, salt, and herbs in the diet of peasants. Honey could be harvested from wild beehives or produced from domestic hives. Salt is essential for health and was needed to preserve food. In the Middle Ages, salt was mined or produced by evaporating sea water. Herbs, the leaves of plants that could be grown in peasant gardens such as sage, dill, or mint, were used to flavor food. Spices from Asia such as cinnamon, pepper, and cloves were expensive imported products available only to the wealthy.

People in the Middle Ages did drink water, contrary to popular modern myths. Water was consumed plain, flavored with vinegar, honey, or spices, and mixed with wine or beer. Medieval sources often reference the drinking of ale or wine, while references to drinking water are rare. But common daily acts are usually omitted from written records. Drinking wine or beer conveyed more prestige than drinking water, which was free and available everywhere, and therefore more likely to be referenced in surviving sources.[13]

Evidence from records of medieval cities demonstrate people of the era understood the dangers of polluted water, even though they lacked modern scientific explanations. Efforts were made to bring clean water into the city and avoid polluting water sources. For example, in thirteenth-century London, a conduit of lead pipes was constructed to provide fresh water from springs outside the city. Those unable to afford access were forced to draw water from existing wells or from the increasingly polluted Thames River. Medieval towns also had early versions of zoning that required polluting industries such as leather tanning and wool fulling be located downstream from the town.

Based on scholars' conclusions about the diet of peasants in the Middle Ages, one might assume their diet was healthful—high in complex carbohydrates and fiber, low in fat and sugar, with an acceptable amount of protein. But four important factors must be considered.

First, the wealth and resources of peasant households varied greatly and these differences directly impacted their daily diet. The amount of land available to a household for growing grains, gardens, orchards, and for livestock pasture, and access to wild foods such as fish or game determined the variety and quantity of food consumed. In general, the less land available to the peasant household, the more limited their diet.

Second, the quality and quantity of the peasant diet varied not just by the wealth and resources of the household, but also by the season. During the harvest season in the autumn, peasants had access to more food and wider choices. But during the winter and spring, choices were limited to what could be stored and preserved. The leanest months were those just preceding the harvest, May and June in England, when the previous year's food was depleted and the new season's fruits, vegetables, and grains were not mature.

Third, because peasant households usually produced just enough for their needs for the year, one disaster could wipe out the year's food supply. Crop damage caused by weather, war, insects, or diseases often caused severe short-term shortages and in the most extreme cases, long-term famine. An exceptionally cold, hot, wet, or dry summer could destroy crops. Soldiers might raid food supplies or deliberately destroy crops and livestock.[14]

For example, historian Christopher Dyer estimated English harvest workers in the early fourteenth century were receiving food allowances that provided 2,000–3,000 calories a day, enough to maintain health. But these workers were toward the top of the hierarchy; many rural peasants earned less. Employment for day laborers was intermittent. Harvest workers who were well fed in August during the harvest may have faced hunger in other seasons or in years that crops failed.[15]

Finally, the health of most medieval peasants probably suffered, often or occasionally, from a lack of calories and essential vitamins and minerals in their diet. Diseases caused by nutritional deficiencies that are rare in the modern Western world—rickets, scurvy, beriberi, and anemia—were common in the pre-industrial era. Tooth loss from poor nutrition was frequent, but they did not suffer from dental problems caused by sugar consumption.

Medieval peasants were unlikely to develop obesity-related health problems or those that accompany a diet high in fat, sugar, and sodium such as high blood pressure and heart disease. These modern health problems were mostly confined to the medieval elite who could afford to eat large quantities of meat, cheeses, and fats, consume excessive amounts of alcohol, and avoid the exercise required by the chores of daily life.[16]

Historians studying the diet of medieval people sometimes present conflicting descriptions of medieval diets, interpreting primary sources differently. While some historians focus on disease caused by nutrition deficiencies and a lack of adequate food among peasants, others perceive an abundant, but monotonous, supply of food.[17] Scholars have been able to determine which foods and nutrients were available in the Middle Ages, but it is very difficult to determine exactly what was consumed, in what quantities, and how it impacted the daily health of medieval children, men, and women.

Furthermore, agricultural productivity was much lower than today. Modern domestic animals, grains, fruits, and vegetables are all the result of hybridization, selective breeding, and genetic engineering and yield at levels unheard of in the pre-industrial era. Domestic livestock was 40–60 percent smaller than modern breeds. Not only did farm animals produce less meat, but also lower yields of milk or eggs. Medieval grain harvests have been estimated to be just three to four times more than the amount of seed planted (3:1–4:1).[18] On the other hand, modern wheat harvests can yield at a ratio of 20:1; oats 15:1; and corn, a grain unknown in medieval Europe but on which the world now depends, can yield at rates as high as 100:1.[19]

Modern Americans consume a very different diet than people in the pre-industrial world. The diet of a medieval peasant was monotonous and dull by today's standards. The same choices, bread, beer, beans, vegetables, and in smaller amounts, cheese, eggs, butter, and maybe meat, varied very little from day to day and from year to year, was high fiber, low fat, and sometimes did not meet nutritional requirements for good health. On the other hand, modern Americans have countless food choices and on average, too many calories. The typical modern diet, also called the Western pattern diet, is high in fats from meat and fried foods, high in refined sugar and carbohydrates from processed foods and sodas, and low in fresh fruits and vegetables, whole grains, seafood, poultry.

Food, Dining, and Social Status

The foods of the wealthy and of average people of the pre-industrial world were distinguished by quantity and variety, as well as the methods used to prepare food and behavior at the table. In peasant households, cooking was just one of many daily chores of wives, mothers, and daughters. Cooked dishes were simple, made over a fire and served from the same pot in which they were prepared.

On the other hand, those sitting at the wealthiest tables were served rare, costly, and sometimes bizarre dishes at lavish banquets with expensive table settings and elaborate etiquette. For example, the Roman emperors Vitellius and Elagabalus were reported to have hosted extravagant banquets featuring brains of pheasants and peacocks, tongues of flamingos, vegetables mixed with gold, onyx, and amber, and rice and fish with pearls served on costly dishes (sources 1 and 2). Not only were these exotic ingredients very expensive and difficult to acquire (it would take a LOT of flamingos to produce a banquet dish full of their tongues), but also a trained cook was required to prepare these delicacies. Only the wealthy could afford the numerous slaves or servants and trained cooks to prepare and serve such meals.

The ingredients, tools, and preparation time required for some dishes automatically made them a high-status food. For example, molded gelatin dishes, both savory and sweet, or jellies, were high-status dishes in the Middle Ages. The

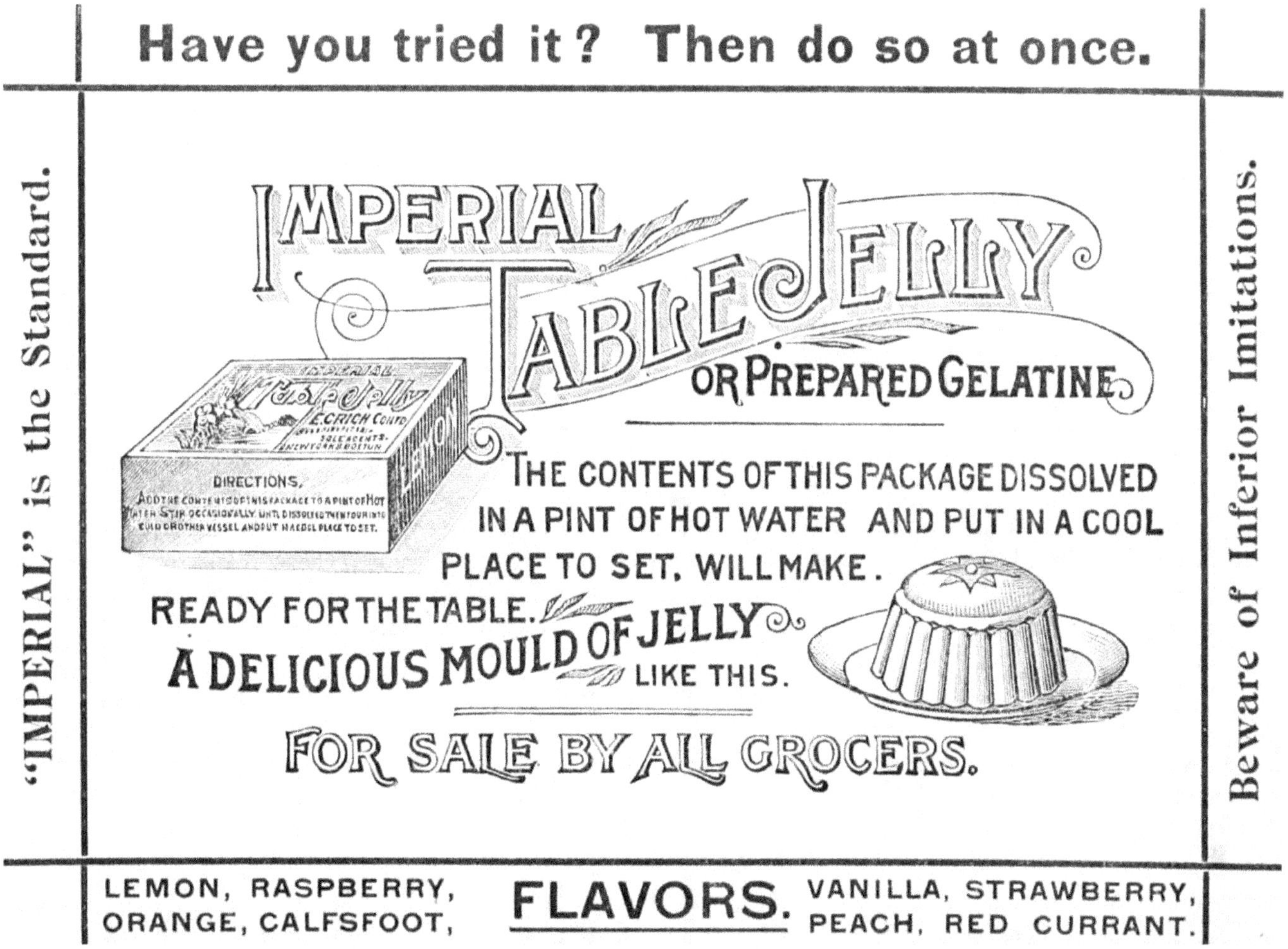

Figure 4.3. A gelled or jellied dish, known today as gelatin, was a work-intensive and high-status food in the pre-industrial era. Collagen was extracted from boiled animal bones, flavored, and molded. Unflavored, dried gelatin became available for purchase in England in the 1840s and in the late 1890s; Charles Knox developed and marketed Knox Gelatin to American home cooks. Today, gelatin is sold under several brand names including Jell-O. The brand featured in this 1891 ad was available in several flavors including calfsfoot, an original source of gelatin.
Advertisement for Imperial Table Jelly or Prepared Gelantine, *The Universal Cookbook* by the Ladies' Aid Society of the First Universalist Church of Englewood, Illinois (Chicago: C. H. Morgan Co, 1891), 17. (Courtesy of Library of Congress and Internet Archive)

ancestor of modern gelatin, the dish required collagen, a substance that causes liquids to coagulate or gel. First, skin, bones, and connective tissues of animals, usually pig or sheep feet, chicken, rabbit, or other parts of domestic animals had to be boiled to produce collagen. The resulting liquid was strained and simmered in clean pots several times. It was flavored with expensive spices, decorated with fruit or other foods, and poured in special decorative molds to set.[20] The medieval peasant had neither the time, tools, nor variety of ingredients to create molded jellies.

In the Middle Ages, table manners for both rich and poor would have been shocking by modern standards. Eating with hands, spoons, and knives out of shared pots or plates was common throughout the Middle Ages in the homes of all social classes. Even in wealthy households, a trencher, a plate made of wood, might be shared between two people. But there were distinctions separating well-bred nobility from commoners.

Geoffrey Chaucer's description of the table manners of the prioress, in the late medieval *The Canterbury Tales* (1387–1400) demonstrates the divide. The prioress, a noble woman, did not drop food from her mouth on her clothing, or leave greasy marks on her cup. She could make pleasant conversation at the table. She did put her fingers in the common dish of sauce; what distinguished her was she didn't make a mess doing it. She was sharing a cup, but not leaving it greasy or dropping bits of chewed food in it. The prioress was unusual, she was a point of contrast to most medieval diners who were messy eaters with food on their mouths, hands, clothes, and table (source 3).

Polite table manners for upper class Renaissance courtiers was described in Giovanni della Casa's book of advice, *Galateo: The Rules of Polite Behavior* (1559). Gentlemen were advised against scratching and belching, using or wearing a toothpick at the table, leaning over the table, eating greedily, filling their mouths too full, and scrubbing teeth with napkins or fingers. Grooming was to be done in private, not at the table or in view of others. Hands should be washed before sitting down at the table. Because della Casa had to warn his upper class readers on what to do and not do at the table suggests that his many contemporaries were doing exactly the opposite of what he advised (source 4).

The shift to table manners acceptable today did not occur until the eighteenth century. New patterns of eating and dining were first adopted by the upper classes and people living in urban areas. Utensils for eating and serving food and how they were used communicated the social status of diners and households. The fork and knife are one such example.

In pre-industrial Europe, forks were serving utensils, usually large, two-pronged utensils used to carve meat. These forks were not designed to put food directly in the mouth. People ate food with their hands, a spoon, or a knife. Knives were sometimes shared, but many people carried their own multi-purpose knife for use at the table or at work. In the sixteenth century, the elite in Italy and France began using a smaller, special fork to put food into their mouths, much as it is used in the modern world. But this practice was slow to catch on among average people throughout the sixteenth and seventeenth centuries.

Americans were slow to adopt the English and French uses of the small, three-pronged fork.[21] In the eighteenth century, many Americans still followed the old practice of eating with a spoon, hands, and stabbing pieces of food with a knife and putting it in their mouths. An advice book published in 1838, with an audience of middle and upper class readers, still advised it was proper in America to put food in the mouth with the blade of a knife. But the author acknowledged some Americans had already adopted the European fashion (source 5). Sources describe frontier families sharing bowls, plates, knives, and noggins (wooden cups) and following pre-industrial methods of cooking and serving food (source 6).

The dining room was another innovation symbolizing the divide between the upper and growing middle classes and the working classes in the eighteenth and nineteenth centuries. Throughout the Middle Ages and Early Modern Period, spaces in the homes of both wealthy and poor were multipurpose. The space where people ate was also used for sleeping, working, or entertaining. Tables and chairs were often makeshift so they could be moved out of the way for other activities.

By the nineteenth century, the presence of dining rooms indicated to guests that the household had the financial means and the good taste to be in the rising middle and upper classes. Status and wealth was evident in matched sets of tables and chairs, and large, elaborate carved sideboards for displaying and storing a variety of specialized serving dishes. Paintings and prints of still-life themes of fruits, vegetables, flowers, and game were needed to decorate the dining room.[22]

How the food was served when guests when invited to dine became more elaborate in the eighteenth and nineteenth centuries in Europe and later in America. In the eighteenth century, for French style of service diners arrived in the dining room to a table already set and ornate dishes filled with food. Typically, four courses were served—soup, two main courses, and dessert. Servants were required to remove the dishes after each course and set the table for the next

No. 2187. CASTER [Decency], $11.00
Satin Embossed, Six No. 26 Bottles.

No. 281. CHASED CASTER [Decently], $8.25
Six No. 11½ Bottles.

Figure 4.4. Castor Sets from an 1889 catalog. A castor set, also called a cruet frame, held salt, pepper, mustard, vinegar, and other condiments. As mass-produced tableware became available, even middle class homes could afford elaborate table settings. The process of electroplating was developed in the early 1800s. Silver-plated tableware gave the appearance of wealth at a lower cost.

In 1846, Catharine Beecher, in *Miss Beecher's Domestic Receipt Book*, recommended to "set the castors in the exact centre of the table. Some prefer to have them on a side-table, and the waiter carry them around, but the table looks better to have them put in the centre. If they are put on the side-table, the celery stand may be placed in the centre of the table." By the late nineteenth century, styles changed and tall, elaborate fruit stands were preferred on the most stylish tables. Many nineteenth-century home goods catalogs are available online. The source of this image is a 471-page catalog featuring hundreds of silver-plated items including fruit stands, card receivers for visiting cards of guests, jewelry, and accessories for the dining room, bedroom, bathroom, and parlor.

13th Annual Illustrated Catalogue of Busiest House I America (Salem, WV: L. J. Flowers, 1889), 41. (Courtesy of Internet Archive) course, but the host and hostess often helped to serve at least some of the food to guests from their positions at the head of the table.

The nineteenth-century Russian style service required more tableware, a wider variety of foods, and more servants. When guests arrived, the table was set with the expensive plates, glasses, and specialized forks, knives, and spoons. The host and hostess no longer helped to serve the food from a large serving dish on the table. Instead, numerous servants and waiters placed individual portions on the plate of each diner. Additional plates, glasses, and silverware were placed on the table by servants for as many as fourteen different courses of the meal.[23] Numerous books and articles on proper dining etiquette were published to advise readers on how to conform to the rules and requirements of polite middle and upper class dining (source 7).

Over the course of the twentieth century, elaborate table settings were simplified. Etiquette for serving the food and eating became less formal. Instead of large formal dinner parties, guests could be entertained at informal buffets, cookouts, or potluck dinners. But etiquette manuals, cookbooks, and household advice continued to communicate messages to readers suggesting one's reputation and status in society depended upon cooking, serving, decorating, eating, and behaving in correct ways when guests were invited to dine (sources 8 and 9).

In the Classroom

During lessons about food and diet, the teacher should be cognizant of the students' concerns about weight and appearance. Nearly one-third of children and youth and two-thirds of adults in the United States are either overweight or obese,[24] and the percentage of American children with obesity has more than tripled since the 1970s.[25] Approximately half of all American adults have one or more preventable, diet-related chronic diseases such as cardiovascular disease and type 2 diabetes,[26] and children with obesity are at higher risk of these and other chronic diseases and are more likely to be bullied, teased, or suffer from depression.[27]

Classroom activities and discussions in which students are required share details about their diet with classmates may not be appropriate. When examples are needed, teachers should share information about their own diet or create hypothetical examples.

In the following activity, students compare and contrast modern diets to those of the pre-industrial world to investigate change over time, not to judge or condemn others. Students, knowingly or unknowingly, may use hurtful or offensive language related to food and diet during classroom discussions. If this occurs, assumptions behind stereotypes must be examined so this type of language is discredited and discouraged. Opportunities to critically examine societal and cultural expectations related to weight and personal appearance may arise and should be addressed in a constructive manner.

Essential Question

What influences our food choices?

Begin the activity by providing images or a short list of foods students are likely to love or hate. Ask them to rate each item on a scale of 1–5, indicating how much they like or dislike that food. Next, ask students to explain *why* they like or dislike a food. Most students will refer to personal tastes.

Introduce the essential questions and explore how food choices are influenced by factors other than personal taste. A popular food advertisement can be introduced to stimulate student discussion. Or, the United States Department of Agriculture Food Guide Pyramid can be used as an example of government impact on food choices. Ask students if salads are for girls and steaks for boys and explore why people might assume it to be true.

Over the following days, ask students to log the food and beverages they consume. Consider forming a partnership with family and consumer science, physical education, biology, or health teachers to create an interdisciplinary project. For example, students might record serving sizes, amounts of protein, fat, and carbohydrates, and calories consumed along with calories burned through physical activity. Many free or inexpensive computer programs are available that make logging food and nutritional assessments quick and easy.

After students have logged their food and beverages, ask them to analyze their lists with the essential question in mind. For example, what foods on their lists are a family or cultural tradition? Are some foods thought to be more appropriate for men or for women? Which items on their lists originated in the local community? What foods or beverages are heavily advertised? What government programs influence school lunch choices? This exploration can be extended over different days, units, or disciplines, depending upon the curriculum and age of the students.

Once students have analyzed their food choices, make comparisons between their diet and that of the pre-industrial era. The information about the diet of an average medieval peasant in this chapter or diet of other historical eras can be provided for comparison. Resources of all types are available documenting the food of most historical eras and cultures. Ask students to consider what foods on their lists would have not been available in the era or region to which comparisons are made and explore the reasons for these differences. Revisit the essential question and explore how food choices in the past were more limited as well as similarities and differences in what influenced food choice.

Be sure to address how temporary or seasonal food shortages, food insecurity, and famine were the same and different in both modern and pre-industrial cultures. In most of the modern world, widespread famine has ceased due to technological advances in agriculture and transportation. But famine has not been eliminated. Modern famines in the twentieth century include those caused by Stalin's policies in the Soviet Union (1932–1933); government failures in Bengal, India, during World War II; Mao Tse-Tung's programs during the Great Cultural Revolution (1958–1961); and the Khmer Rouge in Cambodia (1970s), and those in civil war–torn Africa.

The photographs of Peter Menzel featured in *Hungry Planet: What the World Eats* and *Material World: A Global Family Portrait* are excellent resources for making comparisons to contemporary world cultures. In *Hungry Planet*, families from different nations are depicted in their kitchens with the food they consume in a week. Text and charts provide information about the typical diet in each country, including average caloric intake as well as amounts of sugar and animal products in the diet. In *Material World*, families are photographed with their household belongings. These images demonstrate a powerful message; in some areas of the world, families still consume a pre-industrial diet and live in pre-industrial dwellings.[28]

Few modern Americans face a lifelong struggle for food. Public programs such as the National School Lunch Program and Food Stamp Program prevent starvation. Over the last one hundred years, deficiencies in the essential nutrients in food required for health have decreased and the availability of food has increased. The average daily calorie consumption of Americans has risen from 2,024 calories in 1970 to 2,481 in 2010, an increase of 457 calories per person.[29]

Despite these advances, many living in poverty today face periodic food shortages and may suffer from malnutrition, inadequate or unbalanced amounts of nutrients or calories. Thirteen percent of American households face what is termed *food insecurity*—a lack of access to enough food for an active, healthy life for all members of the household.[30] Most government nutrition programs are designed to be a supplement, not provide for the complete nutrition for a family.

Some live in *food deserts*, poor rural or urban regions where affordable healthful fresh foods are not available. In the United States, people living in the most poverty-dense counties are the most likely to be obese.[31] This seems to be a contradiction and is often misinterpreted. Poverty does not cause obesity; but the challenges of living in poverty are related to high rates of obesity. For example, those living in the poorest areas often more sedentary because lack access to safe outdoor activities, parks, or sports facilities.

Essential Question

What do table manners communicate about an individual? About a culture? About a historical era?

Descriptions of table manners and dining with guests or in public convey a wealth of information about individuals, the wider culture, a historical era, and change over time. The following excerpts span five hundred years. These selected sources provide a glimpse into the diverse sources used by historians to study food-related behavior.

Primary source analysis, or close reading, should focus on an essential question so students reach beyond the obvious and engage in critical analysis. Always ask students to cite details from the text to provide evidence for their conclusions.

The following list of questions can be used to prompt student inquiry.

- What details and facts can be learned about dining behavior of the era? What food was served? What tableware was required? Where are guests entertained? On what occasions? What behavior was expected?
- Was the meal, behavior, or situation representative of every meal eaten by the people described? Or was this a special occasion?

- Does the source represent all groups of people in the historical era? Did everyone in the era eat these foods? Use these manners? Which groups are represented? Are the rules for behavior different for men and women or rich and poor?
- Describe the type of primary source. Descriptive or prescriptive? Real or ideal? A history? A travel account? Fiction? Biography or autobiography? How does the genre of the source impact its meaning?
- What viewpoint is represented by the author? Word choices can signify the author's social status and opinion of groups to which the author does not belong. Details may be exaggerated for effect. The author may choose loaded words that convey a positive or negative meaning to the reader. Is the author making a larger moral or religious argument about the role of manners in society?
- Some dining habits change over time, some stay the same. Does the author explicitly or implicitly condemn or praise past habits or compare old and new practices?
- Compare sources from the same era or culture. What is different? What is the same? What explains the similarities and differences?
- Compare sources from different eras. What manners are new? What manners have fallen out of favor? What caused changes in food or behavior? Why did other foods or behaviors stay the same?

The two following excerpts describe the dining habits of the Roman emperors Vitellius and Elagabalus. Although they reigned nearly one hundred and fifty years apart, the descriptions are similar. Both illustrate lavish dining and eating habits of the elite. Both excerpts also convey the authors' disapproval of dissolute lifestyles.

Vitellius's reign is described in The Twelve Caesars, *a set of twelve biographies from Julius Caesar to Domitian, written in 121 AD by Seutonius. This work is an important primary source about the lives of the early rulers of the Roman Empire. It also follows a distinct style in which the author contrasts the moral habits of some emperors with the immorality of others, linking the success of the empire with the morality of its leader. Seutonius may have exaggerated to make these contrasts. In this excerpt, Vitellius is portrayed as a glutton, someone who eats and drinks excessive amounts.*

This style was adopted by many biographers throughout history. It was used in the Augustan History, *from which the excerpt below about Elagabalus was taken.* Augustan History *is a compilation of thirty biographies of emperors from 117 to 285, written by several different authors, probably in the fourth century. Historians are uncertain about the purpose of this later work and the truthfulness of the information. Elagabalus's rule was short and controversial. The following description of his extravagant dining habits may have been exaggerated to make political or rhetorical point that Rome was abandoning its moral traditions.*

SOURCE 1

Excerpt from the *Life of Vitellius*[32] (ruled April–December 69)

He was chiefly addicted to the vices of luxury and cruelty. He always made three meals a day, sometimes four; breakfast, dinner, and supper, and a drunken revel after all. This load of victuals he could well enough bear, from a custom to which he had inured himself, of frequently vomiting. For these several meals he would make different appointments at the houses of his friends on the same day. None ever entertained him at less expense than four hundred thousand sesterces.

The most famous was a set entertainment given him by his brother, at which, it is said, there were served up no less than two thousand choice fishes, and seven thousand birds. Yet even this supper he himself outdid, at a feast which he gave upon the first use of a dish which had been made for him, and which, for its extraordinary size, he called "The Shield of Minerva." In this dish there were tossed up together the livers of char-fish, the brains of pheasants and peacocks, with the tongues of flamingos, and the entrails of lampreys, which had been brought in ships of war as far as from the Carpathian Sea, and the Spanish Straits.

He was not only a man of an insatiable appetite, but would gratify it likewise at unseasonable times, and with any garbage that came in his way; so that, at a sacrifice, he would snatch from the fire flesh and cakes, and eat them upon the spot. When he traveled, he did the same at the inns upon the road, whether the meat was fresh dressed and hot, or what had been left the day before, and was half-eaten.

sesterces—Roman currency; this is a very large amount of money

SOURCE 2

Excerpt from *The Life of Elagabalus* (Emperor of Rome, 218–222)[33]

He gave summer-banquets in various colors, one day a green banquet, another day an iridescent one, and next in order a blue one, varying them continually every day of the summer. Moreover, he was the first to use silver urns and casseroles, and vessels of chased silver, . . . some of them spoiled by the lewdest designs. . . . Indeed, for him life was nothing except a search after pleasures. He was the first to make *forcemeat* of fish, or of oysters of various kinds or similar shell-fish, or of lobsters, crayfish and squills (*fish*).

He had couches made of solid silver for use in his banqueting-rooms and his bed-chambers. In imitation of *Apicius* he frequently ate camels-heels and also cocks-combs taken from the living birds, and the tongues of peacocks and nightingales, because he was told that one who ate them was immune from the plague. He served to the palace-attendants, moreover, huge platters heaped up with the viscera of mullets, and flamingo-brains, partridge-eggs, thrush-brains, and the heads of parrots, pheasants, and peacocks . . .

He fed his dogs on goose-livers. Among his pets he had lions and leopards, which had been rendered harmless and trained by tamers, and these he would suddenly order during the dessert and the after-dessert to get up on the couches, thereby causing an amusing panic, for none knew that the beasts were harmless. He sent grapes from *Apamea* to his stables for his horses, and he fed parrots and pheasants to his lions and other wild animals. For ten successive days, moreover, he served wild sows' udders, . . . peas with gold-pieces, lentils with onyx, beans with amber, and rice with pearls; and he also sprinkled pearls on fish and truffles in lieu of pepper.

He was accustomed, furthermore, to have dinners served to him of the following kind: one day he would eat nothing at all but pheasant, serving only pheasant-meat at every course; another day he would serve only chicken, another some kind of fish and again a different kind, again pork, or ostrich, or greens, or fruit, or sweets, or dairy-products.

forcemeat—smooth ground meat mixed with fat and seasonings, similar to pâté

Apicius—a first-century Roman gourmet and often believed to be the author of an early cookbook

Apamea—a city in located in modern-day Syria

SOURCE 3

Excerpt from *The Prioress, The Canterbury Tales* (1387–1400) by Geoffrey Chaucer[34]

A prioress was the administrator of a monastic community of nuns. In the Middle Ages, a woman holding this position would have been from the elite class. Compare her manners with those recommended and criticized by the Renaissance courtier below.

> There was also a nun, a *prioress*
> Who, in her smiling, modest was and coy;
> Her greatest oath was but "By Saint Eloy!" . . .
> At table her manners were well taught withall,
> And never let morsels from her lips fall,
> Nor dipped her fingers deep in sauce, but ate
> With so much care the food upon her plate
> That no drop could fall upon her breast.
> In courtesy, she had delight and zest.
> Her upper lip was always wiped so clean
> That on her cup no speck or spot was seen

Of grease, when she had drunk her draught of wine.
Graciously she reached for food to dine.
And certainly delighting in good sport,
She was very pleasant, amiable—in short.
She was in pains to imitate the cheer
Of courtliness, and stately manners here,
And would be held worthy of reverence.

prioress—the administrator of a monastic community of women, or nuns. In the Middle Ages, a prioress was a position of prestige and women in that position would have been from the elite class.

SOURCE 4

Excerpt from *Of Manners and Behaviors* (1558) by Giovanni Della Casa[35]

Giovanni della Casa (1503–1556) was a wealthy courtier from Renaissance era Florence, Italy. The advice on manners in this book was intended for the social world of an elite gentleman.

It is a rude fashion for a man to claw or scratch himself when he sits at the table. And a man should at such time have a very great care to spit not at all . . . We must also beware we do not eat so greedily, that he get the hiccups or belches. Some eat so fast that they annoy the company with their loud blowing and puffing. Likewise you must not rub your teeth with your napkin and much less with your fingers, for these are the habits of a slovenly man. Neither must you openly rinse your mouth with the wine and then spit it out . . . It is a rude fashion to lean over the table, or to fill our mouth so full of meat that your cheeks are blown up.

SOURCE 5

Excerpt from *The Young Lady's Friend* (1838) by Mrs. John Farrar[36]

Eliza Ware Farrar was the daughter of a Massachusetts family, born in France in 1791 and educated in England. She moved to the United States at age twenty-eight. Throughout her book, she makes distinctions between the manners of Europeans and Americans.

When you send your plate for anything, whether by the hand of a servant, or a friend, take off the knife and fork, and lay them down on the cloth, supporting the ends on your bread, or else hold them in your hand, in a horizontal position. If you wish to imitate the French or English, you will put every mouthful into your mouth with your fork, but if you think, as I do, that Americans have as good a right to their own fashions as the inhabitants of any other country, you may choose the convenience of feeding yourself with your right hand, armed with a steel blade; and provided you do it neatly, and do not put in large mouthfuls, or close your lips tight over the blade, you ought not to be considered eating ungenteelly.

When not engaged in eating, do not let your fingers find employment in playing with any of the table furniture, or in making pellets of bread. If you would be very refined, you must avoid blowing your nose at table, or touching your hair, or adjusting combs; those are, in some person's eyes, great offenses. I once heard a gentleman describe a young lady as having every virtue and every charm that could be desired, and then he added with a sigh, "She would be perfect were it not for one thing." I eagerly asked what that was; and he replied, "She blows her nose at dinnertime."

SOURCE 6

Excerpt from *Autobiography of Peter Cartwright, The Backwoods Preacher* (1859) by Peter Cartwright[37]

Peter Cartwright (1785–1872) was a traveling Methodist preacher who visited communities on the American frontier. In this excerpt, he visited an Indiana home in 1823–1824. Note that his account was published over thirty years after the incident occurred.

There was but one chair in the house, and that was called the preacher's chair. The bottom was weak and worn out, and one of the upright back pieces was broken off. We had a hewed *puncheon* for a table, with four holes in it, and four straight sticks put in for legs. The hearth was made of earth, and in the center of it was a deep hole, worn by sweeping. Around this hole the women had to cook, which was exceedingly inconvenient, for they had no kitchen. When we came to the table there were wooden trenchers for plates, sharp-pointed pieces of cane for forks, and tin cups for cups and saucers. There was but one knife besides the butcher knife, and that had the handle off.

puncheon—a slit log or heavy slab of timber with only one smooth, finished side.

SOURCE 7

Excerpt from *How to Set the Table* (1901) by Mrs. Sarah Tyson Rorer[38]

The following was taken from a booklet published by a manufacturer of silver-plated dishes and utensils. The first half of the publication describes the proper way to set a table for breakfast, luncheon, and dinner. The last half is an advertisement and catalog with photographs and prices of the many items required to set a table for polite dining.

A full dinner service in silver consists of:

- a silver soup tureen
- large meat platter with cover
- two vegetable dishes (silver), the tops having moveable handles, allowing them to be used also as dishes
- a silver fish platter
- four sets of knives for fruit, dessert, fish, and meat
- six sets of forks for oyster, fish, meat, salad, game, and dessert
- soup, ice cream and dessert spoons
- a large and a small carving set
- a long gravy spoon, gravy boat, platter, and ladle
- small boat with small ladle for salad dressing
- individual salt spoons
- mustard and horseradish spoon
- extra silver, such as jelly knife, asparagus tongs, ice tongs, salad fork and spoon, cake knife and fork, small sugar tongs
- black coffee service, consisting of three pieces, a pot, sugar and cream jug, with of course, small individual spoons

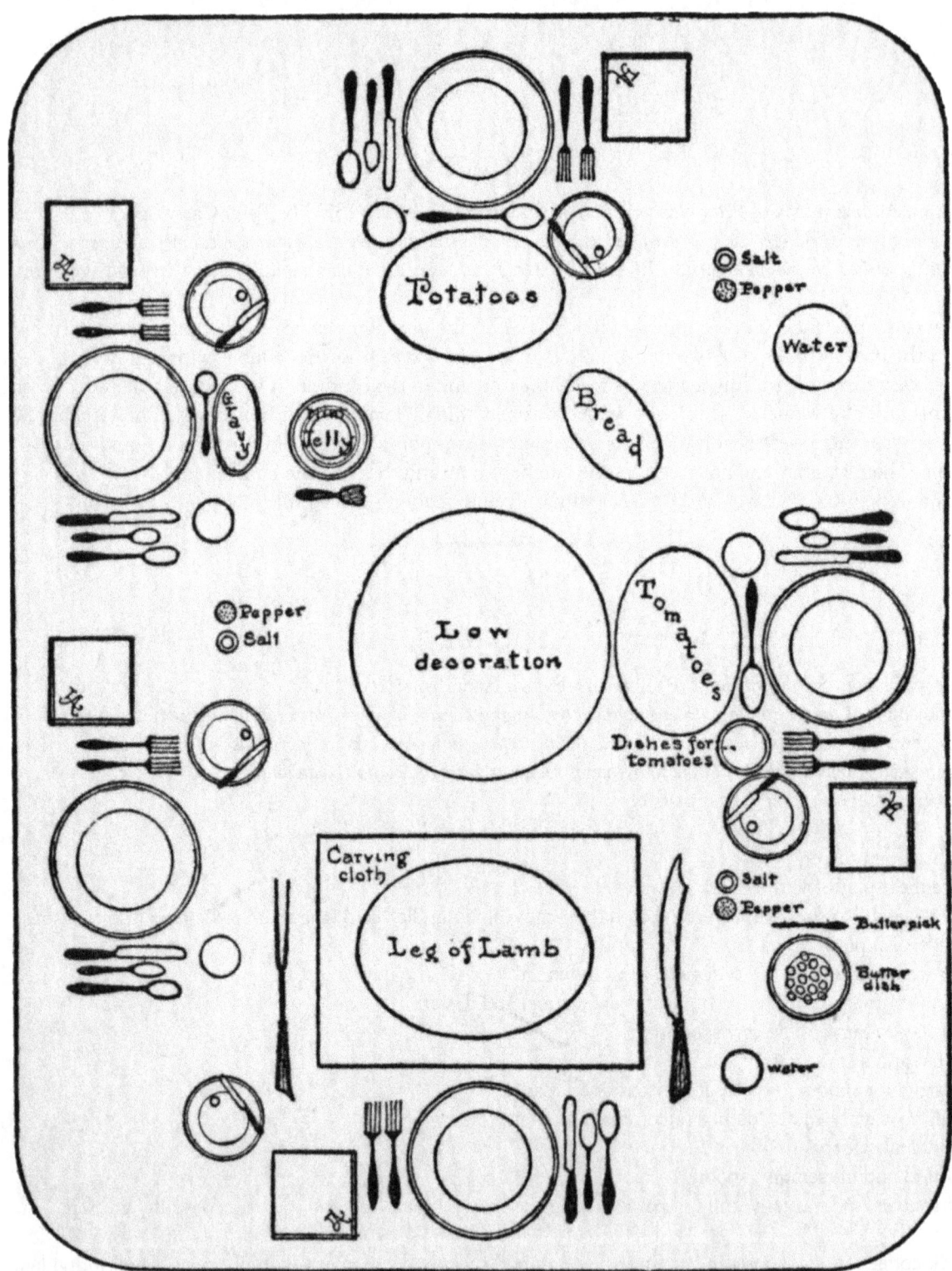

Figure 4.5. Diagram of Table Laid for Home Dinner without Service of a Maid, 1922. Numerous books and articles advised women how to decorate a dining room, set the table, create menus for entertaining, and serve guests. This diagram appeared in a textbook by Lucy Allen, an instructor at the Fannie Farmer's Boston School of Cookery. The book was dedicated to Fannie Farmer and Farmer wrote the introduction. By the time of its publication in 1922, homes were getting smaller, fewer homes employed maids, and dining etiquette was becoming less formal. This 128-page booklet reflects both old and new trends.

Diagram of Table Laid for Home Dinner without Service of a Maid in Table Service. In *Table Service* by Lucy Grace Allen (Boston: Little, Brown and Company, 1922), 61. (Courtesy of Internet Archive)

SOURCE 8

Manners for Teenagers in the 1940s and 1950s.

The following instructional films were created for a teenage audience.

Dinner Party, 1945. Proper table etiquette is portrayed by teenagers at a birthday dinner party. The narrator explains both good and bad behavior during the three-course meal. Length—15 minutes.

https://archive.org/details/DinnerPa1945

Good Table Manners, 1951. A bad-mannered fourteen-year-old is advised by his future self on why he should develop proper manners and how to act at a dinner party. Length—10 minutes.

https://archive.org/details/GoodTabl1951

SOURCE 9

Excerpt from *Amy Vanderbilt's Complete Book of Etiquette, A Guide to Gracious Living*[39]

Amy Vanderbilt was considered an expert on etiquette after the publication of the first edition of her best-selling Amy Vanderbilt's Complete Book of Etiquette *in 1952. This book was updated and re-published several times; the most recent edition in 1995.*

Whether trained servants present platters of peacock's tongues or the hostess herself dishes up a good spaghetti dinner is quite immaterial. If the house looks as if it expected and welcomed guests, if the host and hostess are relaxed and smiling, the guests will feel at home and at ease, no matter what superficial accouterments of entertaining may be missing . . . The truly formal dinner in all of its stiff elegance is not what the average American thinks of as a formal dinner. What we encounter most in the way of special entertaining is the semiformal dinner for which the household puts its best face forward. This is the seated dinner of four to eight guests (who may or may not be in evening dress) or even more, depending on the dining room's ability to contain them all comfortably. Entertaining at home of more than eight at dinner usually must be buffet style or at bridge tables, informally.

Very few homes in the land these days can accommodate the traditional thirty-four guests at one dinner table—or even half that many—in comfort. Who indeed has the space to store all the silver, glassware, and china for such dinner parties, and where are the trained men to serve them, one man to each three guests?

A formal dinner always has a soup course, always fish or seafood (which may come first, as in oysters à la Rockefeller), always hot meat with vegetables as the main dish, a salad, dessert, little cakes (petits fours), and demitasses served in the living room. Each course is served separately.

The informal dinner is not so complicated and consists of an entrée of some kind, which may be hot or cold soup and which may be served in a handled cup, pottery bowl, or cream bowl, whereas at a formal dinner, soup is always in a flat soup dish. The main course may be fish instead of meat, since usually not both are served. Second helpings are often offered. At formal meals, they never are. Salad may well be served at the same time as the main dish rather than as a separate course. There is dessert, and after-dinner coffee is often served at the table with dessert or just following it and is usually poured by the hostess (who adds sugar and cream for those who wish it) and passed around, though it may be poured in the kitchen if there is a waitress and passed on a tray with cream and sugar.

Notes

1. Haber, Barbara, "Culinary History Vs. Food History," in *The Oxford Encyclopedia of Food and Drink in America* (Oxford University Press, 2004), accessed October 2016, http://www.oxfordreference.com.libproxy.eku.edu/view/10.1093/acref/9780195154375.001.0001/acref-9780195154375-e-0242.

2. Sidney W. Mintz, *Sweetness and Power, The Place of Sugar in Modern History* (New York: Elisabeth Sifton Books/Viking, 1985).

3. Christopher Dyer, *Making a Living in the Middle Ages: The People of Britain 850–1520* (New Haven, CT: Yale University Press, 2002), 159, 164, 171.

4. Frances and Joseph Gies, *Cathedral, Forge, and Waterwheel, Technology and Invention in the Middle* Ages (New York: HarperPerennial, 1995), 44–49.

5. C. M. Woolgar, D. Serjeantson, and T. Waldron, "Conclusion," in *Food in Medieval England: Diet and Nutrition*, eds. C. M. Woolgar, D. Serjeantson, and T. Waldron (Oxford: Oxford University Press, 2006), 269, accessed October 2016, eBook Collection, EBSCOhost.

6. Ibid., 268–69.

7. Waldron, Serjeantson, and Woolgar, *Food in Medieval England*, 270–72; Kathy L. Pearson, "Nutrition and the Early-Medieval Diet," *Speculum* 72, no. 1 (January 1997): 3–5.

8. Alan S. C. Ross, "The Assize of Bread," *The Economic History Review*, New Series, 9, no. 2 (1956): 333, doi:10.2307/2591750; James Davis, "Baking for the Common Good: A Reassessment of the Assize of Bread in Medieval England," *The Economic History Review* 57, no. 3 (2004): 465–502. http://www.jstor.org/stable/3698543.

9. Waldron, Serjeantson, and Woolgar, *Food in Medieval England*, 273–74.

10. Richard W. Unger, *Beer in the Middle Ages and the Renaissance* (Philadelphia: University of Pennsylvania Press, 2004), 2–3, http://www.jstor.org/stable/j.ctt3fj2zx.24.

11. Pearson, "Nutrition and the Early-Medieval Diet," 6–7, 9.

12. Waldron, Serjeantson, and Woolgar, *Food in Medieval England*, 271–72, 278–79.

13. James Salzman, *Drinking Water, A History* (New York: Overlook Duckworth, 2012), 79–80.

14. Pearson, "Nutrition and the Early-Medieval Diet," 24–26.

15. Christopher Dyer, *Everyday Life in Medieval England*, (London: Hambledon Continuum, 2000), 96, accessed July 2016, eBook Collection, EBSCOhost.

16. Pearson, "Nutrition and the Early-Medieval Diet," 29–32.

17. Ibid., 1–2.

18. Ibid., 16–18.

19. "Generation System of Seed Multiplication," TNAU Agritech Portal, Seed Technology http://agritech.tnau.ac.in/seed/seed-multiplication.html," Generation, accessed February 2017.

20. Barbara Santich, "The Evolution of Culinary Techniques in the Medieval Era," in *Food in the Middle Ages: A Book of Essays*, ed. Melitta Weiss Adamson (New York: Garland, 1995), 66.

21. Jack Larkin, *The Reshaping of Everyday Life, 1790–1840* (New York: HarperPerennial, 1988), 180–81; David Freeman Hawke, *Everyday Life in Early America* (New York: Harper & Row, 1989), 56.

22. Kenneth L. Ames, *Death in the Dining Room and Other Tales of Victorian Culture* (Philadelphia: Temple University Press, 1992), 44–96.

23. Cathy K. Kaufman, "Dining Rooms, Table Settings, and Table Manners," in *The Oxford Encyclopedia of Food and Drink in America* (Oxford University Press, 2004), accessed January 2017, http://www.oxfordreference.com.libproxy.eku.edu/view/10.1093/acref/9780195154375.001.0001/acref-9780195154375-e-0260.

24. U.S. Department of Health and Human Services and U.S. Department of Agriculture. *2015–2020 Dietary Guidelines for Americans*, 8th ed. (December 2015), chapter 2, accessed April 2017, https://health.gov/dietaryguidelines/2015/guidelines/chapter-2/current-eating-patterns-in-the-united-states/.

25. Center for Disease Control and Prevention, *Childhood Obesity Facts*, accessed April 2017, https://www.cdc.gov/healthyschools/obesity/facts.htm.

26. *2015–2020 Dietary Guidelines for Americans*.

27. Center for Disease Control and Prevention, *Childhood Obesity Facts*.

28. Faith D. Aluisio and Peter Menzel, *Hungry Planet: What the World Eats* (2007, 2008) and Peter Menzel, Charles Mann, and Paul Kennedy, *Material World: A Global Family Portrait* (1995).

29. Drew Desilver, "What's on Your Table? How America's Diet has Changed Over the Decades," Pew Research Center, December 2016, accessed March 2017, http://www.pewresearch.org/fact-tank/2016/12/13/whats-on-your-table-how-americas-diet-has-changed-over-the-decades/.

30. United States Department of Agriculture, *Household Food Security in the United States in 2015*, accessed March 2017, https://www.ers.usda.gov/publications/pub-details/?pubid=79760.

31. James A. Levine, "Poverty and Obesity in the U.S.," *Diabetes* 60 no. 11 (June 2011): 2667–68, accessed April 2017, https://www.ncbi.nlm.nih.gov/pmc/articles/PMC3198075/.

32. Suetonius, *The Lives of the Twelve Caesars*, eds. J. Eugene Reed and Alexander Thomson (Philadelphia: Gebbie & Co., 1889), accessed June 2016, http://www.perseus.tufts.edu/hopper/text?doc=Perseus:abo:phi,1348,019:13.

33. *The Life of Elagabalus*, Part 2 (Loeb Classical Library, 1924), http://penelope.uchicago.edu/Thayer/E/Roman/Texts/Historia_Augusta/Elagabalus/2*.html.

34. Geoffrey Chaucer, *The Canterbury Tales*, accessed April 2017, http://www.librarius.com/canttran/genpro/genpro118-162.htm.

35. Giovanni della Casa, *Galateo, Of Manners and Behaviors*, (Boston: The Merrymount Press, 1914), 108–9, Internet Archive, https://archive.org/details/arenaissancecou00delluoft.

36. Mrs. John Farrar, *The Young Lady's Friend* (Boston: American Stationer's Company/John B. Russell, 1838), 346–47, Internet Archive, https://archive.org/details/youngladysfrien05farrgoog.

37. Peter Cartwright, *Autobiography of Peter Cartwright, The Backwoods Preacher* (Cincinnati: R. P. Thompson, 1859), 251–52, Internet Archive, https://archive.org/details/autobiographyofp01cart.

38. Sarah Tyson Rorer, *How to Set the Table* (Wallingford, CT: R. Wallace and Sons Manufacturing Co., 1901), 19, Internet Archive, https://archive.org/stream/howtosettablebei00rwal#page/18/mode/2up.

39. Amy Vanderbilt, *Amy Vanderbilt's Compete Book of Etiquette, A Guide to Gracious Living* (Garden City, NY: Doubleday & Company, Inc., 1954), 261–63, 271.

CHAPTER FIVE

~

Home Cooking from Scratch

Essential Questions

- What does "home cooking" really mean? How has our perception of "home cooking" changed over time? What drives this change?
- How has technology changed cooking at home?
- What does "pure food" mean? How are perceptions of food impacted by culture, advertising, and government?

Historical cookbooks and recipes are primary source smorgasbords! They illustrate two hundred years of industrialization and changing technology that radically altered food production, preparation, and consumption. Recipes and ingredients tell a place-based story of cultural and regional food traditions. Cookbooks and household advice books demonstrate how the roles and work of women changed in the home. These sources also communicate what their creators thought *ought* to be happening in the kitchen. Historians must assess to what extent readers really followed all of that advice.

The first section of this chapter is a brief history of cookbooks from ancient times to the Civil War. The second section focuses upon the domestic science movement and its goals to reform American cooks in the late nineteenth and early twentieth century. These efforts merged with those of big business to promote and advertise industrially processed foods on a national scale. The work of domestic scientists often became indistinguishable from advertising. The final section spotlights the development of manufactured cooking fats and how these products were promoted, regulated, and rejected or adopted by family cooks.

Each section revolves around objective and subjective meanings of home cooking. In the last two hundred years, cooking at home has changed dramatically. Pre-industrial households produced, preserved, and prepared most of their food from scratch. Modern households purchase ready-to-eat dishes and entire meals that have been produced and processed in factories and restaurants. Since the late nineteenth century, home cooking has been reinterpreted by the food industry to sell new food products and household equipment. An analysis of cookbooks, recipes, and food advertising reveal both continuity and change in the meaning of the phrase and the slippery line between perceptions of a past era and what really happened daily in homes and kitchens.

History of Recipes and Cookbooks—Ancient World to Twentieth Century

Cookbooks are collections of recipes and other advice for preparing food. The word *cookbook* originated in the United States in 1809, a simplification of the English term *cookery-book* used as far back as 1639.[1] While both terms originated after the advent of printing in the fifteenth century, the concept of collecting instructions for cooking was not new. Manuscript collections of recipes survive from the ancient and medieval world and continued to be assembled long after printed cookbooks were widely available. *Recipe* is a word derived from the word *receive*. In historical sources, recipes are often referred to as *receipts*, reflecting the concept that advice and instructions for cooking are received from others.

Figure 5.1. New technology calls for new recipes. In this 1922 advertisement, the reader is reminded that any recipe, old or new, can be prepared on an electric range just as easily as on a gas stove. An electric waffle iron is also featured. Many home cooks used wood or coal-fired cooking stoves until after World War II because gas or electric was not available in their community.

Advertisement for Westinghouse Electric Range in *The Shorewood Cook Book* by the Ladies' Aid society of the Luther Memorial Chapel (Shorewood, WI, 1922), 54. (Courtesy of Library of Congress and Internet Archive)

Collections of recipes in the ancient and medieval world described dishes consumed by the elite and were products of wealthy households. Even though recipe collections have survived from these eras, most cooks learned through practice in a kitchen. As cooks, mostly women, completed this daily household routine, children, mostly girls, watched and assisted their mothers. Even in the kitchens of the wealthy, cooks, working as slaves or paid servants, learned by example or through apprenticeships, not by reading instructions or cookbooks.

The oldest surviving recipes were recorded by Babylonian scribes on three clay tablets, probably in the seventeenth century BC, around four thousand years ago. Much like a modern recipe, these recipes list main ingredients, utensils needed, and steps for preparing the dish. *The Art of Cookery* was believed to have been composed in the fifth century BC by Mithaikos, a Greek living in the colony of Syracuse, Sicily. But only one recipe from this work has survived, quoted in the work of Greek writer Athenaeus around six hundred years later.[2]

The oldest known collection of recipes, *De re coquinaria* (On Cookery), contains more than 450 entries. This work is believed to have been compiled around 400 AD from a variety of previous works on agriculture, household management, a Greek work on proper diet, and two collections of recipes by Apicius (c. 25 BC–37 AD).[3] Numerous manuscripts of medieval recipe collections have survived from the fourteenth and fifteenth centuries. *The Forme of Curye* (The Way of Cookery), a collection of recipes from the fourteenth-century English royal household of Richard II, is just one example.

Collections of recipes, printed in bound volumes that might be called cookbooks, began to appear in Europe after the invention of the printing press in the fifteenth century. *A Noble Book of Cookery* (1500), a collection of an English feudal estate, was one of the first published collections.[4] *The English Huswife* by Gervase Markham[5] was first published in London in 1615 and reprinted multiple times over the following years. This book contained all sorts of household advice and instructions for medical remedies, cooking, baking, brewing, making butter and cheese, and making cloth from wool, hemp, and flax.

Colonial American cookbooks were imported copies or American reprints of English cookbooks. Records of the Virginia Company show that *The English Huswife*, bound in one volume with Markham's *English Husbandman*,[6] were destined for the colonies in 1620. Eliza Smith's *The Compleat Housewife; or, Accomplished Gentlewomen's Companion*, first published in London in 1727, was the first to be reprinted in the American colonies in 1742. It was published for fifty years in America, in eighteen editions.[7]

Not until 1796, twenty years after the American Revolution, did the first truly American cookbook appear, named *American Cookery*. Little is known about the author, Amelia Simmons. The book was inexpensive and included both practical, everyday recipes as well as those intended for special occasions. Many of the recipes were borrowed from British cookbooks, but others incorporated uniquely American ingredients. For example, Simmons included receipts (recipes) using uniquely American ingredients—corn meal, crookneck squash, Jerusalem artichoke, cranberries, and watermelon. She also included original recipes for "Pompkin" puddings, the forerunner of the modern pumpkin pies, and unique American approaches to traditional English dishes such as "minced" or mincemeat pies and gingerbread.[8]

American cookbooks from the first half of the nineteenth century represent several prominent themes—regional cookbooks featuring uniquely American foods; cookbooks that advise the housewife how to save money; recipes and advice about a proper diet or dietary fads; and comprehensive household management manuals that included advice on scientific approaches to cooking and organizing a kitchen.[9]

Each of these themes have parallels in modern culture. A popular example of each of these trends from the nineteenth century is described below. Selections from these works could be paired with modern examples of similar cookbooks, recipes, or advice from modern television, magazines, or the internet. Students can consider how many seemingly new trends have, in fact, have been recycled and popularized throughout the past.

Regional Foods—America's first widely popular cookbook to describe unique regional dishes was Mary Randolph's *The Virginia House-Wife* (1824), reprinted at least nineteen times before the Civil War. Randolph included recipes for dishes with ingredients representing the unique climate of Virginia and influences of Native American and African slave culture. In her recipe for Barbecued Shote, she noted that *shote* was a local word used in southern states for a fat young hog. Chicken Pudding was labeled "A Favourite Virginia Dish." Recipes for uniquely southern breads such as "Apoquiniminc Cakes," a form of beaten biscuits, and sweet potato buns were included. The recipes for "Ochra Soup" and "Gumbo, A West India Dish" used a regional ingredient, okra.[10] Sweet potatoes and okra are plants cultivated in warm climates and both may have been introduced into the American diet by African slaves.

Figure 5.2. In 1920, the Nineteenth Amendment was ratified and American women voted for the first time in a federal election. Old and new converge in this advertisement for bread flour, published in a 1921 Detroit community cookbook. The ad recognizes women's new right to vote but still calls for women to bake their own bread with Henkel's flour. Inexpensive, factory-produced bread was available in the 1920s, but many women continued to bake bread from scratch. Cookbooks, articles, and advertisements for flour stressed the best bread was homemade and women who did not make their own bread were failing in their duties as a wife and mother.
Advertisement for Henkel's flour. *Book of Recipes* by the Woman's Association of Brewster Congregational Church, 2nd ed. (Detroit, MI, 1921), 113. (Courtesy of Library of Congress and Internet Archive)

Cooking on a Budget—Lydia Maria Child's *The Frugal Housewife* (1829) was one of the most popular cookbooks of its day, offering down-to-earth advice for cooking and housekeeping. In the introduction, the author described the reader for which she wrote the book:

> The information conveyed is of the common kind . . . Books of this kind have usually been written for the wealthy: I have written for the poor. I have said nothing about *rich* cooking; those who can afford to be epicures will find the best information in the "Seventy-five Receipts." I have attempted to teach how money can be *saved*, not how it can be *enjoyed*.[11]

In this quote, Child referenced another popular cookbook of her day, *Seventy-Five Receipts for Pastry, Cakes, and Sweetmeats* (1828) by Eliza Leslie. Child provided recipes for "common cakes" and "common pies." Leslie noted in the introduction to her cookbook that her recipes for puddings, custards, cakes, sweet breads, and preserves also saved money and "may be made in the best and most liberal manner at one half the cost of the same articles supplied by the confectioner."[12]

Eliza Leslie (1787–1858) and Lydia Maria Child (1802–1880) were prolific writers, publishing cookbooks, advice books on household management and manners, and fiction for children and adults. Both women were products of upper middle class families, but both faced economic challenges. Leslie's father died when she was fifteen; her mother opened a boardinghouse to support the family. Child's husband did not earn enough money to ensure a middle class lifestyle. Both women were accomplished and serious writers of the era, choosing to write as a career for intrinsic rewards as well as to support their families.[13]

Diet Trends—Special diets were also promoted in early cookbooks. Many household manuals included recipes, special dietary recommendations, and treatments for the sick. Others recommended diets that preferred certain foods and rejected others. Sylvester Graham's *A Treatise on Bread, and Bread-Making* (1837) and William Alcott's *Vegetable Diet: As Sanctioned by Medical Men, and by Experience in All Ages, including a System of Vegetable Cookery* (1849) promoted vegetarianism.

Vegetarianism has been promoted throughout history for moral, religious, or health reasons. But Enlightenment theories about the human body and diet and a new awareness of cruelty to animals combined to give it a new momentum in the nineteenth century. Vegetarianism was endorsed in the United States by Sylvester Graham, a minister, lecturer, and advocate of temperance, and the man after whom whole wheat graham crackers are named. Graham and Alcott combined what they believed were scientific principles with their religious beliefs to promote a new lifestyle.[14] Both represented a wider reforming fervor in the first half of the nineteenth century, a spirit that also led to the establishment of several utopian communities. Strict vegetarianism was the basis on which Amos Bronson Alcott, father of Louisa May Alcott, established the short-lived utopian community Fruitlands (1843–1844).

Comprehensive Household Management—The reforming spirit, scientific knowledge of the era, and practical advice for economy in the household were all combined in the work of Catharine Beecher (1800–1878), one of the most popular authors of household advice books and articles in the nineteenth century. Beecher's *Treatise on Domestic Economy* (1841) and its supplementary receipt book, *Miss Beecher's Domestic Receipt Book* (1846),[15] were different from previous works such as Lydia Maria Child's *The Frugal Housewife*.

Beecher offered more than Child's plain-spoken advice for cooking and daily household chores. Beecher's books described a complete system of proper household management representing the ideals of republican motherhood. Her manual was very popular, revised and republished in fifteen editions, and adopted as a school textbook.[16] In 1869, she coauthored *The American Woman's Home*[17] with her sister, Harriet Beecher Stowe. This book was revised in 1873 and titled *The New Housekeeper's Manual*.[18] The new edition included *The Handy Cookbook* with five hundred recipes.

Advertising, Reform, and Home Cooking—Late 1800s to mid-1900s

In the late 1800s, the work of the new home economics movement merged with the goals of the food industry. Both groups wanted housewives to change the way cooking had been done for generations. Both wanted the housewife to adopt scientific cooking methods, use store-bought foods, and purchase new kitchen technology. Home economists and the food industry often cooperated in the creation of recipes and cookbooks promoting their goals. Old recipes were adapted to include new ingredients or preparation techniques and recipes for completely new dishes were introduced.

The domestic science movement of the late 1800s and early 1900s reflected the social and economic changes of the era and impacted not only cookbooks, but how Americans thought about food and diet. Catharine Beecher's vision of scientific housekeeping, introduced before the Civil War, merged with the work of a new generation of women later in the century. Beecher and the new domestic scientists shared some goals—educating women and making the work of the housewife appreciated, manageable, and up-to-date. But household management as promoted by Beecher served a moral, civic, and religious ideal. The new generation of domestic scientists shifted the focus away from these lofty goals to focus on practical scientific knowledge, industrial organizational principles, new technology, and a role for women outside the home.

Ellen Richards (1842–1911) and other domestic scientists urged housewives to run their homes like well-regulated factories. Leaders in the movement criticized the old, traditional ways of household management, arguing outdated customs lead to poor health and disease. At the same time, domestic scientists were attempting to reform the home; they sought to create a professional sphere outside the home for women, a career track for college-educated women.[19]

The career of Ellen Richards illustrates the struggle of women to have professional careers in the late 1800s. Richards earned an undergraduate chemistry degree, but chemical firms in the 1870s refused to hire women. She entered the newly created Massachusetts Institute of Technology as a "special student" in a segregated lab because the school was hesitant to even admit a woman. Richards went on to become the first women to hold a degree from Massachusetts Institute of Technology in 1873 and ten years later, she became the first woman faculty member in the field of sanitary chemistry.

Not until the turn of the nineteenth century was the work of domestic scientists officially recognized as a profession outside the home. In 1899, Ellen Richards and other domestic scientists, at a series of conferences, selected the name *home economics* to describe the new academic discipline. By 1908, the professional organization American Home Economics Association was founded and dedicated to "the improvement of living conditions in the home, the institutional household, and the community."[20] Home economists published professional journals and taught in newly established departments of home economics at high schools and universities. College-educated home economists, almost exclusively women, worked outside the home in education, industry, and government.[21]

The home economics movement promoted cooking, housekeeping, and sewing schools for women. By the 1870s and 1880s, the rapid industrial changes of the era had inspired educational reform. Industrial education colleges were opened and new vocational education public school programs were developed for men and women. The Boston Cooking School, founded in 1879, is one prominent example. Its motto "Better ways, lighter burdens, more wholesome results" exemplifies the domestic science goals. Like many of these cooking and housekeeping schools, the focus of the middle class white founders was to reform the diet and housekeeping of the poor. Reformers thought if the poor and immigrants could be taught to cook following scientifically, then criminality, poverty, and alcoholism could be reduced.[22]

The booklets *Fifteen Cent Dinners for Workingmen's Families (1878)* and *Twenty-five Cent Dinners for Families of Six (1878)*,[23] represent the efforts of reformers to change the diet of the poor and working classes. Both were published and distributed for free by Juliet Corson, founder of the New York Cooking School. Corson recommended recipes, meals, and tips that could be prepared by working class wives to improve the health of their families. While Corson's background and education put her in the middle class, she recognized the limitations of buying and preparing food on a very limited budget.

Corson also believed a good diet would reduce the temptation of alcohol for the working class. Her work reflected the assumption of the largely middle class temperance movement that the problems of the poor were caused by alcohol consumption, rather than wider structural problems of the era—low wages, dangerous working conditions, and substandard housing. She noted many poor families wasted money daily to purchase beer because they mistakenly believed beer was healthy for men, women, and even children. Corson argued beer consumption should be limited even among men and never consumed by women and children. Her advice was, "What you need when you crave liquor is a good, warm meal."[24]

Corson's booklets represent one of many efforts to reform the diet of the poor. Cooking classes were offered in settlement houses, girls' clubs, city missions, reformatories, and in public schools.[25] Reformers believed through diet, the wider society could be reformed: goals of temperance achieved, problems of labor unrest solved, threats of socialism, communism, and anarchism defeated, and strange customs of immigrants replaced by middle class, white, American values. Sadly, many of these reformers failed to acknowledge immigrants valued their native food culture and the wider

Don't BAKE Bread

═══ *Buy It!* ═══

80,000 MILWAUKEE FOLKS eat ATLAS BREAD every day

"A Golden Crust—A Creamy Taste"

ASK MOTHER–SHE KNOWS!

Figure 5.3. This 1922 advertisement for commercially baked bread says mothers endorse Atlas Bread. In the early twentieth century, branded, factory-produced white bread was marketed as healthier, cleaner, safer, and more convenient than home-made or bread produced in local bakeries. This advertisement appeared in a community cookbook, a published collection of recipes provided by community or club members and sold to raise funds for a club, church, or reform effort.
Advertisement for Atlas Bread in *The Shorewood Cook Book* by the Ladies' Aid society of the Luther Memorial Chapel (Shorewood, WI, 1922), 4. (Courtesy of Library of Congress and Internet Archive)

economic problems faced by the poor limited their diet. As cooking school reformers began to realize the poor were not eager to follow their recommended diet and routines, their focus shifted.[26]

While some cooking schools continued to offer classes in plain cooking for working class women, most changed their focus. Cooking schools offered courses for affluent middle class wives featuring recipes for elaborate meals or programs to prepare women for professional positions. Cooking schools trained teachers and professionals to manage institutional kitchens in schools, hospitals, asylums; run catering businesses; give public lectures about scientific methods for cooking and housekeeping; or create and demonstrate recipes for the food industry.[27] The cookbook authors were middle class, assuming those who read their cookbooks were middle class or aspired to be middle class. The modern cookbook is a product of the domestic science and cooking school movements and reinforces the values of the middle class.

Fannie Farmer's *Boston Cooking School Cook Book* (1896) is often considered the first modern cookbook. The instructions featured exact measurements, ingredient lists, and the recipes were written in an impersonal authoritative voice. The book was so popular it was reprinted every year until 1906. When a revised edition was published, that also continued to be reprinted for years after Farmer's death in 1915. The most recent updated and revised thirteenth edition was published in 1990 and reissued in 1996.[28]

Farmer is often credited with inventing scientific measurements. In fact, patent records, advertisements, cookbooks, and magazines indicate efforts to standardize kitchen measures began in mid-1800s. In 1915, the U.S. Bureau of Standards published an official code stating the exact measure required for kitchen measuring cups and spoons.[29] Farmer did attempt to end confusion about the common use in recipes of "rounded" or "heaping" measuring spoons or cups. She insisted a cook should never round up ingredients because it was imprecise and unscientific. Instead, she advised readers cups, tablespoons, and teaspoons should always be measured level.[30]

Recipes as Advertising

New recipes were an especially effective method for promoting the sales of new or brand name foods and encouraging cooks to incorporate packaged and processed foods in their home cooking. Since the late 1800s, promotional recipes have been included in advertisements, in and on food packages, at live food demonstrations, and in radio and television shows. Food company sponsored recipe contests generated new recipes and the best were published in promotional cookbooks distributed for free or at very low cost. Promotional recipes are reprinted in community cookbooks, extending the likelihood more home cooks will purchase brand name food items.

Well-known cooking teachers and domestic scientists of the era, such as Maria Parola and Janet McKenzie Hill, partnered with food companies to provide recipes encouraging the use of new branded products. Parola and Hill were both active in founding, teaching, and promoting cooking schools, published several cookbooks, and both were a part of the effort to make home economics a recognized profession.

Baker's Chocolate had been publishing promotional recipes since 1876. In 1909, both women contributed their names and expertise to the cookbook *Chocolate and Cocoa Recipes by Miss Parloa and Home Made Candy Recipes by Mrs. Janet McKenzie Hill* (1909) promoting Baker's Chocolate products. By 1912, this popular recipe book was in its twenty-sixth and twenty-seventh editions of over a quarter million copies, and in 1914, editions were printed in French and German. Hill also worked with the United Fruit Company, Knox Gelatin, and other food, appliance, and kitchenware manufacturers.[31]

Convenience and easy food preparation is a primary theme of food advertising that encourages the cook to adapt how and what they cook at home. Advertisers promise their products make cooking at home faster and easier. In the late nineteenth and first half of the twentieth centuries, advertisers addressed the busy housewife, insisting packaged foods and other products were needed so that she could have more time for important activities with the family, in the community, for hobbies, or just well-deserved relaxation. Ads sought to convince cooks that products such as commercially baked bread were just as good as home-made and buying bread would make their lives easier. Even though convenience food products appealed to working women of all ethnicities, food advertising predominately featured white, middle class at-home wives until the last half of the twentieth century.[32]

Although advertisers tried to redefine home-cooking so it included more prepared and packaged foods, women did not always agree. After World War II, when a growing range of packaged, processed, frozen, and prepared foods were available, studies showed women working in and outside the home were not purchasing convenience products to replace all their traditional cooking tasks. The food industry and home economists conducted studies to learn about consumer habits to create more effective advertising campaigns. One such study focused on frozen foods.

Many new frozen foods had been introduced after World War II, but sales were not as expected except for two popular products—frozen orange juice and fish sticks. In the early 1950s, a study discovered the small refrigerators of most homes lacked the freezer space to accommodate numerous frozen foods. Only when people began to move to new homes in the suburbs, with more space for home freezers, did frozen foods and home freezer sales increase.[33]

A study by the *Journal of Marketing*, published in 1950, revealed women perceived the purchase of too many convenience foods as lazy and wasteful. Women who were not cooking from scratch for their families were considered bad wives and negligent mothers. But women preferred cooking to be easy. They did not have the time or did not want to spend long hours in the kitchen. This insight inspired the food industry to reframe how cooking with processed and packaged foods was perceived.

Advertisers and cookbook writers worked to remove the stigma associated with the use of packaged, processed, and convenience foods. The meanings of home cooking and from scratch had to be redefined for the American public. In the 1950s and 1960s, pre-packaged food cuisine showcased new foods and preparation methods framed as home cooking. New recipes and methods were developed in professional test kitchens and popularized in newspapers, magazines, cookbooks, and home economics classes. Quick recipes were re-labeled as creative. Old recipes were glamorized by adding a new, different, or special packaged food product. The new messages about home cooking declared women could cook quickly with packaged products and not feel guilty about failing as a wife or mother.[34]

Two popular cookbooks from the mid-twentieth century exemplify how home cooking and from scratch were redefined. *The Can Opener Cookbook* (1951) promoted this new form of fine dining. Dishes were created from a few canned and prepackaged ingredients and served in an elegant fashion. The author, Poppy Cannon (1905–1975), worked in food advertising, was the food editor of *Ladies' Home Journal* and *House Beautiful,* and the author of several 1950s cookbooks.

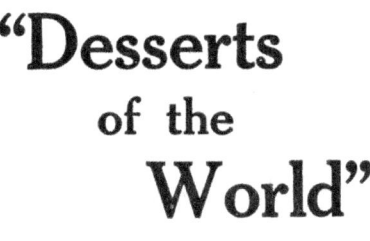

Figure 5.4. The processed and packaged food industry seeks to convince cooks to buy new products and incorporate them into cooking routines. This 1909 advertisement for Jell-O uses several different strategies. Jell-O is easy because "any woman can make it" and recipes are not needed. The statement "every woman likes to serve new recipes" uses the bandwagon technique. Readers can order an inexpensive yet beautiful cookbook of exotic recipes using Jell-O. The woman featured in the advertisement is white, middle class, and at leisure. The smaller image of the child suggests children love Jell-O too. For more about packaged gelatin, see Figure 4.3.
Advertisement, Jell-O, *McClure's Magazine* (December 1909): 114.

She argued the can opener was no longer "the hallmark of the lazy lady and careless wife," but a magic wand that could transform the everyday cook into "the artist-cook, the master, the creative chef."[35]

The *I Hate to Cook Book* (1960) by Peg Bracken also incorporated canned, frozen, and pre-packaged ingredients in quick, easy recipes. But this popular book exemplified a new message in a new era in which women were rejecting old roles. Bracken's commentary did not glorify home cooking as the moral duty of the wife and mother. Instead, she proclaimed that she and many other women hated to cook. Women were tired of being shamed by cookbooks and a wider culture that insisted women should love and perform complicated, traditional home cooking. Bracken assured the reader "it is always nice to know that you are not alone" in rejecting a role society expects.[36] The *I Hate to Cook Book* sold over three million copies in multiple editions.

In the 150 years between the publication of Amelia Simmon's first American cookbook and the 1960s when more and more women began to question traditional roles in the kitchen, the nature of cooking changed dramatically. Simmons, Beecher, and other early nineteenth-century writers advised the housewife how to complete labor-intensive tasks such as cooking using simple tools and materials produced within the household. But by the early twentieth century, the pre-industrial concept of home cooking or cooking from scratch faded as households ceased to be producers of the goods they needed. Home cooking took on new meanings as cooks used ingredients from a can or box and bought whole meals, already prepared and ready to reheat and set on the family table.

Early home economists recognized homemakers could purchase or "consume" new food products and labor saving appliances for the home. Home economists redefined a woman's role in the home as intelligent buying and wise consumption and created a profession for themselves to educate women on how to select, purchase, and use the wide array of newly available products.[37] The home economics movement merged with the food and kitchen appliance industry. Many of the goals of the home economists—sanitation, food purity, health, convenience, and novelty—were adopted by the food industry to sell their products. Well-known home economists worked for the food industry or were happy to identify their names with food and appliance manufacturers to sell "pure," "healthy," and convenient food.

Cookbooks and food advertising convey messages about what is considered "normal" for a society. Several assumptions are prominent in these media from the nineteenth and twentieth centuries. First, the normal family was supposed to be white and middle class. Second, women cooked for the family; men did not. Third, women should be stay-at-home wife and mothers. And finally, "home-cooking" was the best. Even as Americans have become aware that these expectations do not always reflect a wider reality, the messages are still evident in modern culture.

Then and now, all women are not stay-at-home housewives; all families were not white or middle class; and men, as well as women, can cook. Home cooking continues to be redefined by changes in technology, households, and society. For example, from 1965 to 2008 the proportion of men who cooked increased from 29 percent to 42 percent while the proportion of women who cooked declined from 92 percent to 68 percent. Even though men are cooking more than in the past, a 2015 survey found that on an average day, women spent twice as much time preparing food and drinks as men. The consumption of food at home and time spent in food preparation decreased 23 percent across all socioeconomic groups since 1965 and 2008.[38]

Pure, Safe, Wholesome, Healthful—Who Decides?

In the late 1800s, as the food industry began to offer packaged and processed foods, concerns about the safety and purity of purchased food were widespread. Pre-industrial households produced their own food or purchased it locally, giving them direct knowledge of the freshness and purity of meats, dairy products, grains, fruits, and vegetables. But as households shifted to purchasing food produced and processed in distant locations, they had to rely on grocers and the food industry to ensure the quality and safety of food. Highly publicized food scandals of the era caused consumers to question the ethics of the food industry and demand government regulation.

The swill milk scandals that began in the 1850s in New York are just one example of food supply concerns of the era. Distilleries operated dairies where grain byproducts of the brewing process, or swill, was fed to milk cows. The cows lived and were milked in crowded, filthy conditions that encouraged disease. The poor-quality milk was often diluted with water and then "enriched" with flour, plaster of Paris, starch, and other substances to make it appear fresh.[39] Press coverage and public outcry resulted in state government oversight of the New York dairy industry by the 1880s. Other states and cities enacted similar food purity regulations. But at the federal level, while dozens of food and drug purity bills were introduced, very few were passed into law.

Pre-packaged foods that could not be inspected by the customer were especially suspect. Foods preserved in metal cans were one of the earliest packaged foods. Commercially canned foods were introduced in the early 1800s and used to feed troops during wartime. By the late 1800s, new technology made canned food safe and affordable but scandals caused home cooks to question the quality of foods that could not be inspected before purchase. For example, the U.S. Army beef scandal during the Spanish–American War (1898) involved canned meat produced by nationally known meatpacking companies. The canned beef was poorly preserved or spoiled and adulterated with chemicals to disguise the problems.

Beginning in 1889, under the leadership of Harvey Wiley, the United States Department of Agriculture was given the job of investigating the adulteration of foods, drugs, and liquors. Wiley not only tested the quality of foods, but also widely publicized his findings. The work of food purity groups, domestic scientists, and other Progressive era reformers, along with Wiley's findings, coverage in newspaper and magazines, and the publication of the 1906 novel *The Jungle* by Upton Sinclair encouraged federal government involvement in food regulation.

As individuals and reforming groups called for government oversight, many in the food industry were also promoting federal regulation for their own interests. Different and often conflicting local and state regulations and mislabeled foods

R EASONS WHY . . .

NELSON MORRIS & CO'S
Kettle Rendered Pure Leaf Lard

Should be used in preference to all others:

1st. Because it is made from the best quality of Leaf Lard.

2d. Because it is absolutely pure and free from all adulterations.

3d. Because it is the most economical for the consumer on account of being perfectly **pure and unadulterated,** and thus going the **farthest.**

4th. Because it is recommended before all others by **chefs** in the largest and best hotels in the country, who look for **absolutely pure goods** as the most economical, and will buy no other.

5th. Because from the foregoing you cannot fail to see that **it will pay you to use our lard.** So give your butcher or grocer a trial order.

NELSON MORRIS & CO.,
Union Stock Yards, Chicago.

Figure 5.5. Food safety and purity concerns about industrially processed food began long before the publication of *The Jungle* in 1906. This 1891 advertisement for lard addresses many consumer concerns. Nelson Morris and Company leaf lard is "pure and unadulterated," recommended "by chefs in the largest and best hotels," and economical. The reader is encouraged to ask for a trial order of this brand name product from the local butcher or grocer so other lards are not substituted. Leaf lard is the highest grade of lard. Lard was often adulterated with cottonseed oil. See primary source 1 in this chapter for more about "sham lard."

Advertisement for Nelson Morris and Company Pure Lard, *The Universal Cookbook* by the Ladies' Aid Society of the First Universalist Church of Englewood, Illinois (Chicago: C. H. Morgan Co, 1891), 75. (Courtesy of Library of Congress and Internet Archive) hindered interstate trade and complicated national distribution by large food manufacturers. Large food manufacturers, led by H. J. Heinz and Frederick Pabst, were in favor of national legislation because it favored branded, packaged goods with labels over bulk, unbranded food items sold by local grocers.

A major obstacle for national food marketing campaigns was convincing customers to abandon the practice of purchasing generic food from bulk containers from local grocers and instead buy pre-packaged name-brand goods from distant locations and factories. Prior to the late nineteenth century, grocers typically weighed or measured the flour, sugar, coffee, crackers, or other goods from their bulk bins into plain paper bags or packages for each consumer. But highly publicized cases in which local grocers misled customers by substituting cheaper foods, such as manufactured corn syrup for pure molasses, were important in convincing consumers packaged and labeled foods were better choices.[40]

The Pure Food and Drug Act of 1906 prohibited interstate transportation of falsely labeled or adulterated foods and drugs. Items produced and sold within one state continued to be regulated under state and local laws. While this federal law sought to remove deceptively labeled putrid or filthy products from the market, inferior food products with various additives were still legal, if these ingredients were listed on the label. Government regulation of the safety of food, then and now, is a balancing act between serving the interests of individuals and those of food manufacturers.

From Pure to Processed—Butter and Lard to Oleo Margarine and Crisco
The story of two processed cooking fats, margarine and Crisco vegetable shortening, illustrates the transition from cooking fats used throughout history to commercially processed and pre-packaged cooking fats.

Cooking fats and oils are required for cooking and health. Both contain dietary fat, one of the three essential elements in food that along with protein and carbohydrates provide one hundred percent of the energy, or calories required by the human body. Throughout history, a variety of cooking fats have been obtained from plant and animals sources. Commonly used vegetables oils in the modern world include olive, sunflower, cottonseed, rapeseed (canola), peanut, soy, coconut, and palm. Animal fats used in cooking are commonly obtained from the milk of cattle, sheep or other herd animals (butter) or the body fat of pigs (lard), cattle or sheep (suet or tallow), poultry, fish, or wild game. Fats are generally solid at room temperature; oils are liquid. In some recipes, fats and oils are interchangeable; in others, either a solid or a liquid is preferable.

The cooking fats and oils used by cooks in the pre-industrial era were determined by the climate and available technology. For example, Mediterranean cultures preferred olive oil from trees that thrived in that climate and could be extracted through mill or presses available in the ancient world. On the other hand, native people in North America used mostly animal fats because processing oils from available plant sources was nearly impossible. Eskimos had no access to oil-producing plants; therefore, whale blubber and seal fat were used for both food and fuel for lamps. In many pre-industrial cultures of warmer climates, sunflower seeds, peanuts, coconut, and palm kernels were available and could be heated to extract the oil. Not until the 1800s and early 1900s were new techniques developed to extract oil from many more plants such as soybean, corn, and cottonseed.

Butter, other dairy products such as cheese, and in lesser amounts, animal fats, were the primary sources of fat in the diet and for cooking of medieval European peasants. Colonial Americans, with more access to land and thus more space for raising cattle and pigs, used much higher quantities of both animal fats and butter. These fats were produced in the household or purchased from local farmers until after the Civil War.

Animal fats, which do not require refrigeration, were available commercially before the Civil War; by 1840 Cincinnati led the nation in pork processing. Dairy fats require refrigeration. Therefore, commercial dairies served local or regional customers until the late 1800s when national distribution was made possible with refrigerated railway cars. Oils and fats that were solely the product of manufacturing became available in the late 1800s. Margarine, also called oleo or oleomargarine, was first manufactured from animal byproducts and sold as a butter substitute. Crisco was created as a lard substitute and manufactured from cottonseed oil.

Margarine was one of the first successful food substitutes. Margarine is a dyed-yellow fat spread created to look and taste like butter. First developed in 1869 in France, margarine was cheaper and kept longer than butter. The American meat processing industry saw an opportunity to turn previously unusable animal fats into this profitable new product. By 1886, over thirty factories in the United States were producing margarine. Margarine manufacturers claimed it was just as wholesome as butter. Margarine advertising capitalized on food purity scandals involving the dairy industry. Butter was portrayed as a product of filthy barnyards and much more likely to be spoiled when it was sold to the consumer. Margarine was portrayed as a safer food, created in sanitary factories.

The dairy industry fought back, seeking to regulate the sale of margarine by lobbying at the state and national level for the passage of laws to tax and regulate margarine. They demanded labeling laws that made the differences between margarine and butter clear to consumers. Several states passed laws in favor of the dairy industry, restricting how margarine could be labeled and packaged.

The Oleomargarine Act of 1886, the first federal law related to the purity of food, clearly defined the distinctions between butter and margarine, required margarine be clearly labeled, imposed a tax of two cents per pound on margarine, and taxed the manufacturers, wholesalers, and retailers of margarine.[41] The law protected the interests of the dairy industry far more than the interests of consumers. But despite this regulation, margarine sales continued to grow, quadrupling between 1888 and 1902.[42]

In 1902, Congress passed another law raising the tax on dyed-yellow margarine to ten cents per pound while decreasing the licensing fee for white, undyed margarine. Consumers could buy yellow dye capsules to knead into the cheaper white margarine to give the product a buttery-yellow color. Butter continued to outsell margarine nationwide, until World War II rationing, when margarine required fewer ration points than butter. In 1950, President Harry Truman signed the Margarine Act of 1950, ending the federal tax on margarine.[43] Margarine sales grew from the 1940s until the 1970s, while butter sales decreased.

In the 1930s, margarine manufacturers switched from using animal fats to a new type of processed vegetable oil—partially hydrogenated oils. This process of hydrogenation converted liquid vegetable oils to spreadable solids and gave them a longer shelf life and prevented the fats from becoming rancid. The hydrogenation process was commonly used with cottonseed, palm, soy, and corn oils. Commercially produced baked goods and other packaged products using hydrogenated oils stayed fresh longer, thus improving product quality and profits.

Crisco, the brand name for shortening made from cottonseed oil and manufactured by Procter and Gamble, was introduced to the American consumer in 1912. Crisco was marketed as a pure vegetable substitute for lard. The product was inspired by the company's quest to create more profitable products from cottonseed oil, an ingredient already required for the manufacture of their main product—soap.

Procter and Gamble created a new approach for marketing and advertising food products that became an industry standard. The company conducted extensive market research and product testing to overcome two consumer concerns. First, they had to convince consumers that a soap company could make food products that were more pure, more wholesome, and safer than other available cooking fats, especially lard. Second, they had to convince home cooks to change their home cooking routine. Procter and Gamble claimed Crisco produced better results than traditional cooking fats and was much more convenient.

Recipes were an especially effective marketing and advertising tool for convincing consumers to use the new product. Recipes using Crisco appeared in newspaper and magazine advertising and in an eight-page booklet included inside the lid of every can. Product samples were distributed throughout the nation at grocery stores and directly to customers.

Week-long cooking schools were conducted throughout the nation featuring foods using Crisco.[44] Procter and Gamble began mailing *Tested Crisco Recipes*, a free paperback with a hundred recipes and the story of Crisco's discovery and manufacture, to potential customers in 1912. The following year, one could order a hardback edition, *The Story of Crisco*,[45] with 250 recipes, for ten cents. *A Calendar of Dinners* containing 365 menus and 615 recipes went through twenty-six editions by 1925.[46]

By the mid-twentieth century, cooks could choose between butter, lard, various vegetable oils, margarine, and solid vegetable shortenings such as Crisco. Concerns about consuming too much animal fat and cholesterol began to appear in the 1950s, based on the research of Ancel Keys (1904–2004). In 1956, the American Heart Association endorsed this view, cautioning Americans that large quantities of butter, eggs, lard, and beef could lead to heart disease. In the 1950s and 1960s, many Americans switched to margarine and solid vegetable shortening, believing both were healthful alternatives to butter and lard.

In recent decades, new research has caused consumers to reject margarine and vegetable shortening. In the 1990s, trans-fatty acids or trans fats, created in the hydrogenation manufacturing process, were associated with heart disease, making products with hydrogenated oils as likely to contribute to heart disease as animal fats. Since that discovery, margarine manufacturers and the processed food industry have lowered the amount of trans fatty acids in many foods. Between 2003 and 2012, consumer trans-fat consumption decreased about 78 percent. In 2015, the Federal Food and Drug Administration required partially hydrogenated oils, which contain trans fats, be removed from foods by 2018.[47]

Figure 5.6. This 1887 cartoon illustrates the conflicting interests in government food regulation. The monster's three heads represent processed food manufacturers and their new products—glucose syrup, cottonseed oil shortening, and oleomargarine. The farmer represents agricultural interests; he is fighting the fraud of manufacturers who misrepresent their products to compete with cane sugar, lard, and butter. He has injured the oleomargarine head of the monster, a reference to the Oleomargarine Act of 1886 that favored the dairy industry. See Figure 5.7 for more information about corn syrup.
Cover of *Rural New-Yorker*, 46 (May 14, 1887). (Courtesy of Internet Archive)

In the Classroom

Home cooking has changed dramatically since the pre-industrial era to adapt to different foods, technology, tastes, and changing households. While students may not cook or know how to read a recipe, cookbooks, recipes, and advertising can be used as primary sources to examine the past and think critically about the present.

Essential Questions

What does "home cooking" really mean? How has our perception of "home cooking" changed over time? What drives this change?

Cookbooks and food advertising from the late nineteenth and through the twentieth century implied the best food was prepared by women in their roles as wife and mother and served at home. These messages reflected lifestyles of white, middle class households but ignored the reality of cooking and eating of many other groups. In the last fifty years, the themes of food advertising have shifted somewhat to reflect current trends, but still portray idealized imagery to sell products.

In this activity students examine advertising to assess the meaning of home cooking as defined by modern and historical sources. Several relevant examples of historical advertisements, both images and text, are featured in this book. Teachers should assemble a collection of modern advertisements for student analysis. Many resources for historical advertising are available online; visit this book's companion website for additional suggestions.

Community cookbooks are excellent resources for recipes and advertisements. A community cookbook is a collection of recipes provided by community or club members, published and sold to raise funds for a club, church, or reform effort. Publication of this popular genre boomed after the Civil War and continues to be popular today. The Library of Congress provides full text access to dozens of community cookbooks from after the Civil War to the 1920s.[48] Local libraries and archives may also have collections of community cookbooks representing the surrounding community. These unique sources relate how name brand products were adopted for daily use, food traditions in a specific region, the impact of changing technology in daily life, and the transformation of women's roles.[49]

At the beginning of the activity, ask students to consider, individually or in groups, their own definitions of home cooking. Show video clips or display examples of several modern food advertisements. Ask students to analyze what messages are conveyed; the following questions can serve as a guide.

- Who should do the cooking?
- Are the people preparing food male or female?
- Are the people eating the food male or female?
- What social classes are represented? What ethnicities or races?
- What foods or types of food should be eaten? Why?
- What is healthful and what is not?

This activity can be expanded to other advertising techniques common for products other than food such as repetition, claims about a product, associations, bandwagon technique, or promotions.

After students have made conclusions about modern advertising, provide sets of historical advertisements and ask students to identify messages and reoccurring themes. The teacher may choose to provide the following list of common themes in food advertising from the late nineteenth and early twentieth centuries.

- Women show their love for their families through choosing and preparing food.
- The health of husbands and children depend upon home cooking and a wife/mother's choices when preparing food.
- Cooking for a man/husband makes a woman/wife more attractive and feminine.
- Women should cater to the needs of men and children by selecting and preparing the foods men or children prefer.
- Cooking and food choices for the family demonstrate the social status of the family or the family's patriotism.[50]

After students complete their analysis, revisit the essential question.

Essential Question

How has technology changed cooking at home?

In advance, the teacher should obtain modern recipes or purchase boxed or packaged mixes for the following. Each item corresponds with the recipes below from Amelia Simmons's *American Cookery*.

- Roast Stuffed Turkey or instructions from the packaging of a frozen turkey and a box of stuffing mix.
- Mincemeat Pie or a jar of ready-made mincemeat and use the instructions for making a pie on the label
- Home-canning procedures for pears or other fruit or commercially canned pears
- Pudding or instant pudding mix
- Fruit Smoothie or packaged mix
- Cake or cake mix

Introduce the essential question and ask students to list the technology used to prepare food. An example to trigger discussion is the kitchen microwave. Invented in 1945 and purchased by American households in the 1980s and 1990s, the microwave revolutionized how we cook and eat in just a few decades.

Divide students into small groups and provide each group with a set of the recipes from Amelia Simmons's *American Cookery*. Ask students to analyze the recipes using the following questions to prompt discussion:

- Are the recipes for these dishes commonly prepared today?
- Could you follow this recipe and prepare this food? Why or why not?
- What equipment or technology is required to prepare this food?
- Circle unfamiliar ingredients or words.
- In the late eighteenth century, where would the home cook obtain the ingredients for these dishes?

After students have analyzed the recipes, the teacher may need to share the following information and additional information from this chapter about the development of recipes and cookbooks.

- Gill—a unit of measure equal to approximately one pint
- Mince or mincemeat—Mincemeat pies are still prepared for fall or winter holidays in some regions. Historically, mincemeat was prepared when hogs or cattle were slaughtered in autumn when the weather cooled. Less desirable parts of the animals and fat were cooked, mixed with various fruits available at the time or dried fruits, spices, sugar or molasses, brandy, and sometimes vinegar. Sugar, brandy, and vinegar helped to preserve the mixture.
- Pudding—In English and early American cooking pudding was not the modern sweet, dairy-based dessert. Pudding was a heavy bread cooked by steaming or boiling it. The batter was placed in a fabric bag and hung over a pot of water boiling at the hearth. The pudding steamed for several hours and required little attention from the cook. Since the batter was high in butter or lard, the leftovers would keep for several days.
- Syllabub—A drink that combined fresh milk and sweet apple cider. Sweet apple cider was fresh apple juice. Hard apple cider was a fermented drink like beer that was very popular and had a much longer shelf life. The milk, straight from the cow, would have had a high cream content; the froth was whipped cream.

After students have discussed Simmons's recipes, provide each group with the modern recipes or mixes. Ask students to compare the late eighteenth-century recipes with the modern versions using the following questions as a guide for analysis.

- What is the same and different about the ingredients?
- Want is the same and different about the instructions about how to prepare these dishes?
- What is the same and different about the technology required to prepare these dishes?

As a conclusion, ask students to revisit the essential question—How has technology changed cooking at home?

Early American Recipes
from *American Cookery* (1796) by Amelia Simmons
 NOTE: Unique grammar and spelling are as in the original publication.
 1. To Stuff a Turkey
 Grate a wheat loaf, one quarter of a pound of butter, one quarter of a pound salt pork, finely chopped, 2 eggs, a little sweet marjoram, summer savory, parsley and sage, pepper and salt (if the pork be not sufficient), fill the bird and sew up. Some add a gill of wine.
 The same will answer for wild fowl.
 Water fowls require onions.
 The same ingredients stuff a leg of veal, fresh pork or a loin of veal.
 Hang down to a steady solid fire, basting frequently with salt and water, and roast until steam emits from the breast. Put one third of a pound of butter into the gravy, dust flour over the bird and baste with gravy. Serve up with boiled onions and cranberry-sauce, pickles or celery.
 2. Minced Pies
 Scald beefs feet, and clean well (grass fed are best). Put them into a large vessel of cold water, which is changed daily during a week, then boil the feet till tender and take away the bones when cold. Chop fine, to every four pound minced meat, add one pound of beef suet, and four pound of apple raw, and a little fat. Chop all together very fine, add one quart of wine, two pound of raisins, one ounce of cinnamon, one ounce of mace, and sweeten to your taste. Bake three quarters of an hour.
 3. To Preserve Pears, Plums for tarts and pies
 Gather them when full grown, and just as they begin to turn, pick all of the largest out, save about two-thirds of the fruit, to the other third put as much water as you think will cover them, boil and skim them. When the fruit is very soft, drain it through a course sieve; and to every quart of this liquor put a pound and a half of sugar, boil it, and skim it very well; then throw in your fruit, just give them a scald; take them off the fire, and when cold, put them into bottles with wide mouths, pour your syrup over them, lay a piece of white paper over them, and cover them with oil.
 4. A Nice Indian Pudding
 3 pints of scalded milk, 7 spoons fine Indian meal, stir well together while hot, let stand till cooled. Add 7 eggs, half pound of raisins, 4 ounces butter, spice and sugar. Put into a strong cloth, brass or metal vessel, stone or earthen pot, secure from wet and boil 12 hours.
 5. Syllabub—To make a fine syllabub from the cow
 Sweet a quart of cider with sugar, grate nutmeg into it, then milk your cow into your liquor. When you have thus added what quantity of milk you think proper, pour half a pint or more, in proportion to the quantity of syllabub you make, of the sweetest cream you can get all over it. Whip it with a whisk, take off the froth as it rises and put it into your syllabub glasses or pots, and they are fit for use.
 6. A Plain Cake
 Two quarts of milk, 3 pound of sugar, 3 pound of shortening, warmed hot. Add a quart of sweet cider, let this curdle, add 18 eggs, allspice and orange to your taste, or fennel, caraway or coriander. Put in 9 pounds of flour and 3 pints of emptins [*yeast*]. Bake well.

Essential Question

What does "pure food" mean? How are perceptions of food impacted by culture, advertising, and government?
 Americans are uncertain about what foods are healthful. Conflicting information in the media suggests foods are either good or bad. Modern reports describe food product recalls due to contaminants or dangerous bacteria and create uncertainty about the use of pesticides and genetic modification of plants and animals. The results of recent scientific and unscientific studies are reported with little attention to long-term trends in nutritional research. The food industry contributes to the confusion through participation in trade associations and public relations campaigns that promote specific foods.[51] With globalization, food is imported from ever distant locations; quality is difficult to discern.

Concerns about the safety of the food supply are not new. Medieval regulations sought to ensure the purity of flour and beer. Food scandals and the growth of the industrial food industry in the late nineteenth century led to concerns about food adulteration and the sale of spoiled foods. Different levels of government have regulated the food industry throughout time, but regulation has always been a balancing act between protecting interests of consumers and those of business and industry.

The following primary sources, along with figures 5.3, 5.5, 5.6, and 5.7, can be used in the classroom to make comparisons to modern concerns about the food supply. In addition to the essential questions above, students might also consider the following:

- Whose interests should the government protect the most—the health and safety of individuals or the interests of business and industry?
- Should advertisers be held accountable for misleading claims about their products? If so, how?
- Why do individuals and groups perceive the safety and health benefits of foods differently?

SOURCE 1

Excerpts from "Sham Lard and Other Shams," *New York Times*, March 2, 1887[52]

Do Armour & Co. sell cottonseed oil? No: They sell lard, and consumers who buy their lard do not know that in making it one-fifth of the cottonseed oil made in the country was used as an adulterant . . . It is very much cheaper than lard . . . But it is a great swindle to deceive consumers by selling cottonseed oil for cheese or lard as it is oleomargarine for butter.

Millions are employed in the manufacture of glucose . . . But where is there a consumer who asks his grocer for glucose? Like the manufacture of oleomargarine, the manufacture of *glucose* lives by fraud. Glucose serves as an adulterant in sugar, syrups, candies, preserved fruits, honey, and many other articles of food. It is sold for honey to persons who believe they are buying real honey. It is sold for sugar to consumers who pay for cane sugar. It is exported for purpose of adulteration at the rate of more than 3,000,000 pounds a year. And so it is with oleomargarine, as everybody knows. Enormous quantities are still palmed off on swindled consumers in this country.

Glucose—corn syrup. Not to be confused with high-fructose corn syrup, a product first marketed in the 1970s. Both products are made from corn, but have different chemical compositions.

SOURCE 2

Advertisement for Bishop's California Preserves, 1904[53]

Bishop's Preserved Figs or Bishops Sweet Pickled Figs bring to your table the succulent sweetness and delicacy of the ripe white fig—the finest fruit of Southern California.

Bishops Figs are a unique example of what the science of fruit preserving, honestly done, can accomplish. Ripe fruit, pure sugar—that is all. Every jar is guaranteed by $1,000 to contain nothing else.

Housekeepers who know Bishop's James and Jellies will avoid the troublesome preserving season this year. Bishop's have the "home made" flavor, and the thirty varieties give one such opportunity for change as no home preserving can afford.

Ask your best Grocer for Bishop's. A taste of the contents of a single jar will tell you more than words.

Bishop & Company, Los Angeles, California.

Figure 5.7. This 1909 advertisement for corn syrup assures readers this new, manufactured substitute for sugar is "wholesome and digestible" and can be used in any recipe. The reader can order a free Karo Cook Book. In the small print, another use is suggested—"As a spread for bread, you can give children all they want." Corn syrup, also referred to as glucose syrup, was a manufactured substitute for sugar. Corn syrup is chemically different from modern high-fructose corn syrup, a controversial ingredient developed in the 1970s.

Advertisement for Karo Corn Syrup, *McClure's Magazine* (December 1909): 45.

SOURCE 3

Advertisement for Shredded Wheat, 1912[54]

Woman's world and work grow larger with her increasing freedom from household drudgery. Food sense and food knowledge have opened up larger opportunities for intelligent home-management. When cooks fail and servants fail and other duties are pressing hard there is Shredded Wheat Biscuit with which it is so easy to prepare in a few moments, a delicious, nourishing meal without any knowledge of cookery or any housekeeping experience.

Shredded Wheat is ready-cooked and ready-to-serve. Simply heat the Biscuit in the oven for a few moments to restore crispness; then pour over it hot milk and salt or sweeten to suit the taste. It is delicious, and wholesome when served with canned pears or other canned or preserved fruits . . . Made only by The Shredded Wheat Company, Niagara Falls, N. Y.

SOURCE 4

Excerpts from *The Story of Crisco*, 1914[55]

Cooking methods have undergone a market change during the past few years. The nation's food is becoming more and more wholesome as a result of different discoveries, new sources of supply, and the intelligent weighing of values. Domestic Science is better understood and more appreciated . . .

It seems strange to many that there can be anything *better* than butter for cooking, or of greater utility than lard, and the advent of Crisco has been a shock to the older generation, born in an age less progressive than our own, and prone to be content that the old-fashioned things are good enough. But these good folk, when convinced are great enthusiasts. Grandmother was glad to give up the fatiguing spinning wheel. So the modern woman is glad to stop cooking with expensive butter, animal lard and their inadequate substitutes. And so, the nation's cook book has been hauled out and is being revised. Upon thousands of pages, the words "lard" and "butter" have been crossed out and the word "Crisco" written in their place.

The Importance of Giving Children Crisco Foods.

A good digestion will mean much to the youngster's health and character. A man seldom seems to be stronger than his stomach, for indigestion handicaps him in his accomplishment of big things . . . Equip our children with good stomachs by giving them wholesome Crisco foods,—foods which digest with ease . . . They may eat Crisco doughnuts or pie without being chased by nightmares. Sweet dreams follow the Crisco supper.

"A Woman Can Throw Out More with a Teaspoon Than a Man Can Bring Home in a Wagon."

Kitchen expense comes by the spoonful. Think of the countless spoonfuls of expensive butter used daily, where economical Crisco would accomplish the same results at one-third the cost. It should be remembered that one-fifth less Crisco than butter may be used, because Crisco is richer than butter.

SOURCE 5

Advertisement for Fairmont Creamery Company, 1915[56]

BUTTER-FAT
is the only fat from live animals.
All other fat is from dead animals or dead plants. To get the highest food value, and the most delicate flavor in your cake or any baked goods, use
"DIADEM BUTTER"
And
"FAIRMONT CARTON EGGS"

The Domestic Science teachers tell us, that no substitute for butter and eggs (no matter how cheap) has equal food value compared with cost.
The Fairmont Creamery Co.
12th and Jones Streets

SOURCE 6

Brer Rabbit Molasses Advertisement, 1933[57]

Her Saturday Night Gingerbread brought him back to her

Alice, after several years of marriage, began to feel that Jack was getting tired of domesticity and just her. In particular, she thought, his eyes wandered all too often in the direction of pink and white Betty Thorton.

Alice, however had a way with her, too. So she bought an exotic black satin at Dale's which made her figure look like a movie star's.

The next evening, she prepared a dinner of simple delicious dishes, ending with Jack's favorite dessert—Brer Rabbit Gingerbread, heaped high with whipped cream.

It was while Jack was lifting his third forkful of gingerbread to his mouth that he said what Alice had hoped all evening he would say.

"There's something about this dinner, darling, that makes me feel like a pampered prince. Everything is so perfect—and you look like a princess."

Alice though, as she smiled across the table into Jack's worshipful eyes, "It's the gingerbread that did the trick . . . he's as crazy about it as a little boy. There's no molasses flavor like Brer Rabbit."

SOURCE 7

Excerpt from *Single Girl's Cookbook* by Helen Gurley Brown[58]

Helen Gurley Brown is best known as the editor of Cosmopolitan *magazine from 1965–1997 and her book* Sex and the Single Girl, *published in 1962, one year before Betty Friedan's* The Feminine Mystique.

I don't have to tell you what being a good cook can mean in your life. So I will tell you anyway! Cooking is a way to be loved and appreciated by friends and a way to love and appreciate them back. Cooking is also creative and satisfying.

All people aren't born cooks. I wasn't; I'm still struggling as I told you. But I know if I had had this kind of recipe book when I was a single girl, I might have quit being single sooner! Well, maybe I would have. You see, inside its pages are recipes, simple instructions, and guiding philosophies to make you a fabulous cook and the utter darling of a lot of people.

Notes

1. *Oxford English Dictionary Online*, s.v. "cook-book, n." December 2016. http://www.oed.com/view/Entry/40947?redirectedFrom=cookbook.

2. Jean Bottéro, "The Most Ancient Recipes of All," in *Food in Antiquity: Studies in Ancient Society and Culture*, eds. John Wilkins, David Harvey, Michael J. Dobson (Liverpool, UK: Liverpool University press, 1995): 248–55.

3. Phyllis P. Bober, "Apicius," in *Encyclopedia of Food and Culture*, Vol. 1, ed. Solomon H. Katz (New York: Charles Scribner's Sons, 2003), 100–2, accessed February 2017, Gale Virtual Reference Library.

Translation of the recipes attributed to Apicius available at "Antique Roman Dishes – Collection," http://www.cs.cmu.edu/~mjw/recipes/ethnic/historical/ant-rom-coll.html.

4. 1882 edition of *A Noble Book of Cookery* available at Internet Archive, https://archive.org/details/b21529565.

5. 1623 edition of *The English Huswife* available London School of Economics and Political Science Digital Library, http://digital.library.lse.ac.uk/objects/lse:heh898zor.

6. *The English Husbandman* available as The Project Gutenberg EBook, http://www.gutenberg.org/ebooks/22973.

7. Mary Tolford Wilson, "Amelia Simmons Fills a Need: American Cookery, 1796," *The William and Mary Quarterly* 14, no. 1 (January 1957): 17, 19, accessed February 2017, http://www.jstor.org/stable/1917369.

8. Ibid., 20–21.

9. Janice Bluestein, Anne Mendelson, Becky Mercuri, Carol Mighton Haddix, Anne L. Bower, and Alice Ross, "Cookbooks and Manuscripts," in *Oxford Encyclopedia of Food and Drink in America* (Oxford: Oxford University Press, 2004), accessed October 2016, http://www.oxfordreference.com.

10. Mary Randolph, *The Virginia Housewife* (Baltimore: John Plaskitt, 1836), 15, 51, 81, 83, 139, 141, accessed February 2017, Internet Archive, https://archive.org/details/virginiahousewif00randrich.

11. Lydia Marie Child, *The American Frugal Housewife*, 12th ed. (Boston: Carter, Hendee, and Co., 1832), 6, accessed February 2017, Internet Archive, https://archive.org/details/TheAmericanFrugalHousewife.

12. Eliza Leslie, *Seventy-Five Receipts for Pastry, Cakes, and Sweetmeats* (Boston: Munroe and Francis, 1828), iv, accessed February 2017, Internet Archive, https://archive.org/stream/seventyfiverecei00lesl#page/n5/mode/2up.

13. Judith Fetterley, *Provisions, A Reader from 19th-Century American Women* (Bloomington: Indiana University Press, 1985), 70, 159.

14. James C. Whorton, "Vegetarianism," on *Cambridge World History of Food*, Vol. 2, eds. Kenneth F. Kiple and Kriemhild Conee Ornelas (Cambridge, UK: Cambridge University Press, 2000), 1555–59.

15. Catharine Beecher, *Miss Beecher's Domestic Receipt Book* (New York: Harper and Brothers, 1846), Internet Archive, https://archive.org/details/missbeechersdome01beec.

16. Dolores Hayden, *The Grand Domestic Revolution: A History of Feminist Designs for American Homes, Neighborhoods, and Cities* (Cambridge, MA: The MIT Press, 1981), 55–63.

17. Catharine Beecher and Harriet Beecher Stowe, *The American Woman's Home* (New York: J.B. Ford and Company, 1869), Internet Archive, https://archive.org/details/americanwomansho00beecrich.

18. Catharine Beecher, *The New Housekeeper's Manual* and *The Handy Cook-Book* (New York: J.B. Ford and Company, 1873), Internet Archive, https://archive.org/details/cu31924090142138.

19. Sarah Stage, "Ellen Richards and the Social Significance of the Home Economics Movement," in *Rethinking Home Economics, Women and the History of the Profession*, eds. Sarah Stage and Virginia B. Vincenti (Ithaca, NY: Cornell University Press, 1997), 21–25.

20. Carolyn M. Goldstein, *Creating Consumers: Home Economists in Twentieth Century American* (Chapel Hill: The University of North Carolina Press, 2012), 1, accessed February 2017, EBSCOhost eBook Collection.

21. Laura Shapiro, *Perfection Salad, Women and Cooking at the Turn of the Century* (Berkeley: University of California Press, 1986, 2009), 7.

22. Stage, "Ellen Richards," 23.

23. Juliet Corson, *Twenty-Five Cent Dinners* (New York: Published by the Author at the New York Cooking School, 1878), Internet Archive, https://archive.org/details/twentyfivecentdi00cors; Juliet Corson, *Fifteen Cent Dinners for Workingmen's Families* (New York: Published by the Author, 1877), Internet Archive, https://archive.org/details/fifteencentdinne00cors.

24. Corson, *Fifteen Cent Dinners*, 20.

25. Shapiro, *Perfection Salad*, 132.

26. Ibid., 121–30.

27. Ibid., 45–61.

28. Ibid., 106.

29. Nancy Duran and Joe Jaros, "American Measurement: Refining Cups and Spoons for Scientific Cooking in the Late 19th–Early 20th Century," *Journal of Agricultural & Food Information* 11, no. 1 (2010): 16–27, DOI: 10.1080/10496500903436326.

30. Fannie Farmer, *The Original Fannie Famer 1896 Cookbook*, A facsimile of the first edition, 1896 (Baltimore, MD: Ottenheimer Publishers, 1996), 27–29.

31. "Biography of Janet McKenzie Hill" and "Biography of Maria Parloa," Feeding America, The Historic American Cookbook Project, accessed February 2017, http://digital.lib.msu.edu/projects/cookbooks/html/authors/author_hill.html; http://digital.lib.msu.edu/projects/cookbooks/html/authors/author_parloa.html;

Susan Strasser, *Satisfaction Guaranteed: The Making of the American Mass Market* (New York: Pantheon Books, 1989), 131.

32. Katherine J. Parkin, *Food Is Love: Advertising and Gender Roles in Modern America* (Philadelphia: University of Pennsylvania Press, 2006).

33. Laura Shapiro, *Something From the Oven, Reinventing Dinner in 1950s America* (New York: Viking/Penguin, 2004), 10–17.

34. Ibid., 54–68.

35. Poppy Cannon, *The Can Opener Cookbook* (New York: Thomas Y. Crowell Company, 1951), 1.

36. Peg Bracken, *The I Hate to Cook Book* (New York: Harcourt, Brace & World, Inc., 1960), xii.

37. Goldstein, *Creating Consumers*, 3

38. Lindsey P. Smith, She Wen Ng, and Barry M. Popkin, "Trends in U.S. Home Food Preparation and Consumption: Analysis of National Nutrition Surveys and Time Use Studies from 1965–1966 to 2007–2008," *Nutrition Journal* 12, no. 45 (2013), accessed May 2017, https://www.ncbi.nlm.nih.gov/pmc/articles/PMC3639863/; United States Bureau of Labor Statistics, American Time Use Survey, accessed May 2017, https://www.bls.gov/TUS/CHARTS/HOUSEHOLD.HTM.

39. "How We Poison Our Children," *New York Times* (May 13, 1858); "Swill Milk Destroyed," *New York Times* (May 1, 1887). Retrieved from ProQuest Historical Newspapers: *New York Times*.

40. Strasser, *Satisfaction Guaranteed*, 257–60.

41. "Oleomargine Act of 1886," Internet Archive, https://archive.org/stream/358364-oleomargarine-act-of-1886/358364-oleo-margarine-act-of-1886_djvu.txt.

42. Gerry Strey, "The 'Oleo Wars': Wisconsin's Fight over the Demon Spread," *The Wisconsin Magazine of History* 85, no. 1 (Autumn, 2001): 2–15, accessed March 2017, http://www.jstor.org/stable/4636942.

43. Gerry Schremp, *Kitchen Culture: Fifty Years of Food Fads* (New York: Pharos Books, 1991), 51, 83.

44. Strasser, *Satisfaction Guaranteed*, 8–12.

45. Procter & Gamble Company, *The Story of Crisco*, 3rd ed. (Cincinnati: Procter & Gamble Company, 1913, 1914), Internet Archive, https://archive.org/details/storyofcrisco00neil.

46. Marion Harris Neil, *A Calendar of Dinners with 615 Recipes* (Cincinnati: Procter & Gamble, 1921), Internet Archive, https://archive.org/details/calendarofdinner00neiluoft.

47. United States Food and Drug Administration, "The FDA Takes Step to Remove Artificial Trans Fats in Processed Foods" (June 16, 2016), accessed April 2017, https://www.fda.gov/NewsEvents/Newsroom/PressAnnouncements/ucm451237.htm.

48. Library of Congress, Community Cookbooks: Selected Titles from General Collections, https://www.loc.gov/rr/scitech/SciRefGuides/communitycookbooks.html

49. Cynthia Williams Resor, "Using Community Cookbooks as Primary Sources," *Social Education* 75, no. 1 (January/February, 2011): 30–35.

50. Parkin, *Food Is Love*, 8–11.

51. Marion Nestle, *Food Politics* (Berkeley, CA: University of California Press, 2002), 17–21.

52. "Sham Lard and Other Shams," *New York Times* (March 2, 1887), Retrieved from ProQuest Historical Newspapers: *New York Times*.

53. Bishop's California Preserves Advertisement, *Munsey's Magazine*, vol. 31, no. 3 (June 1904), Advertising Section.

54. Shredded Wheat Company Advertisement, *Everybody's Magazine*, vol. 26, no. 4 (April 1912): 16d.

55. Procter & Gamble Company, *The Story of Crisco*, 9–10, 18.

56. Advertisement for Fairmont Creamery Company, *Benson Woman's Club Cook Book* (Douglas Printing Co. 1915), 14, Internet Archive, https://archive.org/stream/bensonwomansclub00omah#page/14/mode/2up

57. Brer Rabbit Molasses Advertisement, *Good Housekeeping* (December 1933): 136.

58. Helen Gurley Brown, *Single Girl's Cookbook* (Greenwich, CT: Fawcett Publications, 1969), 6.

CHAPTER SIX

Education Theories behind the Themes

The savvy teacher will ask, "Are the ideas in this book aligned with current education trends?" This final chapter answers that question with a brief exploration of the pedagogies and standards that serve as a framework: thematic instruction, place-based education, culturally responsive teaching, and national social studies and literacy standards.

Thematic Instruction

Thematic teaching is the selection and highlighting of a theme through a unit, a course, a series of social studies courses, or across disciplines. The theme should be recurrent through history and present in modern life. Themes can be topics, such as food, housing, or family or overarching questions, such as, "Is that really a thing?" The theme and its essential questions should be relevant to students' lives and address important issues within academic disciplines.

Teaching with themes is included in and consistent with many popular instructional approaches such as interdisciplinary or integrated instruction, differentiated instruction, problem-based learning, student choice, and connecting real-world experiences to classroom content. Even though thematic teaching is most often associated with elementary and middle schools, it is possible in a high school setting within an individual course or across the curriculum.

The advantages of thematic teaching are numerous.

- Students learn better when experiencing knowledge in a larger context. Relationships and connections between facts, concepts, and disciplines become more apparent.
- Larger themes and concepts more closely resemble how life is experienced outside the classroom.
- Choosing themes related to students' lives incorporates the needs, interests, and perspectives of the students into classroom instruction.
- Students make connections between seemingly distant and irrelevant events, people, and cultures in the past to their modern lives.
- Students critically analyze their own culture and community as well as national and international media, events, and trends through new eyes.
- The disciplinary tools of literacy and the social sciences stressed in current teaching standards—questioning, analysis, critical reading, and writing—can be incorporated in a more meaningful way.
- Thematic instruction may inspire students to become more interested in history and other academic subjects.
- Teachers may discover new professional inspiration while exploring themes relevant to both the classes they teach and their personal interests.

Place-Based Education

Place-based education is an interdisciplinary approach to education that immerses students in the history, culture, landscapes, and experiences of their own communities with a special focus on service projects.[1] Sadly, place-based education is often overlooked in social studies because teachers, pressured by textbooks, curricula, and standards with a national or international focus, feel there is little time to examine local issues when a few thousand years of political and historical narrative must be covered.

Even materials that promote place-based education, such as this book, must focus upon the big picture rather than the local community, to reach a wider audience. Despite this limitation, the themes of food, housing, and family have relevance to students as individuals and to students' communities and cultures, both in the past and the present. While food, family, and housing have local relevance, learning more about these topics on the local level may require additional reading and research by the teacher.

In the previous chapters, historical items such as houses or furniture or forks are examined as objective relics of the past and subjective symbols of social status or gender. Communities can be explored using the same framework. The geographic concept of *place*, at the heart of place-based education, has three aspects representing the objective and subjective—location, locale, sense of place.[2]

All places have an absolute *location*, a fixed coordinate on the surface of the planet. Locations are usually communicated using latitude and longitude. Students can easily determine the absolute location, or latitude and longitude, of their dwelling, school, or community using global positioning system (GPS) receivers, often included in modern cell phones. Location is objective and rarely contested. People with different values or different experiences can hardly disagree about the latitude/longitude reference for a town, or its dot on a road map. But the next two aspects, locale and sense of place, are shifting sands of meaning.

The second aspect of place, *locale*, is the actual setting in which people carry on their lives. Settings consist of objects—roads, buildings, trees, walls, furniture, doors, or pictures on the wall. When people describe their dwelling or the community, they usually list the most prominent characteristics, or the locale. But people experience buildings and communities differently. For example, if next door neighbors are asked to describe the locale of their community by listing the five most prominent landmarks, the lists will likely be different. People see the landmarks of their community every day, but ascribe very different levels of importance to the objects because of their experiences.

Ask students to draw a mental map of the school, labeling the five most important locations in the school. Each student's perception of the school will be represented somewhat differently on their maps. The principal's office, library, cafeteria, classrooms, detention center, counselor's office are elements of a school's locale everyone can see, but students' experiences will determine which ones are memorable and which ones are not.

The third aspect of place is a *sense of place*, a phrase geographers use to describe a person's subjective and emotional attachment to a location and locale. This book explores a place called *home*. Home might be a happy safe place for some or associated with violence, abuse, or a struggle for survival for others. Sense of place does not only originate in the minds of individuals. Concepts of place or home are influenced by the wider culture. Place is a *social construct*, an idea appearing natural and obvious to the group of people who agree it is true, but it may not represent reality when examined closely.

Perceptions of communities, as well as houses, food, and family, are socially constructed. For example, small towns are often described as ideal locations for homes and families and common terms and phrases used to describe them are a part of a wider, American social construct of an ideal community called "small town America." Phrases like "people are friendly" and "people know and help their neighbors" are commonly used to describe this utopian place.

"Small town values" has become a common and controversial phrase in modern political commentary. This phrase can have positive connotations or suggest negative qualities such as closed-mindedness. When "small town America" is held up as an ideal, the unspoken implication is big city America is a negative opposite that should be avoided. These constructs are often unquestioned and accepted as reality, but upon closer examination, the claims may be overly positive, stereotypical, and ignore harsh realities. Everyone in a small town is not friendly and helpful and newcomers and minority groups may be shunned. On the other hand, many helpful, friendly people live in cities too.

In the previous chapters, the focus has been on daily life of everyday people, not the politically powerful. But the concept of place often encompasses perceptions of power that should be examined in the classroom. The architecture, maintenance, and location of residential neighborhoods convey messages of power or lack of power. The visibility of grand historical homes as tourist sites and the absence or invisibility of the historical homes of average people creates a skewed view of life in the past for students.

As students examine historical dwellings of the powerful or elite in their community, focus attention on the roles of worker households whose labor enabled construction, the craftspeople who built the homes, and the servants who maintained these estates, as well as the power the elite had over these average people. Great houses are often named for the man who built them. Explore the contributions of women—the wives, mothers, daughters, and servants—who lived in the house and oversaw, cleaned, and maintained these great houses. Search for historical homes and neighborhoods of working people, servants, and slaves.

Placed-based education asks students to explore their community, the locations in it, and the meanings attached to those locations by different groups of people so that students develop an awareness and appreciation for the experiences of their neighbors. This parallels the inquiry approach described in the previous chapters that asks students to examine their own lives and culture through the study of the daily life in the past. Both recognize and respect that different people have different experiences, the concept at the core of culturally responsive teaching.

Culturally Responsive Teaching

Culturally responsive teaching stresses the importance of recognizing the uniqueness of the cultures and social status of all groups of students, rather than assuming all come from or must conform to a dominant culture or national ideal. In culturally responsive classrooms, students of all backgrounds are not just introduced to differences; they are also asked to analyze why, when, and how these differences occurred and consider the implications of differences in economic, political, and social situations.[3] In other words, students wear two pairs of "glasses"; they consider the curriculum through their own cultural framework, or lenses, and through a set of critical lenses that provides a wider perspective.

This book promotes a culturally responsive approach to social history. Students are adding a third set of lenses—social history glasses. Students explore how daily routines in the past were a response to *historical* realities and cultural expectations for men, women, and children; just as modern differences are a product of unique circumstances and cultures. Historical concepts are measured against the present. Discussion and critical analysis takes place on three levels; students compare and contrast human experiences in the past, in modern culture, and their own lives.

Discussion of modern, controversial topics can be difficult for students and for teachers. A culturally responsive approach to history has an additional advantage. Students can hone their skills at critical analysis using distant, historical circumstances, allowing them to consider their own values and beliefs without feeling threatened.

Culturally responsive teaching and examining historical themes related to modern issues requires a classroom atmosphere in which students can learn about and examine similarities and differences in a neutral setting. Teachers must examine their own conceptions of food, home, and family, and recognize that while their experiences can provide another insight, they may be very different from those of their students. Furthermore, if students simply repeat or adopt historical stereotypical views of sex, gender, social class, race, and ethnicity without question, the goal of critical analysis is never achieved. The teacher must provide a model for and guide students in critical analysis of the objective, the subjective, the real and ideal meanings of historical and modern food, housing, and family.

Aligning to Standards

Social studies standards vary from state to state, therefore the most current publication of the National Council of Social Studies, *College, Career, and Civic Life (C3) Framework for Social Studies State Standards: Guidance for Enhancing the Rigor of K–12 Civics, Economics, Geography, and History*,[4] provides an organizational framework for this thematic approach. The four-dimension Inquiry Arc promotes both critical analysis and content-specific learning. The entire publication is available for free online, so there is no need to review its contents in detail. But key aspects of the four dimensions (in italics below) are important to note.

Developing questions and planning inquiries is the first dimension in *College, Career, and Civic Life (C3) Framework*; student inquiry is focused upon compelling and supporting questions. A compelling question is a renaming of Jay McTighe and Grant Wiggins's essential question. According to McTighe and Wiggins, essential questions are overarching questions with three important characteristics—they reflect the key inquiries within a discipline, can be applied over multiple units or disciplines, and serve as a conceptual framework for learning both concepts and discrete facts.[5] These three characteristics also support thematic instruction. Thematic instruction requires a focus beyond the content, especially for themes as broad as food, family, and housing.

The second dimension, *applying disciplinary tools and concepts*, is related to both literacy skills and the specific skills used by historians. Inquiry, however, does not occur in a vacuum; historians must have a deep and wide knowledge within their field of study. Each chapter includes a broad historical summary. But the wide scope of food, housing, and family necessitated a specific historical focus. European and United States history was chosen not because it is the only important history, but because it was the area in which the author had the most knowledge. Each theme has relevance and importance far beyond of the context of Western civilization.

Third, so students can become adept at *evaluating sources and using evidence*, each chapter includes primary sources focused on the chapter's essential questions.

Finally, the *C3 Framework* Inquiry Arc engages students in *communicating conclusions and taking informed action*. Communication of conclusions can take many forms, both written and oral, inside and outside the classroom. But taking informed action on events of the past can be a challenge. The action component of social history can involve studying the history of family, food, and housing in the local community or state; analyzing the theme in one's personal or family life; investigating the theme in the modern world locally, nationally, or internationally; or using what is learned to act within the classroom, school, or community.

The *C3 Framework* was written to closely align with the *Common Core State Standards for English Language Arts and Literacy in History/Social Studies, Science, and Technical Subjects*.[6] Like social studies standards in some states, this document has become controversial in recent political debates and has been adopted and un-adopted in states across the nation. Trends come and go quickly in education but one thing remains constant—good teaching is good teaching and students will always need to learn how to read, write, speak, and listen. Many resources are already available describing literacy strategies appropriate for every grade level and every type of reader and writer. Therefore, choosing teaching strategies that best meet the needs of your students and local and state curriculum requirements is left up to your professional judgment.

Notes

1. Center for Place-Based Learning and Community Engagement, "What Is Place-Based Education?" http://promiseofplace.org/what_is_pbe.

2. Tim Creswell, *Place: A Short Introduction* (Malden, MA: Blackwell Publishing, 2004), 7.

3. Geneva Gay, *Culturally Responsive Teaching: Theory, Research, and Practice*, 2nd ed. (New York: Teachers College Press, 2010); Concha Delgado Gaitan, *Building Culturally Responsive Classrooms* (Thousand Oaks, CA: Corwin Press, 2006), 144.

4. National Council of Social Studies, *College, Career, and Civic Life (C3) Framework for Social Studies State Standards: Guidance for Enhancing the Rigor of K-12 Civics, Economics, Geography, and History*, 2013, https://www.socialstudies.org/c3.

5. Jay McTighe and Grant Wiggins, *Essential Questions: Opening Doors to Student Understanding* (Alexandria, VA: Association for Supervision & Curriculum Development, 2013).

6. Common Core Standards Initiative, "English Language Arts Standards," http://www.corestandards.org/ELA-Literacy/.

Works Cited

Ames, Kenneth L. *Death in the Dining Room and Other Tales of Victorian Culture*. Philadelphia: Temple University Press, 1992.

Ariés, Philippe. *Centuries of Childhood: A Social History of Family Life*. Translated by Robert Baldick. New York: Vintage Books, 1962.

Bayard, Ferdinand-M. *Travels of a Frenchman in Maryland and Virginia with a Description of Philadelphia and Baltimore, in 1791*. Translated and edited by Ben C. McCary. Williamsburg, VA: Ben C. McCary, 1950. Accessed April 2017. Hathi Trust Digiial Library. https://babel.hathitrust.org/cgi/pt?id=mdp.39015027057820;view=1up;seq=6.

Beecher, Catharine and Harriet Beecher Stowe. *The American Woman's Home*. New York: J.B. Ford and Company; Boston: H.A. Brown & Co. 1869. Internet Archive. https://archive.org/details/americanwomansho00beecrich.

Beecher, Catharine. "How to Redeem Woman's Profession From Dishonor." *Harper's New Monthly Magazine* 31 (November 1865): 710–16.

———. *Miss Beecher's Domestic Receipt Book*. New York: Harper and Brothers, 1846. Internet Archive. https://archive.org/details/missbeechersdome01beec.

———. *The New Housekeeper's Manual* and *The Handy Cook-Book*. New York, J.B. Ford and Company, 1873. Internet Archive. https://archive.org/details/cu31924090142138.

Bellamy, Edward. *Looking Backward: 2000–1887*. Accessed July 2016. Project Gutenberg Ebook. http://www.gutenberg.org/ebooks/624.

Bem, Sandra Lipsitz. *The Lenses of Gender: Transforming the Debate on Sexual Inequality*. New Haven, CT: Yale University Press, 1993.

"Biography of Janet McKenzie Hill" and "Biography of Maria Parloa." Feeding America, The Historic American Cookbook Project. Accessed February 2017. http://digital.lib.msu.edu/projects/cookbooks/html/authors/author_hill.html; and http://digital.lib.msu.edu/projects/cookbooks/html/authors/author_parloa.html.

Bluestein Janice, Anne Mendelson, Becky Mercuri, Carol Mighton Haddix, Anne L. Bower, and Alice Ross. "Cookbooks and Manuscripts." In *The Oxford Encyclopedia of Food and Drink in America*. Oxford University Press, 2004. Accessed October 2016, http://www.oxfordreference.com.

Bober, Phyllis P. "Apicius." In *Encyclopedia of Food and Culture*. Vol. 1, Edited by Solomon H. Katz. New York: Charles Scribner's Sons, 2003. Accessed February 2017. Gale Virtual Reference Library.

Bottéro, Jean "The Most Ancient Recipes of All." In *Food in Antiquity: Studies in Ancient Society and Culture*. Edited by John Wilkins, David Harvey, Michael J. Dobson. 248–55. Liverpool, UK: Liverpool University Press, 1995.

Bowes, Kim, Mariaelena Ghisleni, Cam Grey, and Emanuele Vaccaro. "Excavating the Roman Peasant." *Expedition Magazine* 53 no. 2 (July 2011): 4–12. Accessed June 2016. http://penn.museum/documents/publications/expedition/PDFs/53-2/bowes.pdf.

Bracken, Peg. *The I Hate to Cook Book*. New York: Harcourt, Brace & World, Inc., 1960.

Brown, Helen Gurley. *Single Girl's Cookbook*. Greenwich, CT: Fawcett Publications, 1969.

Bureau of Labor Statistics. "24 percent of employed people did some or all of their work at home in 2015." July 8, 2016. Accessed November 2016. https://www.bls.gov/opub/ted/2016/24-percent-of-employed-people-did-some-or-all-of-their-work-at-home-in-2015.htm.

Campbell, Helen Stuart. *Household Economics: A Course of Lectures in the School of Economics of the University of Wisconsin*. New York: G.P. Putnam's Sons, 1896. Internet Archive. https://archive.org/stream/householdeconomi00camp#page/222/mode/2up.

Cannon, Poppy. *The Can Opener Cookbook*. New York: Thomas Y. Crowell Company, 1951.

Cartwright, Peter. *Autobiography of Peter Cartwright: The Backwoods Preacher*. Cincinnati: R. P. Thompson, 1859. Internet Archive. https://archive.org/details/autobiographyofp01cart.

Catling, Chris. "How the Black Death Prompted a Building Boom." *Current Archaeology* 279 (June 2013): 12–19.

Center for Disease Control and Prevention. "Childhood Obesity Facts." Accessed April 2017. https://www.cdc.gov/healthyschools/obesity/facts.htm.

Center for Place-Based Learning and Community Engagement. "What Is Place-Based Education?" http://promiseofplace.org/what_is_pbe.

Chaucer, Geoffrey. *The Canterbury Tales*. Accessed April 2017. http://www.librarius.com/canttran/genpro/genpro118-162.htm.

Chew, Lee. "The Biography of a Chinaman." *The Independent* 55, no. 2829 (February 19, 1903): 417–23. HathiTrust Digital Library. https://babel.hathitrust.org/cgi/pt?id=inu.32000000688715;view=1up;seq=463.

Child, Lydia Marie. *The American Frugal Housewife*. 12th ed. Boston: Carter, Hendee, and Co., 1832, Internet Archive. https://archive.org/details/TheAmericanFrugalHousewife.

Chiles, Rosa Pendleton. "John Howard Payne: American Poet, Actor, Playwright, Consul and the Author of 'Home, Sweet Home.'" *Records of the Columbia Historical Society*. Vol. 31/32 (1930): 209–97. Accessed April 2017. http://www.jstor.org/stable/40067449.

Clarence, Louise. "Domestic Service." *Far and Near* (1891): 24–26.

Clark, Clifford Edward Jr. *The America Family Home, 1800–1860*. Chapel Hill: The University of North Carolina Press, 1986.

Common Core Standards Initiative. "English Language Arts Standards." http://www.corestandards.org/ELA-Literacy/.

Cott, Nancy F. *The Bonds of Womanhood: 'Woman's Sphere' in New England, 1780–1835*. New Haven, CT: Yale University Press, 1997. eBook Collection. EBSCOhost

Coontz, Stephanie. *Marriage, A History: How Love Conquered Marriage*. New York: Penguin Books, 2005.

———. *The Way We Never Were: American Families and the Nostalgia Trap*. New York: Basic Books, 1992, 2000.

Corson, Juliet. *Fifteen Cent Dinners for Workingmen's Families*. New York: Published by the Author, 1877. Internet Archive. https://archive.org/details/fifteencentdinne00cors.

———. *Twenty-Five Cent Dinners*. New York: Published by the Author at the New York Cooking School, 1878. Internet Archive. https://archive.org/details/twentyfivecentdi00cors.

Cowan, Ruth Schwartz. *More Work for Mother: The Ironies of Household Technology from the Open Hearth to the Microwave*. New York: Basic Books, 1983.

Creswell, Tim. *Place: A Short Introduction*. Malden, MA: Blackwell Publishing, 2004.

Cummings, Abbott Lowell. "Inside the Massachusetts House." *Readings in American Vernacular Architecture*. Edited by Dell Upton and John Michael Vlach. 219–39. Athens: University of Georgia Press, 1986.

"Curious Kentuckians." *New York Times*, August 7, 1886. Retrieved from ProQuest Historical Newspapers: *New York Times*.

Davis, James. "Baking for the Common Good: A Reassessment of the Assize of Bread in Medieval England." *The Economic History Review* 57, no. 3 (2004): 465–502. http://www.jstor.org/stable/3698543.

della Casa, Giovanni. *Galateo: Of Manners and Behaviors*. Boston, The Merrymount Press, 1914. Accessed January 2017. https://archive.org/details/arenaissancecou00delluoft.

Desilver, Drew. "What's on Your Table? How America's Diet Has Changed Over the Decades." Pew Research Center. December 2016. Accessed March 2017. http://www.pewresearch.org/fact-tank/2016/12/13/whats-on-your-table-how-americas-diet-has-changed-over-the-decades/.

Douglass, Frederick. *My Bondage and Freedom*. New York: Miller, Orton & Mulligan, 1855. Documenting the American South. http://docsouth.unc.edu/neh/douglass55/douglass55.html.

Downing, Andrew Jackson. *The Architecture of Country Houses*. New York: D. Appleton & Company, 1851. Internet Archive. https://archive.org/details/architectureofco00down.

Dubois, W. E. B. *The Philadelphia Negro: A Social Study*. New York: Schocken Books, 1899. Internet Archive. https://archive.org/details/philadelphianegr001901mbp.

Duran, Nancy and Joe Jaros. "American Measurement: Refining Cups and Spoons for Scientific Cooking in the Late 19th–Early 20th Century." *Journal of Agricultural & Food Information* 11 no. 1 (2010): 16–27, DOI: 10.1080/10496500903436326.

Dyer, Christopher Dyer. *Making a Living in the Middle Ages: The People of Britain 850–1520*. New Haven, CT: Yale University Press: 2002.

———. *Everyday Life in Medieval England*. London: Hambledon Continuum, 2000. Accessed July 2016. eBook Collection. EBSCOhost.

Endres, Kathleen L. and Therese Lueck, eds. *Women's Periodicals in the United States: Social and Political Issues*. Historical Guides to the World's Periodicals and Newspapers. Westport, CT: Greenwood, 1996.

Erbes, Scott. "Manufacturing and Marketing the American Bungalow: The Aladdin Company, 1906–20." In *The American Home: Material Culture, Domestic Space, and Family Life*. Editor Eleanor Thompson. 45–69. Winterthur, DE: Henry Francis Du Pont Winterthur Museum, 1998.

Estate Inventory of Moses Hiatt. 1802. Garrard County Court Clerk Archive. Garrard County Court House, Lancaster, Kentucky.

Farmer, Fannie. *The Original Fannie Famer 1896 Cookbook*. A facsimile of the first edition, 1896. Baltimore, MD: Ottenheimer Publishers, 1996.

Farrar, Mrs. John (Elizabeth Ware). *The Young Lady's Friend*. Boston: American Stationer's Company/John B. Russell, 1838. Internet Archive. https://archive.org/details/youngladysfrien05farrgoog.

Fetterley, Judith Flanders. *The Making of Home: The 500-Year Story of How Our Houses Became Our Homes*. New York: Thomas Dunne Books, 2014.

Flynn, Peter. "How Bridget Was Framed: The Irish Domestic in Early American Cinema, 1895–1917." *Cinema Journal* 50, no. 2 (Winter 2011): 1–20. www.jstor.org/stable/41240691.

Fossier, Robert Fossier. *Peasant Life in the Medieval West*. Translated by Juliet Vale. Oxford, UK: Basil Blackwell, 1988.

Fry, Richard and Rakesh Kochhar. "Are You in the American Middle Class?" Pew Research Center. May 11, 2016. Accessed October 15, 2016. http://www.pewresearch.org/fact-tank/2016/05/11/are-you-in-the-american-middle-class/.

Gaitan, Concha Delgado. *Building Culturally Responsive Classrooms* (Thousand Oaks, CA: Corwin Press, 2006), 144.

Gay, Geneva. *Culturally Responsive Teaching: Theory, Research, and Practice*. 2nd ed. New York: Teachers College Press, 2010.

Geist, Claudia and Philip N. Cohen. "Headed Toward Equality? Housework Change in Comparative Perspective." *Journal of Marriage & Family* 73, no. 4 (2011): 832–44. Accessed August 27, 2016. Education Source. EBSCOhost.

Ghisleni, Mariaelena, Emanuele Vaccaro, Kim Bowes, Antonia Arnoldus, Michael MacKinnon, and Flavia Marani. "Excavating the Roman Peasant: Excavations at Pievina." *Papers of the British School at Rome* 79 (2011): 95–145. Accessed June 2016. http://www.jstor.org/stable/41725305.

Gies, Frances and Joseph. *Cathedral, Forge, and Waterwheel, Technology and Invention in the Middle Ages*. New York: HarperPerennial, 1995.

Gilbert, Dennis. *The American Class Structure in an Age of Growing Inequality*. 9th ed. Thousand Oaks, CA: Sage, 2015.

Gilliam, Jan K. "The Evolution of the House in Early Virginia." In *The American Home: Material Cultures, Domestic Space, and Family Life*. Edited by Eleanor McD Thompson. 177–96. Winterthur, DE: Henry Francis du Pont Winterthur Museum, 1998.

Goldstein, Carolyn M. *Creating Consumers: Home Economists in Twentieth Century America*. Chapel Hill: The University of North Carolina Press, 2012. Accessed February 2017. EBSCOhost. eBook Collection.

Grund, Francis Joseph. *The Americans: In Their Moral, Social, and Political Relations*. Boston: Marsh, Capen and Lyon 1837. Internet Archive. https://archive.org/stream/americansintheir00grun#page/236/mode/2up.

Gunter, Mary Alice, Thomas H. Estes, and Jan Schwab. *Instruction: A Models Approach*. 3rd ed. Boston: Allyn and Bacon, 1999.

Haber, Barbara. "Culinary History Vs. Food History." In *The Oxford Encyclopedia of Food and Drink in America*. Oxford University Press, 2004. Accessed October 2016. http://www.oxfordreference.com.

Hawke, David Freeman. *Everyday Life in Early America*. New York: Harper & Row, 1989.

Hayden, Dolores. *The Grand Domestic Revolution: A History of Feminist Designs for American Homes, Neighborhoods, and Cities*. Cambridge, MA: The MIT Press, 1981.

Herlihy, David. *Medieval Households*. Cambridge, MA: Harvard University Press, 1985.

Hood, Ernie. "Dwelling Disparities: How Poor Housing Leads to Poor Health." *Environmental Health Perspectives* 113, no. 5 (May 2005): A310–A317. Accessed October 2016. https://www.ncbi.nlm.nih.gov/pmc/articles/PMC1257572/.

Horton, George. "Home." *Mansford's Magazine* 37, no. 4 (April 1893): 237. Accessed April 2017. Google Books.

"How to Sweep a Room." *Scribner's Monthly* 9, no. 1 (November 1874): 118–19, Accessed July 2016. http://ebooks.library.cornell.edu/cgi/t/text/pageviewer-idx?c=scmo;cc=scmo;rgn=full%20text;idno=scmo0009-1;didno=scmo0009-1;view=image;seq=124;node=scmo0009-1%3A18;page=root;size=100.

"How We Poison Our Children." *New York Times* (May 13, 1858). Retrieved from ProQuest Historical Newspapers: *New York Times*.

Isager, Signe and Jens Erik Skydsgaard. *Ancient Greek Agriculture: An Introduction*. London: Taylor & Francis Routledge, 1992.

Johns, Elizabeth. *American Genre Paintings: The Politics of Everyday Life*. New Haven, CT: Yale University Press, 1991.

Katzman, David M. *Seven Days a Week: Women and Domestic Service in Industrializing America*. New York: Oxford University Press, 1978.

Kaufman Cathy K. "Dining Rooms, Table Settings, and Table Manners." In *The Oxford Encyclopedia of Food and Drink in America*. Oxford University Press, 2004. Accessed January 2017. http://www.oxfordreference.com.libproxy.eku.edu/view/10.1093/acref/9780195154375.001.0001/acref-9780195154375-e-0260.

Kellogg Susan and Steven Mintz. "Family Structures." In *Encyclopedia of American Social History*. Vol. 3. Edited by Mary Kupiec Cayton, Elliott J. Gorn, and Peter W. Williams. 1925–1944. New York: Charles Scribner's Sons, 1993.

Kerber, Linda. "The Republican Mother: Women and the Enlightenment-An American Perspective." *American Quarterly* 28, no. 2 (1976): 187–205.

Kniffen, Fred B. "Folk Housing: Key to Diffusion." In *Readings in American Vernacular Architecture*. Edited by Dell Upton and John Michael Vlach. 3–57. Athens: University of Georgia Press, 1986.

Kotchemidova, Cristina. "Why We Say 'Cheese': Producing the Smile in Snapshot Photography." *Critical Studies in Media Communication* 22, no. 1 (March 2005): 2–25.

Lancaster, Clay. *The American Bungalow in Common Places: Readings in American Vernacular Architecture*. Edited by Dell Upton and John Michael Vlach. 79–106. Athens: University of Georgia Press, 1986.

Larkin, Jack. *The Reshaping of Everyday Life: 1790–1840*. New York: HarperPerennial, 1988.

Leslie, Eliza. *Seventy-Five Receipts for Pastry, Cakes, and Sweetmeats*. Boston: Munroe and Francis, 1828. Accessed February 2017. Internet Archive. https://archive.org/stream/seventyfiverecei00lesl#page/n5/mode/2up.

Levine, James A. "Poverty and Obesity in the U.S." *Diabetes* 60 no. 11 (June 2011): 2667–2668. Accessed April 2017, https://www.ncbi.nlm.nih.gov/pmc/articles/PMC3198075/.

The Life of Elagabalus. Part 2. Loeb Classical Library, 1924. http://penelope.uchicago.edu/Thayer/E/Roman/Texts/Historia_Augusta/Elagabalus/2*.html.

Matt, Susan J. "You Can't Go Home Again: Homesickness and Nostalgia in U.S. History." *The Journal of American History* 94, no. 2 (September 2007): 469–97. Accessed March 2017. http://www.jstor.org/stable/25094961.

Matthews, Glenna. *"Just a Housewife": The Rise and Fall of Domesticity in America*. New York: Oxford University Press, 1987.

McAlester, Virginia S. and Lee McAlester. *A Field Guide to American Houses*. New York: Alfred A. Knopf, 2006.

McTighe, Jay and Grant Wiggins. *Essential Questions: Opening Doors to Student Understanding*. Alexandria, VA: Association for Supervision & Curriculum Development, 2013.

Mintz, Sidney W. *Sweetness and Power: The Place of Sugar in Modern History*. New York: Elisabeth Sifton Books/Viking, 1985.

Mintz, Steven and Susan Kellogg. *Domestic Revolutions: A Social History of American Family Life*. New York: The Free Press, 1988.

Murtha, Hillary. "Man, Machine and Refined Dining in the Victorian Era." *Food for Thought: Essays on Eating and Culture*. Edited by Lawrence C. Rubin. 15–30. Jefferson, NC: McFarland, 2008.

National Council of Social Studies. *College, Career, and Civic Life (C3) Framework for Social Studies State Standards: Guidance for Enhancing the Rigor of K-12 Civics, Economics, Geography, and History*, 2013, https://www.socialstudies.org/c3.

Nestle, Marion. *Food Politics*. Berkeley, CA: University of California Press, 2002.

"Oleomargine Act of 1886." Internet Archive. https://archive.org/stream/358364-oleomargarine-act-of-1886/358364-oleomargarine-act-of-1886_djvu.txt.

Oliver, Paul. *Dwellings: The Vernacular House World Wide*. London, UK: Phaidon Press Limited, 2003.

Parkin, Katherine J. *Food Is Love: Advertising and Gender Roles in Modern America*. Philadelphia: University of Pennsylvania Press, 2006.

Pearson, Kathy L. "Nutrition and the Early-Medieval Diet." *Speculum* 72, no. 1 (January 1997): 1–32. Accessed October 2016. www.jstor.org/stable/2865862.

Petersilie, Karl W. and L. M. Brown. "'Tis Home Where the Heart Is." Notated Music. Philadelphia: George Willig, 1847. Library of Congress. Accessed May 2017. https://www.loc.gov/item/sm1847.430850/.

Pettengill, Lillian. *Toilers of the Home: The Record of a College Woman's Experience as a Domestic Servant*. New York: Doubleday, Page & Company, 1903. Internet Archive. https://archive.org/details/toilershomereco00pettgoog.

Procter & Gamble Company. *The Story of Crisco*. 3rd ed. Cincinnati: Procter & Gamble Company, 1913, 1914. Internet Archive. https://archive.org/details/storyofcrisco00neil.

Randolph, Mary. *The Virginia Housewife*. Baltimore: John Plaskitt, 1836. Internet Archive. https://archive.org/details/virginiahousewif00randrich.

Resor, Cynthia Williams. "Using Community Cookbooks as Primary Sources." *Social Education* 75, no. 1 (January/February 2011): 30–35.

Riis-Carstensen, Leifa. "Using Cow Thermal Energy to Heat Homes in Winter." *Mother Earth News* (November/December 1982). Accessed July 2016, http://www.motherearthnews.com/homesteading-and-livestock/cow-thermal-energy-to-heat-homes-zmaz82ndzgoe.

Rorer, Sarah Tyson. *How to Set the Table*. Wallingford, CT: R. Wallace and Sons Manufacturing Co., 1901. Internet Archive. https://archive.org/stream/howtosettablebei00rwal#page/18/mode/2up

Ross, Alan S. C. "The Assize of Bread." *The Economic History Review, New Series* 9, no. 2 (1956): 332–42. doi:10.2307/2591750.

Salmon, Lucy Maynard. *Domestic Service*. New York: The Macmillan Company, 1897. Internet Archive. https://archive.org/details/domesticservice01salmgoog.

Salzman, James. *Drinking Water: A History*. New York: Overlook Duckworth, 2012.

Santich, Barbara. "The Evolution of Culinary Techniques in the Medieval Era. In *Food in the Middle Ages: A Book of Essays*. Edited by Melitta Weiss Adamson. 61–81. New York: Garland, 1995.

Sayer, Liana C. "Gender, Time and Inequality: Trends in Women's and Men's Paid Work, Unpaid Work and Free Time." *Social Forces* 84, no. 1 (2005): 285–303. Accessed August 27, 2016. *Criminal Justice Abstracts with Full Text*. EBSCOhost.

Schlereth, Thomas J. *Victorian America: Transformations in Everyday Life, 1879–1915*. New York: HarperCollins, 1991.

Schremp, Gerry. *Kitchen Culture: Fifty Years of Food Fads*. New York: Pharos Books, 1991.

Schweitzer, Robert A. and Michael W. R. Davis. *America's Favorite Homes: Mail-Order Catalogues as a Guide to Popular Early 20th Century Houses*. Detroit: Wayne State University Press, 1990.

Sedgwick, Catharine Maria. *Live and Let Live, or Domestic Service Illustrated*. New York: Harper and Brothers, 1837. Internet Archive. https://archive.org/details/liveandletliveo00sedggoog.

"Servants." *New York Times*. September 20, 1874. ProQuest Historical Newspapers: *New York Times*.

"Sham Lard and Other Shams." *New York Times*. March 2, 1887. ProQuest Historical Newspapers: *New York Times*.

Shapiro, Laura. *Perfection Salad: Women and Cooking at the Turn of the Century*. Berkeley: University of California Press, 1986, 2009.

———. *Something from the Oven: Reinventing Dinner in 1950s America*. New York: Viking/Penguin, 2004.

Sheppard, June A. "Vernacular Buildings in England and Wales: A Survey of Recent Work by Architects, Archaeologists and Social Historians." *Transactions of the Institute of British Geographers* 40 (December 1966): 21–37. Accessed June 2016. http://www.jstor.org/stable/621566.

Sigalos, Lefteris. "Housing People in Medieval Greece." *International Journal of Historical Archaeology* 7, no. 3 (September 2003): 195–221. Accessed June 2016. http://www.jstor.org/stable/20853025.

Smith, Lindsey P., She Wen Ng, and Barry M. Popkin. "Trends in U.S. Home Food Preparation and Consumption: Analysis of National Nutrition Surveys and Time Use Studies from 1965–1966 to 2007–2008." *Nutrition Journal* 12, no. 45 (2013): 12–45. Accessed May 2017. https://www.ncbi.nlm.nih.gov/pmc/articles/PMC3639863/.

Smith, Louise Palmer. "The Princess Biddy." *Putnam's Monthly Magazine of American Literature, Science and Art* 15, no. 25 (January 1870): 114–17. Accessed July 2016. http://ebooks.library.cornell.edu/cgi/t/text/pageviewer-idx?c=putn;cc=putn;rgn=full%20text;idno=putn0015-1;didno=putn0015-1;view=image;seq=116;node=putn0015-1%3A1;page=root;size=100.

Stage, Sarah. "Ellen Richards and the Social Significance of the Home Economics Movement." In *Rethinking Home Economics: Women and the History of the Profession*. Edited by Sarah Stage and Virginia B. Vincenti. 17–33. Ithaca, NY: Cornell University Press, 1997.

Stambaugh, John. *The Ancient Roman City*. Baltimore: The Johns Hopkins University Press, 1988.

Stilgoe, John. *Common Landscape of America, 1580 to 1845*. New Haven, CT: Yale University Press, 1982.

———. *Borderland, Origins of the American Suburb, 1820–1939*. New Haven, CT: Yale University Press, 1988.

Strasser, Susan. *Never Done: A History of American Housework*. New York: Pantheon Books, 1982.

———. *Satisfaction Guaranteed: The Making of the American Mass Market*. New York: Pantheon Books, 1989.

Strey, Gerry. "The 'Oleo Wars': Wisconsin's Fight over the Demon Spread." *The Wisconsin Magazine of History* 85, no. 1 (Autumn, 2001): 2–15. Accessed March 2017. http://www.jstor.org/stable/4636942.

Suetonius. *The Lives of the Twelve Caesars*. Edited by J. Eugene Reed and Alexander Thomson. Philadelphia: Gebbie & Co., 1889. Accessed June 2016. http://www.perseus.tufts.edu/hopper/text?doc=Perseus:abo:phi,1348,019:13.

Sutherland, Daniel E. *Americans and Their Servants: Domestic Service in the United States from 1800s to 1920*. Baton Rouge: Louisiana State University Press, 1981.

———. *The Expansion of Everyday Life, 1860–1879*. New York: HarperCollins, 1989.

"Swill Milk Destroyed." *New York Times*. May 1, 1887. ProQuest Historical Newspapers: New York Times.

"'Tis home where the heart is." Library of Congress. Accessed May 2017. https://www.loc.gov/item/amss.hc00027d/.

"*Toilers of the Home*—Lillian Pettengill—Everybody's." Undercover Reporting, Deception for Journalism's Sake: A Database. Accessed July 2016. http://sites.dlib.nyu.edu/undercover/toilers-home-lillian-pettengill-everybodys.

Tosh, John. *A Man's Place: Masculinity and the Middle-Class Home in Victorian England*. New Haven, CT: Yale University Press 1999. Accessed September 5, 2017. eBook Collection. EBSCOhost.

Trollope, Frances. *Domestic Manners of the Americans*. London: Whittaker, Treacher & Company; New York, 1832. Internet Archive. https://archive.org/details/domesticmannerso00troliala.

Tucker, Mrs. H. P. "Help on the Farm." *Transactions of the Wisconsin State Agricultural Society, including a full report of the state agricultural convention, held in February 1873, and numerous practical papers and communications*. Wisconsin State Agricultural Society. vol. XI (1872–1873): 430–33. Accessed July 2016. http://digicoll.library.wisc.edu/cgi-bin/WI/WI-idx?type=turn&entity=WI.WSASv11.p0437&id=WI.WSASv11&isize=M.

Unger, Richard W. Unger. *Beer in the Middle Ages and the Renaissance*. Philadelphia: University of Pennsylvania Press, 2004. http://www.jstor.org/stable/j.ctt3fj2zx.24.

U.S. Census Bureau. "American Housing Survey 2013 National Summary Tables." General Housing Data-All Housing Units, Table C-01-AH. Accessed October 2016. https://www.census.gov/programs-surveys/ahs/data/2013/ahs-2013-summary-tables/national-summary-report-and-tables---ahs-2013.html.

U.S. Census Bureau. United States Bureau of Labor Statistics, American Time Use Survey. Accessed May 2017. https://www.bls.gov/TUS/CHARTS/HOUSEHOLD.HTM.

U.S. Department of Agriculture. "Household Food Security in the United States in 2015." Accessed March 2017. https://www.ers.usda.gov/publications/pub-details/?pubid=79760.

U.S. Department of Health and Human Services and U.S. Department of Agriculture. *2015–2020 Dietary Guidelines for Americans*. 8th Edition. December 2015 Accessed April 2017. https://health.gov/dietaryguidelines/2015/guidelines/chapter-2/current-eating-patterns-in-the-united-states/.

United States Food and Drug Administration. "The FDA Takes Step to Remove Artificial Trans Fats in Processed Foods." June 16, 2016. Accessed April 2017. https://www.fda.gov/NewsEvents/Newsroom/PressAnnouncements/ucm451237.htm.

Urban Andrew. "Irish Domestic Servants, 'Biddy' and Rebellion in the American Home, 1850–1900." *Gender & History* 21, no. 2 (August 2009): 263–86. doi:10.1111/j.1468-0424.2009.01548.x.

Vanderbilt, Amy. *Amy Vanderbilt's Compete Book of Etiquette: A Guide to Gracious Living*. Garden City, NY: Doubleday & Company, Inc., 1954.

Van Vorst, Mrs. John (Bessie). "The Woman of the People." *Harpers* (May 1903): 871–75. Accessed July 2017. Harpers Archive Online.

Votaw, Albert N. "The Hillbillies Invade Chicago." *Harper's Magazine* (February 1958): 64–68.

Van Wormer, Katherine S., Charletta Sudduth, and David W. Jackson. *The Maid Narratives: Black Domestics and White Families in the Jim Crow South*. Baton Rouge: Louisiana State University Press, 2012. Accessed July 2016. eBook Collection, EBSCOhost.

Welter, Barbara. "The Cult of True Womanhood: 1820–1860." *American Quarterly* 18, no. 2 (Summer 1966): 151–74. doi:10.2307/2711179.

Whorton, James C. "Vegetarianism." In *Cambridge World History of Food*, Vol. 2, Edited by Kenneth F. Kiple and Kriemhild Conee Ornelas. 1555–1559. Cambridge, UK: Cambridge University Press, 2000.

Wilson, Mary Tolford. "Amelia Simmons Fills a Need: American Cookery, 1796." *The William and Mary Quarterly* 14, no. 1 (January 1957): 16–30. Accessed February 2017. http://www.jstor.org/stable/1917369.

Woolgar, C. M., D. Serjeantson, and T. Waldron. "Conclusion." In *Food in Medieval England: Diet and Nutrition*. Edited by C. M. Woolgar, D. Serjeantson, and T. Waldron. Oxford: OUP Oxford, 2006. Accessed October 2016. eBook Collection. EBSCOhost.

"*The Woman Who Toils*—Bessie and Marie van Vorst—Everybody's." Undercover Reporting, Deception for Journalism's Sake: A Database. Accessed July 2016. http://sites.dlib.nyu.edu/undercover/woman-who-toils-bessie-and-marie-van-vorst-everybodys.

Index

activities for classroom, 16–19, 34–39, 55, 76–78, 101–4
advertising, 12, *14*, 15, *16*, *23*, *31*, 37, *49*, *54*; food advertising, 67, 73, 76–77, 81, 87, 88, 90, 91, 93–96, *93*, *95*, *97*, 98–99, 101, 103–7, *105*
African Americans, 15, 48, 50, 53–54, 62–63, 89
agency, 18, 53
agricultural productivity, 68, 72, 77
Aladdin Company, 22, *23*, 32
Alcott, Louisa May, 91
Alcott, William, 91
ale. *See* beer
American Cookery, 89, 102–3
American Heart Association, 99
American Home Economics Association, 92
American Revolution, 19, 39, 48, 89
The American Woman's Home, 51, 52, 91
ancient Europe, 7, 8, 25–26, 68, 87, 89, 98; cookbooks/recipes, 87, 89; housing, 25–26; households/family, 8, 9
anthologist/anthropology, 6, 67
antiquarian, defined, 67
apartments (housing), 70, 8, 21, 22, 26, 52, 53
Apicius, 79, 89
archaeology, 25–26, 68, 70
architecture continuum, 21–24. *See also* vernacular architecture
architecture. *See* house architecture
The Art of Cookery, 89
Austin, Hilary Mac, 18
Autobiography of Peter Cartwright, 81

Baker's Chocolate, 94
balloon framing, 32
bathrooms, 24, 35, 53, *54*
beds/bedrooms, 24, 28, 29, 30, 33, 34, 35, 40, 41, 60. *See also* privacy.
Beecher, Catharine, *52*, 52–53, 57, 75, 91, 92, 95
beer, 70, 71, 72, 92, 102, 104

Bellamy, Edward, 52, 59
Better Homes and Gardens, 32
Bingham, George Caleb, 34
Boston Cooking School, 92, 93
Boston Cooking School Cook Book, 93
Bracken, Peg, 95
bread, 53, 56, 57, 70, 72, 80, 89, 90, 91, 93, 94, 102, 105, 107. *See also* food, grains
Brown, Helen Gurley, 107
bungalow, 22, 23

Calendar of Dinners, 99
calories, 70, 71, 72, 76, 77, 98
Campbell's soup advertising, *49*, 15
The Can Opener Cookbook, 94
Cannon, Poppy, 94
The Canterbury Tales, 74, 79
carbohydrates, 70, 72, 76, 98
Cartwright, Peter, 81
Chaucer, Geoffrey, 74, 79
Child, Lydia Maria, 91
children: food for, 92, 95, 101, *105*, 106; role in family/household, 5, 8, 10, 12, *14*, 15, *16*, 21, 24, 29, 30, *51*, 57, 89
Chinese, domestic servant, 63
Chocolate and Cocoa Recipes by Miss Parloa and Home Made Candy Recipes by Mrs. Janet McKenzie Hill, 94
Christian influence: in art, 34; on family/housing, 9, 12, 15, 52, 57
class. *See* social class
College, Career, and Civic Life (C3) Framework for Social Studies State Standards, 113–14
Common Core State Standards, 114
compelling question. *See* essential question
The Compleat Housewife, 89
convenience food. *See* food
cookbook, 79, 107; as primary source, 11, 68, 76, 87, 101, 102; community, 88, 90, 93, 94, 97, 101; history of,

121

87–91, 95–96; home economics movement, 91–93, 95–96; promotional, 94–95, *95*, 106; student activities, 101–3
cooking: schools, 53, 59, 82, 92–93, 94, 99; hearth or fireplace, 10–11, 26, 40, 69, 70, 81, 102
Corson, Juliet, 92
Crisco, 98–100, *100*, 106
cult of domesticity, 12, 13, 48
cult of true womanhood. *See* cult of domesticity
cultural construct, 21, 36
culturally responsive teaching, 2, 3, 111, 113

dairy. *See* food
De re coquinaria (On Cookery), 89
della Casa, Giovanni, 74, 80
dining rooms, 24, 30, 41, 74, 75, 82, 83
disease related to diet/food/water, 29, 68, 72, 76, 92, 99
dog, 29, *51*, 34, 47, *71*, 79
domestic science, 106, 107; domestic science movement, 52–53, 60, 87, 91–94, 96
Domestic Service (research study), 53, 60
domestic work: training in schools, 53, 57, 59, 60, 82, 92–93, 94, 99. *See also* housework/household chores
domestic worker, 8, 9, 10, 13, 18, 30, 34, *35*, 47, 49, *51*, 54, 58, 45–65, 69, 73, 74, 76, 80, 83, 89, 106, 113, *82*
Douglass, Frederick, 41
Downing, Andrew Jackson, 32
Dutch Republic, 33–34
dwellings. *See* housing
Dyer, Christopher, 72

economist / economics, 8, 67
Ehrenreich, Barbara, 55
Elagabalus, Roman emperor, 73, 78, 79
electric power. *See* municipal services
elite: social class (wealthy, upper class), 6, 11; domestic labor/service in elite households, 45, 45, 48, 52, 57, 59, 60, 73; cookbooks/recipes, 67, 89; dining etiquette, 74, 76, 78–80; family, 6, 7, 8, 9; food, 67, 68, 71, 72, 73–74; housing, 11, 22, 24, 25, 27, 30, 32, 113; women, 13
enculturation, 36–37
The English Husbandman, 89
The English Huswife, 89
essential question, 2, 5, 16, 17, 21, 35, 36, 37, 39, 45, 56, 67, 76, 77, 87, 101, 102, 103, 104, 111, 113, 114
ethnicity/race, 1, 113; domestic service, 45, 48, 50, 53, 55, 57–59, 62–63; family/household, 9–10, 13, 36; food, 67, 68, 94, 101
etiquette. *See* manners
Examining the Evidence, Seven Strategies for Teaching with Primary Sources, 18

Fallingwater (house), 22
familial generation, defined, 18–19
family, 5–20; portraits, student activity, 17–18; primary source images, 6, 7, *10*, 14, *16*, 17–18, 29, 35, 47, *51*, 69, *71*; American slave, 9–10, *10*, 39; as a subjective/idealized concept, 1–2, 5, 11, 17; defined, 5–6; economy/economic activities, 6–11, 15; middle class, 5, 12–15, *16*; Native American, 9; roles in society, 6–8; stages/life cycle, 9
famine. *See* food shortage
Farmer, Fannie, 82, 93
Farrar, Eliza Ware (Mrs. John Farrar), 80
Fat. *See* food
The Feminine Mystique, 15, 107
Fifteen Cent Dinners for Workingmen's Families, 92
Filtering/filtering down of housing, 22–23
folk architecture. *See* vernacular
food: children. *See* children, food for; desert, 77; insecurity, 77; purity, 87, 96–100, *100*, 103–7; regulation, 67, 70, 96, 98–99, *100*, 104; scandals, 96–100; service at the table, 74–76, 82; shortage, 68, 69, 72, 77; substitutes, 98–100, *100*; as related to sex/gender, 68, 76, 89, 90, 92–96, 101, 107; convenience, 53, 93, 94, 96; dairy/milk/cheese/butter, 9, 28, 29, 69, 70, *71*, 72, 79, 89, 96, 98–99, *100*, 102, 103, 104, 106; fat/cooking fat/oil, 69, 70, 72, 76, 79, 87, 89, 98–100, *100*, 102, 103, 106; fruit/vegetables, 9, 35, 68, 71, 72, 73, 74, 81, 83, 89, 91, 96, 102, 103, 104, 106; grains, 9, 68, 69, 70, 72, 96; interdisciplinary study of, 67–68; meat (beef, pork, mutton, poultry), 9, 69, 70, 72, 74, 79, 80, 81, 83, 89, 96, 98; processed/manufactured, 15, 67, 72, 87, 94, 95, 96–100, 97, *100*, 103–7, *105*; spices/herbs/seasonings, 9, 68, 69, 71, 74, 75, 79, 102, 103; *See also* sugar/sweeteners
Food Stamp Program, 77
fork, 40, 63, 74, 76, 80, 81, 112
The Forme of Curye (The Way of Cookery), 89
Fourierist community 52; *See also* utopian communities, 52
Freidan, Betty, 15, 107
The Frugal Housewife, 91
Fruitlands, 91

gas power. *See* municipal services
gelatin, 53, 73–74, *73*, 95
gender, defined, 12
genealogy, 19
genre painting, 29, 32–34, *33*, 35, 78
Graham, Sylvester, 91
grain. *See* food, grains
Greece, ancient, 7; households/family, 88–89; housing, 25–26

hall and parlor house, *27*, 27–28
The Handy Cookbook, 91
hearth/fireplace. *See* cooking
Heinz, H. J., 98
help, defined, 48. *See also* domestic worker
The Help (novel and movie), 53
Hill, Janet McKenzie, 94
Hine, Lewis, *16*
Historical American Buildings Survey, 28, 39

"home cooking," 87, 91; redefining, 94–96, 99, 101–3
home economics. *See* domestic science
"Home sweet home" (poem/song), 37–38
home, as a subjective/idealized concept, 1–2, 21, 32, 36–38, 45–46, *47*, 48, *51*, 112–13
house architecture, 21–24
house inventory, 34, 39–40
household: as related to family, 7–11, 13–17; defined, 6, 8; manuals/advice, 11, 13, *14*, 50, 52, 76, 87, 89, 91; objects/goods, 24, 29–30, 33–34, 69, 77; preindustrial, 24–27, 46–48; portrayal in primary source texts and images, 18, 33–34, 36–37; size, 24
housewife, history of word, 9–10, 15, 45–46, 50, 92
housework/household chores, 24, 45–50, 56–59, 73, 106
housework, history of concept, 10–11, 15, 45, 52
housing, 21–44; mass produced, 21–24, 29; pre-industrial, 7, 10, 24–30, *27*, *28*, 29, *33*, 69, *71*; rural, 25–29; urban, 25, 26, 32, 33–34, 52, 53, 11
Howland, Marie Stevens, 52
Hungry Planet: What the World Eats, 77
husbandry, history of concept, 9–10, 15, 45–46
Hutterites, 15
Hydrogenation, 99

I Hate to Cook Book, 94
I house, 27–28, *28*
immigrant/immigration, 15, 22, 48, 50, 53, 92
Industrial Revolution/ industrialization, 2, 5; impact on domestic service, 48, 53; impact on family/households, 10, 11, 17, 18; impact on food/diet, 68, 87; impact on housework, 45; impact on housing, 22, 24, 32
Inquiry Arc, 113–14
inquiry learning. *See* activities for the classroom
interdisciplinary instruction, 2, 3, 35, 68, 76, 111–13
Irish domestic servants, 50, 57, *58*, 62–63
"Is that really a thing?" 1, 3, 111

Jell-O, 53, *73*, 95; *See also* gelatin
Johnson, Eastman, 34, *29*
The Jungle, 96, 97

Kerber, Linda, 12
Keys, Ancel, 99
kitchens, 24, 26, 29, 30, 35, 37, 41, 46, 53, 56, 57, 59, 61, 77, 81, 83, 87, 89, 93, 94
knife, 24, 28, 39, 40, 41, 42, 71, 80, 81
Knox gelatin, 53, *73*, 94; *See also* gelatin
Krimmel, John Lewis, 34

Ladies' Home Journal, 32, 94
laws/government regulation, 8, 9, 25, 62, 67, 70, 71, 96, 98–99, 100, 104
Leslie, Eliza, 91
literacy skills/instruction, 111, 114
lithograph, 34, 37, 46

Live and Let Live; or, Domestic Service Illustrated, 52
Looking Backward 2000–1887, 52, 59

The Maid Narratives, 53
maid. *See* domestic worker
Mallon, Mary, 50; *See also* Irish domestic servant
manners, 1, 3, 11, 13, 25, 30, 36, 52–53, 62, 63, 67, 68, 73–83, 91
marriage, 6, 7, 8, 9, 11, 13, 15, 24, 48, 50, 53, 107; history of, 98–100, *100*
Maria Theresa, Holy Roman Empress, 6
Markham, Gervase, 89
meat. *See* food
media, mass media, 2, 5, 8, 11, 13, 15, 21, 32, 37, 89, 96, 103, 111
medieval/Middle Ages, 7, 15, 98; cookbooks/recipes, 89; diet, 68–72; domestic service, 46; food regulations, 104, 70; housing, 26–27; peasant, 25, 26–27, 68–72, 74; table manners, 74, 78–80
men, role in family/household, 13–15, 96
Menzel, Peter, 77
middle class, 5, 11–12, 13, 74, 91, 92–93, 94, 96, 101; defined, 11–12; dining, 74, 76, *75*; domestic service, 45–46, 48, 50–52, 58; housing, 22, 25, 30, 32, 33–34, *33*, 37; sex/gender expectations, 12–15, *14*, *35*, 46, *47*, 50, 95, 96; food/cookbook themes, 91–94, *95*, 96, 101
middling sort. *See* middle class
mincemeat, 89, 102, 103
Mintz, Sidney, 68
Miss Beecher's Domestic Receipt Book, *75*, 91
Mötley Crüe, 37
Mount, William Sidney, 34
municipal services (electric, gas, water), 11, 22, 24–25, 29, 32, 36, 53, 54, 59, 88

National Historic Register, 39
National School Lunch Program, 77
Native Americans, 9, 89
The New Housekeeper's Manual, 91
Nickel and Dimed: On (Not) Getting By in America, 55
Nineteenth Amendment, *90*
A Noble Book of Cookery, 89
normal/norm, 5, 16–17, 96
nostalgia, 5, 21, 37, 48, 50

obesity. *See* disease
objective concepts, 1, 2, 11, 17, 21, 87, 112, 113
oleo. *See* margarine
Oleomargarine Act of 1886, 99, *101*
Oneida Community/ Perfectionists, 15, 52
organ, parlor. *See* piano
outhouse, 24, 29, 54

Pabst, Frederick, 98
Papa's Own Girls, 52

parlors, 26, 28, 30, *31*, 41, 62
Parola, Maria, 94
peasant, 18, 62; defined, 26; housing/households, 9, 25–27, 40; diet/food/cooking, 68–72, 73, 74, 77, 98
Pettengill, Lillian, 55, 60–61
piano, 30, *31*, 34
place, geographic concept defined, 112
place-based education, 2, 3, 111, 112–13
plumbing, 24, 25, 29, 32, *54*; See also municipal services
porches. 28, 29, 30, 32, 42
pre-industrial era: dining habits/manners, 73–74; domestic service, 46–48, 69; food/diet, 68–72, 98, 69, *71*; household/family, 6, 7, 10, 8–11, 29, 33, 47; housing, 7, *10*, 24–30, *27*, *28*, *29*, *33*, 69, *71*; primary source images, 6, *10*, *27–28*, *29*, *33*, 69, *71*; primary source texts, 39–41, 55–56, 78–80, 103
primary source: analysis, 1, 2, 8, 12, 17, 18, 21, 22, 32, 26, 67, 68, 72, 87; documents, 38–42, 55–63, 78–83, 103, 104–107; images, 6, 7, *10*, 14, *16*, *23*, *27*, *28*, *29*, *31*, *33*, *35*, *46*, *47*, *49*, *51*, *54*, *58*, 69, *71*, *73*, *75*, *82*, *88*, *90*, *93*, *95*, *97*, *100*, *105*; prescriptive, 1, 13, 37, 78
privacy, in the household, 24, 26, 29–30
privy. See outhouse
probate inventory. See house inventory
Procter and Gamble, 99, 106
protein, 69, 70, 72, 76, 98
Pure Food and Drug Act of 1906, 98

race/ethnicity. See ethnicity/race
Randolph, Mary, 89
recipes, 103; as primary sources, 87, 101, 102–3; history of, 87–91; home economics movement, 91–93, 95–96; promotional/advertising, *49*, 94, 95, 99
republican motherhood, 12–13, 45, 48, 91
Resor, Cynthia Williams, 121
Richards, Ellen, 53, 92
Roman/ancient Rome, 7, 8, 9, 12; banquets, 73, 78–79; households/family, 8–9; housing, 25–26

Salmon, Lucy Maynard, 53, 60, 61
school/schooling, 8, 15, *16*, 34, 52, 53, 55, 57, 59, 60, 77, 82, 91, 92–94, 112
Sears and Roebuck, 22, 32
Sedgwick, Catherine, 52
separate spheres, 13, *51*, 52
servant problem, 48–63
servant. See domestic worker
Seventy-Five Receipts for Pastry, Cakes, and Sweetmeats, 91
sewer. See municipal services
sewing. See textile production
sex: defined, 12; division of labor, 9–13, 15, 29, 36–37, 45–46, 48, 50–60, 68, 87, 89, 92–93, 95, 96, 101
Shakers, 15, 52, 121
Simmons, Amelia, 89, 95, 102–3

Sinclair, Upton, 96
Single Girl's Cookbook, 107
slavery, 8, 9, *10*, 25, 26, 39, 40–41, 45, 46, 48, 50, 55, 61, 62, 73, 89, 113
sleeping arrangements, 24, 26, 30, *33*, 34, 41, 60; See also privacy
Smith, Eliza, 89
social class: classroom activities that address social class, 1, 16–18, 34–42, 55–63, 76–83, 101, 113; defined, 11–12; See also middle class, working class, elite
social generation, defined, 18–19
social history, 1–3, 24, 53, 113–14
social status, defined, 11–12; See also social class
sociologist/sociology, 6, 62, 67
Spencer, Lilly Martin, 34, *35*
spinning. See textile production
spittoons, 34
standards, for teaching, 111, 113–14
stereotypes, 50, 52, 58, 76
The Story of Crisco, 99, 106
stove, for cooking/heat, 7, *10*, 29, 34, *35*, 46, 88
Stowe, Harriet Beecher, *51*, 52, 91
student activities. See activities for the classroom
subjective/idealized concepts, 1–2, 5, 11, 17, 21, 87, 112–13
suffrage, 15, *51*, 52
sugar/sweeteners, 68, 70, 72, 77, 81, 83, 100, 102, 103, 104, *105*
syllabub, 102, 103

table manners, 67, 68, 74, 77–80
taxes/taxation, 6, 8, 67, 68, 70, 99
Taylor, Frederick, 53
temperance/temperance movement, 15, 70, 91, 92
Tested Crisco Recipes, 99
textile production, 9, 10, 28, *29*, 34, 40, 48, 92, 106
thematic instruction, 2, 3, 35, 111–13
Thompson, Kathleen, 18
trans-fatty acids/trans fats, 99
A Treatise on Bread and Bread-Making, 91
Treatise on Domestic Economy, 52, 91
Trollope, Frances Milton, 40, 55–56
Truman, Harry, 99
Twenty-Five Cent Dinners for Families of Six, 92
Typhoid Mary. See Mallon, Mary

U.S. Census Bureau, 6, 17, 24
United States Food and Drug Administration, 99
utopian communities, 15, 25, 52, 59, 91, 112

Van Vorst, Bessie, 55, 61
Vanderbilt, Amy, 83
Vegetable Diet: As Sanctioned by Medical Men, 91
vegetable oil. See food, fat
vegetarianism, 91

vernacular architecture, 21–24, 32, 27
The Virginia House-Wife, 89
Vitellius, Roman emperor, 73, 78–79
water service. *See* municipal services
water: consumption, 71; preindustrial supply, 9, 10, 26, 29, 36, 53, 71
weaving. *See* textile production
Western pattern diet, 72
Wiley, Harvey, 96

women: food/cooking, 67, 68, 76, 81, 87, 89, 90, 93, 94–96, 95, 101; household chores, 45–46, 48, 50–62, *51*, *54*, *58*, 92, 113; role in family, 8–13, 45
women's movement, 1960s–1970s, 15, 95, 107
working class, 11, 13, 15, 18; domestic service, 17, 46, 50, 52; food, 92, 93; housing, 11, 26, 32, 74
Wright, Frank Lloyd, 22

The Young Lady's Friend, 80

About the Author

Cynthia Williams Resor taught high school social studies and sixth grade before deciding to pursue her dream of obtaining a PhD in history. She is currently a professor at Eastern Kentucky University and has taught undergraduate and graduate teacher education courses, social studies for teachers, medieval history, U.S. history survey courses, humanities, and led study abroad classes. She has also conducted a wide variety of professional development sessions, published several articles in various journals related to history and social studies education, and served as a history consultant for a Teaching American History grant.

Cynthia loves history, especially the history of daily life and ordinary people, and she is always trying to spread her enthusiasm about history inside and outside of the classroom. She worked as a costumed interpreter, a "fake" Shaker, at the Shaker Village at Pleasant Hill in central Kentucky, and loves to surprise her students by appearing in class in historical costumes. She is obsessed with genealogy and local history and makes her students visit local historical sites. She forces her family and friends to visit old cemeteries and take vacations with her that revolve around historical themes and locations. She lives in an old house, collects old stuff, names her dogs and chickens after historical people, and is probably a dangerous driver because she listens to historical novels in the car. Her dream job is to be the tour guide with a time traveling machine.

Her love of food, recipes, and old houses can be attributed to the time she spent with her grandmothers, to whom this book is dedicated. Her first glimpse into daily life of average people in the pre-industrial past came from the experiences of her grandmothers.

www.ingramcontent.com/pod-product-compliance
Lightning Source LLC
Chambersburg PA
CBHW080541300426

44111CB00017B/2825